BARRON'S

PRAXIS®

CORE EXAMS

Core Academic Skills for Educators

READING (5712)

WRITING (5722)

MATHEMATICS (5732)

COMBINED TEST

(Reading, Writing, and Mathematics) (5751)

2ND EDITION

Dr. Robert D. Postman
Professor and Dean
Nationally Recognized
Test Preparation Expert

BARRON'S

®PRAXIS is a registered trademark of Educational Testing Service (ETS). This publication is not endorsed or approved by ETS.

To my wife Liz,
the most beautiful woman

All inquiries should be addressed to:
Barron's Educational Series, Inc.
250 Wireless Boulevard
Hauppauge, New York 11788
www.barronseduc.com

ISBN: 978-1-4380-0971-1

Library of Congress Control Number: 2017944531

PRINTED IN THE UNITED STATES OF AMERICA
9 8 7 6 5 4 3 2 1

10%
POST-CONSUMER
WASTE
Paper contains a minimum
of 10% post-consumer
waste (PCW). Paper used
in this book was derived
from certified, sustainable
forestlands.

Contents

PART III: PRACTICE CORE TESTS WITH ANSWERS EXPLAINED

Preface

This completely updated and expanded edition shows you how to do your absolute best on the Core Praxis Teacher Certification examinations. Hundreds of prospective teachers field-tested preliminary versions of this book, and dozens of experienced teachers and subject matter specialists reviewed the book to ensure that it provides you with the subject matter preparation and practice tests you need.

The practice tests in this book have the same question types and the same question-and-answer formats as the real tests. The practice tests also have the look and feel of the real thing.

My wife Liz, a teacher, was a constant source of support, and she made significant contributions to this book. I hope she accepts my regrets for the lost months and believes my promises that it won't happen again. My children Chad, Blaire, and Ryan, and my grandson Quinn, have also been a source of support as I worked on this and other books.

I can attest that Barron's is simply the best publisher of test preparation books. The editorial department spared no effort to ensure that this book will be most helpful to you.

Samantha Karasik, my editor at Barron's, did a masterful job with a mammoth and complex manuscript. Samantha and I have worked on other books and, as usual, many of the special touches are due to her caring attention.

Special thanks to the undergraduate and graduate students who field-tested this book and to those at the Educational Testing Service. Special thanks also to Benjamin, Edith, and Pamela, who would have liked seeing their names in a book. I am also grateful to experts at state education departments for taking the time to talk with me about the teacher certification requirements in their states.

I wish you well as you pursue a rewarding and fulfilling teaching career.

Robert D. Postman

PART I
Core Tests and Strategies

Core Computer-Delivered Tests (5712, 5722, 5732, 5751)

1

TEST INFO BOX

Most chapters begin with a Test Info Box. Read it for information about these tests.

The Educational Testing Service (ETS) offers the Core tests. Contact ETS for registration forms, admission tickets, testing accommodations, and test scores.

You can register online. All Core tests are computer delivered.

Educational Testing Service
Box 6501
Princeton, NJ 08541-6051
Website: *www.ets.org/praxis/about/core*
609-771-7395
TTY 609-771-7714
FAX (609) 530-0581 (24 hours)
E-mail: *praxis@ets.org*

The Core Tests
Computer-delivered

Reading (5712)
Writing (5722)
Mathematics (5732)
Combined Test (Reading, Writing, and Mathematics) (5751)

READ ME FIRST!

This section explains the steps you should take when beginning your test preparation. Read it before continuing.

What's Going on with the Core Academic Skills for Educators (Core)?

Teacher certification examinations have been around for years. Recently, states have focused on the reading, writing, and mathematics skills tested by the computer-delivered Core tests.

The Good News

The good news is that the Core tests focus on a central core of reading, writing, and mathematics skills. In this book, you will learn how to prepare successfully for each test.

CORE TESTS—THE INSIDE STORY

The computer-delivered Core tests were developed by the Educational Testing Service in conjunction with a number of states. The Core tests consist of three separate tests: (1) Reading, (2) Writing—multiple-choice and constructed responses, and (3) Mathematics.

Some questions may be part of a field test and do not count toward your score. You will not know which questions these are. Treat every question as though it counts.

Core Tests Summary

Computer-delivered Only		
Reading (5712)	56 multiple-choice questions	85 minutes
Writing (5722)	40 multiple-choice questions 2 typed responses	40 minutes 30 minutes each
Mathematics (5732)	56 multiple-choice questions*	85 minutes
Combined (5751)	All three tests	5 hours

*A few mathematics multiple-choice questions may be replaced by numeric entry questions.

What Are the Tests Like?

The computer-delivered Core tests assess reading, writing, and mathematics skills. The Core is a computer-based multiple-choice test with two typed responses.

You take the computer-delivered Core tests on the scheduled days set by ETS. You sit in a cubicle in front of a computer screen while a video camera mounted overhead records your actions. The computer selects all the items before you take the test. You use a mouse and a keyboard to enter your answers directly on the test screen. You type your responses.

A special "mark tool" lets you mark a question so that you may return later to answer the question or change your answer. A review screen shows the questions you have answered, those marked for return, and those not seen at all.

A basic on-screen calculator is available during the mathematics test. You will be provided with scrap paper to use during the test.

> ### QUESTION TYPES
>
> **MOST MULTIPLE-CHOICE:** These are standard multiple-choice items with five answer choices and one correct answer. The answer choices will appear within ovals.
>
> **MULTIPLE-CHOICE WITH MORE THAN ONE CORRECT ANSWER:** These items may have more than one correct answer. The answer choices for these items will appear in a box rather than an oval.
>
> **NUMERIC ENTRY:** For these questions, you will be asked to type your answer in a box. You can also use the calculator and transfer your answer directly from the on-screen calculator to the box by clicking on "Transfer Display."

READING (5712)

The 85-minute reading test has 56 multiple-choice items. You indicate your answer by clicking an oval. A few items may have several correct answer choices. For questions that may have more than one correct answer, you will click on the appropriate box or boxes. According to ETS, test items are partitioned approximately as follows: 35 percent Key Ideas and Details; 30 percent Craft, Structure, and Language Skills; and 35 percent Integration of Knowledge.

WRITING (5722)

The writing test has a 40-minute multiple-choice section with usage, sentence correction, revision in context, and research skills items and two 30-minute constructed responses. There is one Argumentative constructed response and one Informative/Explanatory (Source-Based) constructed response. You type your responses in the space provided on the computer screen.

MATHEMATICS (5732)

The 85-minute mathematics test has 56 items. All but a few will be multiple-choice. Some of these may have several correct answer choices. You will indicate your answer by clicking on an oval if there is only one correct answer or a box if there may be more than one correct answer. Other items may ask you to type a numeric answer or to transfer a numeric answer from your calculator.

CORE TEST CENTERS

The following website will help you find the test centers nearest to you:

www.ets.org/praxis/register/centers_dates

The Core computer-based tests are available at Prometric® test centers, universities, and other test locations. The test centers I visited were simple but appropriate. These centers are in the test administration business, and schedules are tight. Most test centers administer hundreds of other tests, including the GRE and the MCAT. Security is a big deal, so be aware that you are being "watched."

Test Center Video

There is a brief ETS video, that can be accessed at the website below, that shows you what to expect at a test center:

www.ets.org/s/praxis/flash/prometric/18204_praxis-prometric-video.html

CORE TEST REGISTRATION

Use the following website to register for your test:

www.ets.org/praxis/register

You will also find other information, including special test arrangements and how frequently you may take a test.

Where to Send Your Scores

The *Praxis® Information Bulletin* lists a code for each organization that can receive scores. You may feel that you should wait until you know you have gotten a passing score before sending it in. That is not necessary. You will just slow down the process and incur extra expense. Certification agencies do not use these scores for evaluative purposes. They just need to see a passing score, and ETS reports only your highest score.

PASSING THE CORE TESTS

This section reviews Core scoring and gives you some information about what it takes to get a passing score.

Raw Scores and Scale Scores

Your raw score is the number of items you answer correctly, or the number of points you actually earn. Your scale score converts your raw score to a score that can be compared to those of everyone else who has taken that test.

It works this way. Test items, test sections, and different forms of the test have different difficulty levels. For example, an item on one form might be harder than a comparable item on another form. To make up for this difference in difficulty, the harder item might earn a 0.9 scale point, while the easier item might earn a 0.8 scale point. A scale score can be compared to the scale score on all forms of a test.

This is the fair way to do it. To maintain this fairness, Core scores are reported to you as scale scores. All the scores discussed here are scale scores.

CORE SCALE SCORING

The scoring for each Core test is summarized below. The table shows the scale score for each test at the first quartile, second quartile, and third quartile. The lower the quartile, the lower the score.

Quartile	Reading	Writing	Mathematics
First (75% of scores are higher)	160	158	140
Second (50% of scores are higher)	172	166	156
Third (25% of scores are higher)	184	172	168

Current passing scores with approximate percentiles for most states are shown below. Check for the most recent state requirements at *www.ets.org/praxis/states*.

    Reading (5712): 156—Below the 25th percentile
    Writing (5722): 162—About the 38th percentile
    Math (5732): 150—About the 40th percentile

Comparatively, the Mathematics Core is the most difficult, followed by the Writing Core and then the Reading Core.

CORE PASSING RAW SCORES

It is tricky to figure out the raw score you will need to get a passing scale score. A passing raw score may vary from one test version to another. Even ETS does not know the conversion of a raw score to a scale score until after the test has been given. The passing raw scores on tests released by ETS vary widely.

This means we have to be cautious. However, this is information readers often request, so we will help as best we can. Please remember that these are just estimates. ETS may adjust its scaling, or the Core versions it designs may be harder or easier. The test you take may be a harder or easier version. Any of these things will significantly reduce the meaning of these estimates.

Of course, the idea is to do your best. Remember that you can pick up raw score points by using the fundamental test strategies. Eliminate every answer you know is incorrect. Never leave an answer blank. You will also see that a good essay score can significantly reduce the writing multiple-choice raw score you will need.

So here it is—ESTIMATES. There is absolutely no assurance that they will apply to the test you take. The best approach is to assume you will have to do better than these guidelines indicate.

Generally speaking, a multiple-choice raw score of 70 percent correct is a good score for most test takers. An essay score of 8 points out of 12 points is also a good score for most test takers. Here are our recommended goals for most state passing score requirements:

> **MATHEMATICS**—65 percent correct
>
> **READING**—75 percent correct
>
> **WRITING**—8 of 12 essay points and 65 percent of the multiple-choice points

> Now that you're familiar with the Core computer-delivered tests and how they are scored, be sure to take a quick peek at the two Practice Core tests at the end of this book as well as the online Practice Core test. This online test, which contains Reading, Writing, and Mathematics sections as well as detailed answers and explanations, can be accessed on your computer, smartphone, or tablet. To access the online test, go to:
>
> *barronsbooks.com/tp/praxis/core*
>
>

Core Test-Preparation and Test-Taking Strategies

2

TEST INFO BOX

This chapter shows you how to set up a test preparation schedule and shows you some test-taking strategies that will help you improve your score. The important strategies are discussed below.

MULTIPLE-CHOICE

Eliminate and then guess. There is no penalty for wrong answers. Never leave any answer blank.

Suppose a multiple-choice test has 40 items with five answer choices. Eliminate three incorrect answer choices on all the items, guess every answer, and, on average, you would get 20 correct, although your actual score may be higher or lower.

Multiple-choice questions that have more than one correct answer will have boxes rather than ovals for the answer choices.

Consider working backward from the answers.

CONSTRUCTED RESPONSE

General Guidelines

There are two 30-minute responses—Argumentative and Informative/Explanatory (Source-Based). The approaches to each response are somewhat different. The writing review section provides specific steps for each response and scored sample responses.

WRITE AN OUTLINE. THEN TYPE THE RESPONSE: Handwrite your brief outline on scrap paper.

TOPIC PARAGRAPH: Begin the written assignment with an introduction to orient the reader to the topic. The first paragraph should clearly state the main idea of your entire written assignment.

TOPIC SENTENCE: Begin each paragraph with a topic sentence that supports the main idea.

DETAILS: Provide details, examples, and arguments or references to support the topic sentence.

CONCLUSION: End the written assignment with a paragraph that summarizes your main points.

PROVEN TEST-PREPARATION STRATEGIES

Here are several strategies and steps to follow as you prepare for the test. These strategies take you right up to test day.

Get Yourself Ready for the Test

Most people are less tense when they exercise. Set up a *reasonable* exercise program for yourself. The program should involve exercising in a way that is appropriate for you 30 to 45 minutes each day. This exercise may be just as important as other preparation.

Prepare with another person. You will feel less isolated if you have a friend or colleague to study with.

Follow This Study Plan

Begin working four to ten weeks before the test. Review the description of each test you have to take and then take each appropriate review quiz. Use the answer key to mark the review quiz. Each incorrect answer will point you to a specific portion of the review.

Use the subject matter review indicated by the review quiz. Don't spend your time reviewing things you already know.

Take the targeted test after the review of each chapter is complete. It will let you know what further review may be necessary. Complete your review two weeks before the test. Then, complete the first practice test in the book. Take the test under exact test conditions.

Grade your own test or have someone do it for you. Either way, review each incorrect answer and read all the explanations. Every answer is explained in detail.

TWO WEEKS TO GO

Be sure you are registered. Take the second practice test in the book at about the same time of the day that you will take the real test.

ONE WEEK TO GO

Take the online practice test at about the same time of the day that you will take the real test.

FIVE DAYS TO GO

Make sure you

- have your admission ticket.
- know where the test is given.
- know how you're getting there.

THREE DAYS TO GO

Visit the test site, if you haven't done so already. There are many stories of those who could not find the center and missed an appointment.

TWO DAYS TO GO

Confirm your transportation to the test site.

ONE DAY TO GO

- Talk to someone who makes you feel good, or do something enjoyable and relaxing.
- Get a good night's sleep.

TEST DAY

- Dress comfortably.
- Eat the same kind of breakfast you've been eating each morning.
- Get together things to bring to the test, including your registration ticket and identification forms.
- Get to the site about 10 to 15 minutes before the start time. Remember to leave time for parking and walking to the test site.
- Check in.
- Let the test center director know if there are problems with your cubicle or computer.
- Follow the test-taking strategies in the next section.

Test Day Necessities

- **Admission ticket**
- **Completed forms**
- **Identification**

PROVEN TEST-TAKING STRATEGIES

It's Not What You Know That Matters, It's Just Which Answer You Mark

An impersonal machine scores every item except the essay. The machine just senses whether the correct answer oval is filled in. That is the way the test makers want it. If that's good enough for them, it should be good enough for you. Concentrate on marking the correct answer.

Use the Scrap Paper

Use the scrap paper provided at the test center. Use it to do calculations, to jot down possible answers, and to write reminder notes.

Some Questions Are Distracters

Some questions include the words "not," "least," or "except." You are being asked for the answer that doesn't fit with the rest. Be alert for these types of questions.

Work Backward from the Answers

Back solving is particularly useful for answering mathematics questions. This strategy is discussed in detail in the mathematics section, page 182.

They Show You the Answer

Every multiple-choice test shows you the correct answer for each question. The answer is staring right at you. You just have to figure out which one it is.

Some Answers Are Distracters

When a test writer writes a test question, he or she often includes distracters. Distracters are incorrect answers that look like correct answers. It might be an answer to an addition problem when you should be multiplying. It might be a correct answer to a different question. It might just be an answer that catches your eye. Watch out for this type of incorrect answer.

If you get the right answer but mark the wrong answer, the machine will mark it wrong. We told you that marking the right answer was what mattered.

Eliminate the Incorrect Answers

If you can't figure out which answer is correct, then decide which answers can't be correct. Choose the answers you're sure are incorrect. Keep track on the scrap paper. Only one left? That's the correct answer.

Guess, Guess, Guess

If there are still two or more answers left, then guess. Guess the answer from those remaining. Never leave any item blank. There is no penalty for guessing.

Use the Tutorial

There is an untimed tutorial before each test that shows you how to use the computer, how to indicate your answer, and how to use the "mark tool" and review page. Pay careful attention to the tutorial. It will speed things up when you take the test. Take as much time as you need.

Mark Every Item You Might Come Back To

Before you skip an item, mark it with the "mark tool." Mark each item you answer if you think you may want to come back to it.

Use the Review Screen

Before you finish the test, check the review page to be sure you have answered each item. You can use the review screen to check your progress during the test. Be sure to answer every item.

Your Written Responses Are Graded Holistically

Holistic scoring means the raters assign a score based on their informed sense about your writing. Raters have a lot of answers to look at, and they do not do a detailed analysis. The ETS sends your essay to readers over the Internet. Representatives of ETS show the readers the topics for the test and review the types of responses that should be rated 1–6. The rating guidelines for the Informative/Explanatory (Source-Based) and Argumentative essays are on pages 56–57. The readers are trained to evaluate the responses according to the ETS guidelines.

Each written assignment is evaluated twice, without the second reader knowing the evaluation given by the first reader. If the two evaluations differ by more than one point, other readers review the assignment.

Readers have a tedious, tiring assignment. Think about those readers as you write. Write a response that makes it easy for them to give you a high score.

You will find detailed steps for writing essays on pages 82–83.

Most of all, practice as much as you can! Be sure to visit *barronsbooks.com/tp/praxis/core* to take the online practice test!

PART II
Core Subject Matter Preparation

Reading (5712)

3

USING THIS CHAPTER

This chapter prepares you to take the computer-delivered Core reading comprehension test. Choose one of these approaches.

- **I WANT VOCABULARY AND READING HELP.** Review the entire chapter and take the targeted test at the end.
- **I JUST WANT READING HELP.** Read Strategies for Passing the Reading Test beginning on page 17. Take the targeted test at the end of the chapter.
- **I WANT TO PRACTICE READING ITEMS.** Take the targeted test at the end of the chapter.

VOCABULARY REVIEW

You cannot read if you do not know the vocabulary. You do not have to know every word in the dictionary. Follow this reasonable approach to developing a good vocabulary for these tests.

CONTEXT CLUES

Many times you can figure out a word from its context. Look at these examples. Synonyms, antonyms, examples, or descriptions may help you figure out the word.

1. The woman's mind wandered as her two friends **prated** on. It really did not bother her though. In all the years she had known them, they had always <u>babbled</u> about their lives. It was almost comforting.
2. The wind **abated** in the late afternoon. Things were different yesterday when the wind had <u>picked up</u> toward the end of the day.
3. The argument with her boss had been her **Waterloo**. She wondered if the defeat suffered by Napoleon <u>at this famous place</u> had felt the same.
4. The events swept the politician into a **vortex** of controversy. The politician knew what it meant to be spun around like a toy boat in the <u>swirl of water</u> that swept down the bathtub drain.

    Passage 1 gives a synonym for the unknown word. We can tell that *prated* means babbled. *Babbled* is used as a synonym of *prated* in the passage.

    Passage 2 gives an antonym for the unknown word. We can tell that *abated* means slowed down or diminished because *picked up* is used as an antonym of *abated*.

    Passage 3 gives a description of the unknown word. The description of Waterloo tells us that it is the place where Napoleon suffered defeat.

    Passage 4 gives an example of the unknown word. The example of a *swirl of water* going down the bathtub drain gives us a good idea of what a *vortex* is.

ROOTS

A root is the basic element of a word. The root is usually related to the word's origin. Roots can often help you figure out the word's meaning. Here are some roots that may help you.

Root	Meaning	Examples
bio	life	biography, biology
circu	around	circumference, circulate
frac	break	fraction, refract
geo	earth	geology, geography
mal	bad	malicious, malcontent
mater, matr	mother	maternal, matron
neo	new	neonate, neoclassic
pater, patr	father	paternal, patron
spec	look	spectacles, specimen
tele	distant	telephone, television

PREFIXES

Prefixes are syllables that come at the beginning of a word. Prefixes usually have a standard meaning. They can often help you figure out the word's meaning. Here is a list of prefixes that may help you figure out a word.

Prefix	Meaning	Examples
a-	not	amoral, apolitical
il-, im-, ir-	not	illegitimate, immoral, irreversible
un-	not	unbearable, unknown
non-	not	nonbeliever, nonsense
ant-, anti-	against	antiwar, antidote
de-	opposite	defoliate, declaw
mis-	wrong	misstep, misdeed
ante-	before	antedate, antecedent
fore-	before	foretell, forecast
post-	after	postfight, postoperative
re-	again	refurbish, redo
super-	above	superior, superstar
sub-	below	subsonic, subpar

STRATEGIES FOR PASSING THE READING TEST

This section gives a detailed approach to answering the literal and figurative reading items on the computer-delivered Core.

You do not have to understand the entire passage. In fact, the most common error is to read the entire passage before reading the questions. Do not do that. It just wastes time. You only have to know enough to get the correct answer. Less than half, often less than 25 percent, of the details in a passage are needed to answer a question.

> A great way to develop a strong vocabulary is to read a paper every day and a news magazine every week, in addition to the other reading you are doing. There are also several inexpensive books, including *1,100 Words You Need to Know* and *Pocket Guide to Vocabulary* from Barron's, which may help you develop your vocabulary further.

THE READING COMPREHENSION STUDY PLAN

All reading questions call for either literal or figurative responses. There are examples and tips for answering each type. Then you will learn about the five steps for taking the Core reading test.

Next come passages and questions to try out. All the questions have explained answers. Do not skip anything. Do not look at the answers until you have answered all of the questions.

CORE READING QUESTION TYPES

This is how ETS classifies the three categories of reading items:

Key Ideas and Details

These questions usually ask for the stated main idea of a passage or about details in the passage.

Craft, Structure, and Language Skills

These questions are usually related to word or phrase meaning, the unstated purpose of a passage, the author's reason or purpose for writing the passage, or the general organization of the passage.

Integration of Knowledge and Ideas

These questions may ask you to draw an inference or implication or to identify the author's point of view, attitude, or reason for mentioning something. In addition, you will be asked about the meaning of a word in quotation, and to compare or contrast two paragraphs. The more difficult questions will ask about which listed statement would support or diminish the author's argument or would provide an alternate explanation.

It is not always easy to categorize questions. That is OK because there are really two categories of reading questions—literal comprehension and figurative comprehension. Literal questions typically ask directly about the passage. Figurative questions typically ask you to interpret, extend, and apply ideas in the passage. The test does not identify these categories.

> Let me repeat, do not begin by reading the passage in detail. In fact, that kind of careful reading will almost certainly get you into trouble. Only read in detail after you have read a question and you are looking for the answer.

Correct Answers

It all comes down to finding the correct answer. The correct answer will be the best choice available among the choices listed. The correct answer will be based on the passage, not on what you may know is true or think is true.

Literal Comprehension

MAIN IDEA (MAIN PURPOSE)

These questions are the main focus of reading comprehension. Main idea and main purpose questions ask you to identify the topic of the passage or part of the passage, or the main reason the author wrote the passage or part of that passage.

Main idea questions often include the words "main idea":

Which of the following describes the main idea of the passage?

Main purpose questions also often include the words "primary purpose":

The primary purpose of this passage is . . .

Find the central idea of the passage to answer these questions. What was the author really trying to get at? Why did the author write the passage?

Some main ideas may not be directly stated in the passage. However, the main idea or purpose must be from the passage. It cannot be what you think the author might have in mind.

SUPPORTING DETAILS

Authors give details to support the main idea. These details may be facts, opinions, experiences, or discussions.

Here are some examples of supporting details questions:

Which of the following does the author use to support the main idea in the passage?

Which of the following details is not found in this passage?

To explain [a statement] in the passage the author writes . . .

When the passage describes the outcomes of [an event] it mentions . . .

The answer choices will usually include statements or summaries of statements found in the passage. Read the question carefully to be sure what details are asked for.

Answer choices frequently include details you know to be true but that are not found in the passage. Eliminate those. The correct answer will be found in the passage.

VOCABULARY QUESTIONS

A passage has lots of words and phrases. Vocabulary questions typically ask you to show that you know the meaning of one of those words or phrases.

Here are some examples of vocabulary questions:

Which of the following words is a synonym for (the word) in line 99 of the passage?

Which of the following gives the best definition of (word) in line 99 of the passage?

All of the following gives the best meaning for the (phrase/word) in line 99 EXCEPT . . .

The vocabulary section of this book (beginning on page 16) gives a vocabulary review. It also includes ways to identify words from their context. A word in context is not always a strict dictionary definition. Word meaning can be literal or figurative.

Here is an easy example. The author writes, "Stand up for what you believe in." The question asks about the meaning of "stand up." One of the answer choices is (A) "stand up straight." Another choice is (B) "take a position." The main dictionary definition is "stand up straight." However, that is not what these words mean in context. The words mean "take a position." That is the correct answer.

That is not to say that a literal definition will always be wrong, or often wrong. It does mean that you should think about the word's meaning in context.

ORGANIZATION

These questions ask you about the way a passage or part of a passage is organized. It sounds hard, but the answer choices are just plain language descriptions. It is usually more a matter of common sense than any specialized knowledge.

Organization questions are just what you would think they would be:

Which of the following choices best describes the way the passage is organized?

There may be some moderately difficult words in the choices for these types of questions. Use the vocabulary skills you will learn in this chapter to tackle those words if they occur.

Figurative Comprehension

INFERENCE

An inference question asks you to identify something that can be reasonably implied or inferred from a passage. The answers to inference questions will not be directly stated in the passage.

Inference questions look like this:

> Which choice below can be inferred from this passage?
>
> What can be inferred about [name or event] from lines ___-___ in the passage?

Test writers try to write five choices for which only one is clearly the "most correct" inference. They usually do a good job. However, sometimes other apparently reasonable inferences appear.

> Choose an inference based on the passage. Do not make a choice just because it is true—you will find choices like that. Do not make a choice because it has some other emotional appeal. The inference has to be based on information in the passage.

EVALUATE SUPPORTING DETAILS

Some of these questions may ask you to decide whether details support the main idea. Other times, the questions introduce other details and ask you to determine if they would strengthen or weaken the author's argument.

Evaluate supporting details questions look like this:

> Which of the following statements, if added to the passage, would best support (weaken) the author's argument?
>
> Which of the following information would be needed to fully support the author's claim?

A main idea, a position, or a claim needs appropriate support from details. Think about the author's claim or argument. Think about what in the argument convinces you, and about what information is questionable or missing.

Strengthening or weakening an argument does not mean to prove or disprove that argument. Here is an example:

> An author writes, "All my shoes are black." Then someone says, "Did I see you wearing brown shoes the other day?" The second statement weakens the first. It does not disprove it. The second statement may be wrong, or it may be meant as a joke, or lots of other things. However, the second statement is enough to make us think and enough to weaken the author's statement.

ATTITUDE (ASSUMPTIONS)

These questions ask about a position or point of view the author holds that is revealed in a passage. Questions about attitude frequently have one word answers, while questions about assumptions typically have more detailed answer choices.

Attitude questions are what you would expect.

What is the author's attitude or assumption about [some idea or fact]?

Look for a statement in the passage that includes judgment terms such as "bad," "good," "well-thought-out," "I guess," or "questionable," or terms that reveal the author has a preexisting opinion or point of view.

MAKING PREDICTIONS

These questions ask you to identify predictions that can be made from the information in the passage. A prediction is a statement about something that will happen. The questions may also ask you to identify something that a person may say or do based on information in the passage.

Here is an example that could lead to a prediction:

Derek loves to go out on his boat, but he did not go out yesterday because the waves were over three feet. It is reasonable to predict that Derek would not go out on his boat in the future if the waves were over three feet.

Making predictions questions look like this:

Which of the statements below is the author most likely to agree with?

Do not choose an answer because it seems correct (it may be the correct answer to a different question) or because you agree with it. The answer must be predictable from information in the passage.

> Making a prediction is not the same as saying you are absolutely sure. In the example, Derek might go out on the boat in special circumstances. The waves might be over three feet, but a friend might be out on a boat and need help. It is possible that Derek would go out on his boat under those circumstances. However, we would not predict that based on the information in the passage.

DRAWING CONCLUSIONS

These questions ask you to assume that everything in the passage is correct and then to draw a conclusion from that information. Drawing a conclusion usually means forming a logical inference based on two pieces of information. These two pieces of information may not appear near one another in the passage.

Here is a simple example that could lead to a conclusion:

Whenever Liz meets someone she knows she always talks to him or her. (The first bit of information means talking.) Later we could read that when Liz talks to someone she knows she always shakes his or her hand.

We can conclude that if Liz met someone she knows she would shake his or her hand. We can't conclude that if she shakes hands with someone, then she knows him or her. That conclusion is not supported by the passage.

Drawing conclusions questions look like this:

Based on the information in the passage, which of the following is the most reasonable conclusion?

Do not choose an answer just because it is correct or because you agree with it. The answer must flow logically from the information in the passage.

STEPS FOR ANSWERING READING QUESTIONS

This section describes five steps for answering any Core reading question. You will learn how to apply the steps, and then you will see the steps applied to sample passages. Immediately following the steps are 20 reading items with detailed explanations, and then a Targeted Reading Comprehension Test.

Reading About Reading

Reading seems to be a natural process. Reading about reading and about steps to taking reading tests can seem contrived and confusing. However, we know that these steps and techniques work.

FIVE STEPS FOR TAKING A READING TEST

During a reading test, follow these steps:

STEP 1 Skim to find the topic of each paragraph.

STEP 2 Read the question and the answers.

STEP 3 Identify the question type, if possible.

STEP 4 Eliminate incorrect answers.

STEP 5 Scan the details to find the answer.

STEP 1 **Skim to Find the Topic of Each Paragraph**
Your first job is to find the topic of each paragraph. The topic is what a paragraph or passage is about.

The topic of a paragraph is usually found in the first and last sentences. Read the first and last sentences just enough to find the topic. Use scrap paper to write the topic.

READING SENTENCES

Every sentence has a subject that tells what the sentence is about. The sentence also has a verb that tells what the subject is doing or links the subject to the complement. The sentence may also contain a complement that receives the action or describes what is being said about the subject. The words underlined in the following examples are the ones you would focus on as you preview.

1. The famous educator John Dewey founded an educational movement called progressive education.

2. Sad to say, we have learned American school children of all ages are poorly nourished.

You may occasionally encounter a paragraph or passage in which the topic can't be summarized from the first and last sentences. This type of paragraph usually contains factual information. If this happens, you will have to skim the entire paragraph.

STEP 2 **Read the Question and the Answers**

Now read the questions—one at a time. Read the answers for the question you are working on. Be sure that you understand what each question and its answers mean.

Before you answer a question, be sure you know whether it is asking for a fact or an inference. If the question asks for a fact, the correct answer will identify a main idea or supporting detail. The correct answer may also identify a cause and effect relationship among ideas or be a paraphrase or summary of parts of the passage. Look for these.

If the question asks for an inference, the correct answer will identify the author's purpose, assumptions, or attitude, and the difference between fact and the author's opinion. Look for these elements.

STEP 3 **Identify the Question Type, if possible**

Do your best to identify the question type. It may help you find the answer.

STEP 4 **Eliminate Incorrect Answers**

Read the answers and eliminate the ones that you absolutely know are incorrect. Read the answers literally. Look for words such as *always, never, must, all*. If you can find a single exception to this type of sweeping statement, then the answer cannot be correct. Eliminate it.

STEP 5 **Scan the Details to Find the Answer**

Once you have eliminated answers, compare the other answers to the passage. When you find the answer that is confirmed by the passage—stop. That is your answer choice. Follow these other suggestions for finding the correct answer.

Who Wrote This Answer?

People who write tests go to great lengths to choose a correct answer that cannot be questioned. That is what they get paid for. They are not paid to write answers that have a higher meaning or include great truths.

Test writers want to be asked to write questions and answers again. They want to avoid valid complaints from test takers like you who raise legitimate concerns about their answers.

Try to think like the person who wrote the test.

A Vague Answer Can Be Correct

How can a person write a vague answer that is correct? Think of it this way. If I wrote that a person is 6 feet 5 inches tall, you could get out a tape measure to check my facts. Since I was very specific, you are more likely to be able to prove me wrong.

On the other hand, if I write that the same person is over 6 feet tall you would be hard pressed to find fault with my statement. So my vague statement was hard to argue with. If the person in question is near 6 feet 5 inches tall, then my vague answer is most likely to be the correct one.

Do not choose an answer just because it seems more detailed or specific. A vague answer may just as likely be correct.

APPLYING THE STEPS

Let's apply the five steps to Passage A and item 1.

Passage A

> Many vocational high schools in the United States give off-site work experience to their students. Students usually work in local businesses part of the school day and attend high school the other part. These programs have made American
>
> *Line* vocational schools world leaders in making job experience available to teenage
> *(5)* students.

1. According to this paragraph, American vocational high schools are world leaders in making job experience available to teenage students because they

   Ⓐ have students attend school only part of the day.
   Ⓑ were quick to move their students to schools off-site.
   Ⓒ require students to work before they can attend the school.
   Ⓓ involve their students in cooperative education programs.
   Ⓔ involve their students in after-school part time work.

STEP 1 Skim to find the topic of each paragraph. Both the first and last sentences tell us that the topic is vocational schools and work experience.

STEP 2 Read the question and the answers. Why are American vocational high schools the world leaders in offering job experience?

STEP 3 Identify the question type, if possible. This is a supporting details question.

STEP 4 Eliminate incorrect answers. Choice (C) is obviously wrong. It has to do with work before high school. Choice (B) is also incorrect. This has to do with attending school off-site. This leaves choices (A), (D), and (E).

STEP 5 Scan the details to find the answer. Scan the details and find that parts of choice (A) are found in the passage. In choice (D) you have to know that cooperative education is another name for off-site work during school. There is no reference to the after-school work found in choice (E).

It is down to choice (A) or choice (D). Choice (A) contains only part of the reason that vocational high schools have gained such acclaim. Therefore, choice (D) is the correct answer.

Here's how to apply the steps to Passage B and item 2.

Scrap Paper   **Passage B**

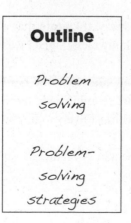

> Problem solving has become the main focus of mathematics learning. Students learn problem-solving strategies and then apply them to problems. Many tests now focus on problem solving and limit the number of computational problems. The problem-solving movement is traced to George Polya who wrote several problem-solving books for high school teachers.
>
> Problem-solving strategies include guess and check, draw a diagram, and make a list. Many of the strategies are taught as skills, which inhibits flexible and creative thinking. Problems in textbooks can also limit the power of the strategies. However, the problem-solving movement will be with us for some time, and a number of the strategies are useful.

2. According to this passage, a difficulty with teaching problem-solving strategies is:

     Ⓐ The strategies are too difficult for children.
     Ⓑ The strategies are taught as skills.
     Ⓒ The strategies are in textbooks.
     Ⓓ The strategies are part of a movement.
     Ⓔ Problem solving is for high school teachers.

STEP 1 Skim to find the topic of each paragraph. The topic of the first paragraph is problem solving. You find the topic in both the first and last sentences. Write the topic next to the paragraph. The topic for the second paragraph is problem-solving strategies. Write the topics on scrap paper.

Now look at the question. If the question is about problem solving "in general," start looking in the first paragraph for the answer. If the question is about strategies, start looking in the second paragraph for the answer.

STEP 2 Read the question and the answers. The answer will be a difficulty with teaching problem solving.

STEP 3 Identifying the question type, if possible. This is a supporting details question.

STEP 4 Eliminate incorrect answers. Choice (A) cannot be right because difficulty is not mentioned in the passage. Choice (E) cannot be correct because it does not mention strategies at all. That leaves choices (B), (C), and (D) to consider.

STEP 5 Scan the details to find the answer. The question asks about strategies so look immediately to the second paragraph for the answer. The correct answer is (B). Choice (C) is not correct because the passage does not mention strategies in textbooks. There is no indication that choice (D) is correct.

The correct answer is choice (B).

Try Them Out

Here are passages with a full range of question types. You will see completely different examples on the Core you take.

You are looking for the best answer from among the ones listed, even if you can think of a better answer. The correct answer is supported by the passage. You should not pick an answer just because it is true or because you agree with it.

You can look back to remind yourself what the question types are. You cannot look ahead at the answers. Looking ahead at the answers will deny you important experiences, and it may well hurt your performance on the Core.

Use scrap paper to jot down the answers you know are incorrect. Select the correct answer.

Apply the five steps to these practice passages. Darken the letter of the correct answer. Follow the directions given below. The answers to these questions are found on pages 33–39. Do not look at the answers until you complete all 20 items.

USE THIS PASSAGE TO ANSWER QUESTIONS 3–7.

Today's students have hand-held calculators that can graph one or even many equations. Students can even type in several equations and the calculator will "solve" them. This is the best way just to see a plotted graph quickly.

Line
(5) This is the worst way to learn about graphing and equations. The calculator can't tell the students anything about the process of graphing and does not teach them how to plot a graph.

Left to this electronic graphing process, students will not have the hands-on experience needed to see the patterns and symmetry that characterize graphing and equations. They may become too dependent on the calculator and be unable to reason *(10)* effectively about equations and the process of graphing.

It may be true that graphing and solving equations is taught mechanically in some classrooms. There is also something to be said for these electronic devices, which give students the opportunity to try out several graphs and solutions quickly before deciding on a final solution.

(15) For all their electronic accuracy and patience, these graphing calculators cannot replace the process of graphing and solving equations on your own. For mastery of equations and graphing comes not just from seeing the graph automatically displayed on a screen, but also comes from a hands-on involvement with graphing.

3. The main idea of the passage is that

Ⓐ a child can be good at graphing equations only through hands-on experience.
Ⓑ teaching approaches for graphing equations should be improved.
Ⓒ accuracy and patience are the keys to effective graphing instruction.
Ⓓ the new graphing calculators have limited ability to teach students about graphing.
Ⓔ graphing calculators provide one of the best possible ways to practice graphing equations.

4. According to this passage, what negative impact will graphing calculators have on students who use them?

Ⓐ They will not have experience with four-function calculators.
Ⓑ They will become too dependent on the calculator.
Ⓒ They can quickly try out several graphs before coming up with a final answer.
Ⓓ They will get too much hands-on experience with calculators.
Ⓔ The teachers will not know how to use the electronic calculator because they use mechanical aids.

5. According to the passage, which of the following is a major drawback of the graphing calculator?

Ⓐ It graphs many equations with their solutions.
Ⓑ It does not give students hands-on experience with graphing.
Ⓒ It does not give students hands-on experience with calculators.
Ⓓ This electronic method interferes with the mechanical method.
Ⓔ It does not replace the patient teacher.

6. The passage includes information that would answer which of the following questions?

Ⓐ What are the shortcomings of graphing and solving equations as it sometimes takes place?
Ⓑ How many equations can you type into a graphing calculator?
Ⓒ What hands-on experience should students have as they learn about graphing equations?
Ⓓ What is the degree of accuracy and speed that can be attained by a graphing calculator?
Ⓔ What level of ability is needed to show mastery of equations and graphing?

7. The description of a graphing calculator found in this passage tells about which of the following?
Select all that apply.

A The equations that can be graphed
B The approximate size of the calculator
C The advantages of the graphing calculator

On July 2, 1937, during her famed journey across the Pacific Ocean to complete flying around the world, noted aviator Amelia Earhart disappeared. Speculation remains about the cause and validity of her elusive disappearance, and Earhart's whereabouts remain a mystery. As one of the first female aviators to attempt an around-the-world
Line
(5) flight, Earhart solidified her reputation as one of the most daring women of her day. Having achieved a series of record-breaking flights—such as surpassing the women's altitude record of 14,000 feet in 1922 and venturing solo across the Atlantic Ocean in 1932—this trailblazer not only paved the way for women aviators but advocated independence, self-reliance, and equal rights for all women.

(10) Billed as the "First Lady of the Air" or "Lady Lindy" (Charles A. Lindbergh's female counterpart), Earhart challenged gender barriers and influenced women's position in the nascent aviation industry. She was a founding member and president of the Ninety-Nines, an international organization of women pilots. In 1932, after completing her solo flight across the Atlantic Ocean, President Herbert Hoover
(15) presented Earhart with the National Geographic Society's gold medal, an honor never before bestowed to a woman. She was also the first woman to receive the National Aeronautical Association's honorary membership.

8. Which of the following is most likely an assumption made by the author of this passage?

    Ⓐ Amelia Earhart was an American spy captured by Japanese forces.
    Ⓑ Charles Lindbergh would not have disappeared had he been the pilot on this mission.
    Ⓒ Amelia Earhart's daring nature caused her to crash on her flight.
    Ⓓ Amelia Earhart may not have died when she disappeared.
    Ⓔ Amelia Earhart may have flown too high and passed out, leading to her disappearance.

9. Which of the following statements, if added to the passage, would weaken the author's statement that Amelia Earhart's whereabouts are unknown?

    Ⓐ A strong storm was reported by a ship along the flight route that Amelia Earhart was following.
    Ⓑ The last person to see Amelia Earhart's plane, a Lockheed Vega, reported that the plane seemed very heavy as it lifted off.
    Ⓒ A search pilot reported signs of recent human habitation on a deserted island along the flight route that Amelia Earhart took.
    Ⓓ Further research on the radio in Amelia Earhart's plane revealed that all the radios in that version of the Lockheed Vega often failed.
    Ⓔ Fred Noonan, a noted aviator and navigator, was with Amelia Earhart as she made this flight across the Pacific Ocean.

10. The author's attitude toward Amelia Earhart can best be described as

    Ⓐ condescending.

    Ⓑ reverential.

    Ⓒ unsettled.

    Ⓓ abhorrent.

    Ⓔ impartial.

11. This passage indicates that Earhart would most likely agree with which of the following?

    Ⓐ Good planning is the secret to any successful endeavor.

    Ⓑ Experience is the quality that is most likely to serve you well in times of trouble.

    Ⓒ Life is full of unexpected events and outcomes.

    Ⓓ The recognition of America's leaders is the best reward for effort.

    Ⓔ In this life, a woman is as capable of success and achievement as any man.

———————————

USE THIS PASSAGE TO ANSWER QUESTIONS 12–18.

Thousands of different types of rocks and minerals have been found on Earth. Most rocks at Earth's surface are formed from only eight elements (oxygen, silicon, aluminum, iron, magnesium, calcium, potassium, and sodium), but these elements are combined in a number of ways to make rocks that are very different.

Line

(5)   Rocks are continually changing. Wind and water wear them down and carry bits of rock away; the tiny particles accumulate in a lake or ocean and harden into rock again. Scientists say the oldest rock ever found is more than 3.9 billion years old. Earth itself is at least 4.5 billion years old, but rocks from the beginning of Earth's history have changed so much from their original form that they have become new

(10)   kinds of rock.

Rock-forming and rock-destroying processes have been active for billions of years. Today, in the Guadalupe Mountains of western Texas, you find limestone, a sedimentary rock, that was a coral reef in a tropical sea about 250 million years ago. Half Dome in Yosemite Valley, California, about 8,800 feet above sea level, is composed of

(15)   quartz monzonite, an igneous rock that solidified several thousand feet deep in the ground. A simple rock collection captures the enormous sweep of the history of our planet.

12. What is the main purpose of this passage?

Ⓐ To provide information that rocks are continually changing

Ⓑ To emphasize that Earth is made of rock from the tallest mountains to the floor of the deepest ocean

Ⓒ To examine that there are thousands of different types of rocks and minerals that have been found on Earth

Ⓓ To prove that in a simple rock collection of a few dozen samples, one can capture an enormous sweep of the history of our planet and the process that formed it

Ⓔ To provide information on the oldest rock that has ever been found dating back more than 3.9 billion years ago

13. Which of the following words or phrases is the best substitute for the word *accumulate* in line 6?

Ⓐ Disperse

Ⓑ Renew

Ⓒ Break down

Ⓓ Gather

Ⓔ Float

14. According to the passage, most rocks at Earth's surface are formed from

Ⓐ oxygen, silicon, calcium, and potassium.

Ⓑ aluminum, iron, and magnesium.

Ⓒ one of eight elements.

Ⓓ elements combined in a number of ways.

Ⓔ what were once coral reefs.

15. What is the author's reason for mentioning that rocks are continually changing?

Ⓐ To make the reading more technical

Ⓑ To provide a visual description

Ⓒ To provide the reader with a physical description of rocks

Ⓓ To allow the reader to have a clearer understanding about the formation of rocks

Ⓔ To provide information to the reader as to why all rocks look different

16. Which of the following is the best description of the organization of this passage?

 Ⓐ An overall description is followed by some specific examples.

 Ⓑ A discussion of one topic ends up with a discussion of an entirely different topic.

 Ⓒ Specific examples are given followed by an explanation of those examples.

 Ⓓ A significant question is raised followed by possible answers to that question.

 Ⓔ A theory is expressed and then examples and counterexamples of that theory are presented.

17. It can be reasonably inferred from the passage that the author

 Ⓐ believes only what the author can personally observe.

 Ⓑ is open to accepting theories presented by others.

 Ⓒ believes science is a mixture of fact and fiction.

 Ⓓ knows how Earth itself was created.

 Ⓔ has an advanced degree in geology.

18. Which of the following statements from the paragraph most convincingly supports the main idea?

 Ⓐ Thousands of different types of rocks and minerals have been found on Earth.

 Ⓑ Today, in the Guadalupe Mountains of western Texas you find limestone, a sedimentary rock, that was a coral reef in a tropical sea about 250 million years ago.

 Ⓒ Wind and water wear them down and carry bits of rock away; the tiny particles accumulate in a lake or ocean and again harden into rock.

 Ⓓ Earth itself is at least 4.5 billion years old.

 Ⓔ A simple rock collection captures the enormous sweep of the history of our planet.

Line

(5)

(10)

The potential for instruction provided by cable television in the classroom is eclipsed by the number of educational practitioners who remain uninformed about the concept or who lack proficiency in the use of protocols and strategies necessary to optimize its benefits. Teachers, trainers, and educational administrators nationwide would benefit from structured opportunities, rather than trial and error, to learn how to maximize the potential of the medium. Cable television in the classroom can introduce real events into instruction by reporting the news from a perspective with which young people are familiar. Broadcasts received by television satellite can present issues as opportunities in which young people can play an active role, rather than as overwhelming problems no one can solve. By incorporating current events and televised symposia learners are exposed to perspectives beyond their teacher's own view and can explore truth without sensationalism or condescension. Thus cable television access in the classroom allows learners to make informed judgments about the content under study.

19. Which of the following conclusions can reasonably be drawn from this passage?

(A) The potential for television in the classroom is more important than the opposition against it.

(B) A lack of understanding of appropriate strategies is the reason cable television in the classroom has not been fully implemented.

(C) The reason cable television in the classroom has not been accepted goes beyond being informed about this instructional tool.

(D) Cable television in the classroom ensures that the teacher's views will receive his or her appropriate attention.

(E) Learners have the ability and the capability, themselves, to make informed decisions about any content area that might be under study.

20. If the analysis of this passage were applied to introducing a completely different type of vacuum cleaner, one might infer that success would most likely be a function of

(A) effectiveness.

(B) cost.

(C) name.

(D) size.

(E) advertising.

Answers Explained

Do not read this section until you have completed the practice passages. Here's how to apply the steps. Use this Step 1 for items 3–7. Complete your own Step 1 for the remaining passages.

STEP 1 Skim to find the topic of each paragraph. Write the topic on scrap paper. Suggested topics are shown next to the following selection. Your topics do not have to be identical, but they should accurately reflect the paragraph's content.

Scrap Paper

> ## Outline
>
> 1. *Graphing Calc.*
>
> 2. *Problem w/ Graphing Calc.*
>
> 3. *Why It's a Problem*
>
> 4. *Good Points*

Passage

Today's students have hand-held calculators that can graph one or even many equations. Students can even type in several equations and the calculator will "solve" them. This is the best way to just see a plotted graph quickly.

This is the worst way to learn about graphing and equations. The calculator can't tell the students anything about the process of graphing and does not teach them how to plot a graph.

Left to this electronic graphing process, students will not have the hands-on experience needed to see the patterns and symmetry that characterize graphing and equations. They may become too dependent on the calculator and be unable to reason effectively about equations and the process of graphing.

It may be true that graphing and solving equations is taught mechanically in some classrooms. There is also something to be said for these electronic devices, which give students the opportunity to try out several graphs and solutions quickly before deciding on a final solution.

For all their electronic accuracy and patience, these graphing calculators cannot replace the process of graphing and solving equations on your own. Mastery of equations and graphing comes not just from seeing the graph automatically displayed on a screen, but also from a hands-on involvement with graphing.

Apply Steps 2 through 5 to each of the questions.

3. **STEP 2** Read the question and the answers. You have to identify the main idea of the passage. This is a very common question on reading tests. Remember that the main idea is what the writer is trying to say or communicate in the passage.

STEP 3 Identify the question type, if possible. This is a main idea question.

STEP 4 Eliminate incorrect answers. Choices (B) and (C) are not correct. Choice (C) is not at all correct based on the passage. Even though choice (B) may be true, it does not reflect what the writer is trying to say in this passage. Choice (E) is also not the correct answer. You might be able to imply this answer from the paragraph, but it is not the main idea.

STEP 5 Scan the details to find the answer. As we review the details we see that both choice (A) and choice (D) are stated or implied in the passage. A scan of the details alone does not reveal which is the main idea. You must determine that on your own.

The correct answer is choice (D). The author certainly believes that choice (A) is true, but uses this point to support the main idea.

4. **STEP 2** Read the question and the answers. This is a straightforward comprehension question. What negative impact will calculators have on students who use them? The second and third paragraphs have topics related to problems with calculators. You will probably find the answer there.

STEP 3 Identify the question type, if possible. This is a main idea question.

STEP 4 Eliminate incorrect answers. Choice (E) is obviously incorrect. The question asks about students. This answer is about teachers. Choice (C) is not a negative impact of graphing calculators. Scan the details to find the correct answer from choices (A), (B), and (D).

STEP 5 Scan the details to find the answer. The only detail that matches the question is in paragraph 3. The author says that students may become too dependent on the calculators. That is the answer.

Choice (B) is the correct answer.

5. **STEP 2** Read the question and the answers. This is another straightforward comprehension question. This question is somewhat different from Question 2. Notice that the question asks for a drawback of the calculator. It does not ask for something that is wrong with the calculator itself. The topics indicate that we will probably find the answer in paragraph 1 or paragraph 2.

STEP 3 Identify the question type, if possible. This is a supporting details question.

STEP 4 Eliminate incorrect answers. Choice (C) is obviously wrong. Graphing calculators do give students hands-on experience with calculators. Be careful! It is easy to mix up choice (C) with choice (B). Choice (A) is a strength of the calculator and is also incorrect. Now move on to the details.

STEP 5 Scan the details to find the answer. Choices (B), (D), and (E) remain. The details in paragraph 2 reveal that the correct answer is choice (B).

Choice (B) is the only absolutely correct answer.

6. **STEP 2** Read the question and the answers. This is yet another type of reading comprehension question. You are asked to identify the questions that could be answered from the passage.

STEP 3 Identify the question type, if possible. This is an evaluate supporting details question.

STEP 4 Eliminate incorrect answers. Choices (B), (D), and (E) are not correct. None of this information is included in the passage. This is not to say that these questions, particularly choice (E), are not important. Rather it means that the answers to these questions are not found in this passage.

STEP 5 Scan the details to find the answer. Both choices (A) and (C) are discussed in the passage. However, a scan of the details reveals that the answer to choice (C) is not found in the passage. The passage mentions hands-on experience, but it does not mention what types of hands-on experience students should have. There is an answer for choice (A). Graphing is taught mechanically in some classrooms.

Choice (A) is the correct answer. One are more of these answers are correct. answered from the passage. The answer is not related to the writer's main idea, and this may make it more difficult to answer.

7. **STEP 2** Read the question and the answers. One or more of these answers are correct. You are given several choices. You must decide which combination of these choices is the absolutely correct answer.

STEP 3 Identify the question type, if possible. This is an evaluate supporting details question.

STEP 4 Eliminate incorrect answers. You can eliminate choice (A). It is not addressed in the passage.

STEP 5 Scan the details to find which of the original three statements is (are) true.

     A No, there is no description of which equations can be graphed.
     B Yes, paragraph 1 mentions that the calculators are hand-held.
     C Yes, paragraph 4 mentions the advantages.

Both choices (B) and (C) are correct.

8. **STEP 2** Read the question and the answers. You have to identify an assumption.

STEP 3 Identify the question type, if possible. This is an assumption question.

STEP 4 Eliminate incorrect answers. Always try to eliminate at least one answer. Eliminate choice (A). There is nothing here at all about this assumption.

STEP 5 Scan the details to find the answer. Choice (D) is the correct answer. The author assumes that Amelia Earhart may not have died when she disappeared. The author never states it, but the author questions the validity of her disappearance and calls her whereabouts a mystery. Although choice (A) is a popular theory among some people, there is no mention of this assumption in this passage. There is nothing in the passage about Lindbergh, other than that Amelia Earhart was "Lady Lindy" (Charles A. Lindbergh's female counterpart), so eliminate choice (B). Choices (C) and (E) are incorrect because there is nothing in the passage to indicate any reason for her disappearance.

9. **STEP 2** Read the question and the answers. You have to find the statement that would weaken the author's argument that Earhart's whereabouts are unknown. Remember weaken does not mean disprove.

STEP 3 Identify the question type, if possible. This is an evaluate supporting details question.

STEP 4 Eliminate incorrect answers. Eliminate choices (B) and (D) because each contains information about why Earhart's plane may have encountered trouble but not about her whereabouts.

STEP 5 Scan the details to find the answer. The reports of human habitation on a deserted island (choice (C)) is the only statement that would weaken that argument, although it would not by itself disprove the statement. The other statements are incorrect: A strong storm (choice (A)), a heavy plane (choice (B)), a malfunctioning radio (choice (D)), and a second member of her crew (choice (E)) do not provide any information about her whereabouts. Do not be tempted by the specific information about Earhart's plane found in choices (B) and (D).

10. **STEP 2** Read the question and the answers. You have to understand how the author feels about Earhart.

STEP 3 Identify the question type, if possible. This is an attitude question—it says it is.

STEP 4 Eliminate incorrect answers. Eliminate choice (D), abhorrent. It is a negative word and the author thinks the world of Earhart.

STEP 5 Scan the details to find the answer. Choice (B) is correct. Reverential means to honor and respect. That is obviously how the author feels toward her. Choice (A) is incorrect because condescending means to look down on, someone or something. Choice (C) is incorrect because the author was settled in his opinion of Earhart. Choice (D) was eliminated. Abhorrent means to have strong negative feelings. Choice (E) is incorrect because impartial means to have no strong views about someone. This author had very positive feelings about Earhart.

11. **STEP 2** Read the question and the answers. You have to identify what Earhart would say about something.

STEP 3 Identify the question type, if possible. This is a making predictions question.

STEP 4 Eliminate incorrect answers. Eliminate choice (D). This passage is mainly about Earhart's disappearance, not about recognition or rewards.

STEP 5 Scan the details to find the answer. Choice (C) is correct. This passage is about Earhart's disappearance, and if she were able to draw anything from that, it would be the uncertainty of life. The other choices are incorrect because none of them meant anything on that fateful day that she likely crashed into the Pacific Ocean. Be careful of the emotional appeal of choice (E). This is true, but it is not what we would predict from this passage.

12. **STEP 2** Read the question and the answers. You have to identify which answer best summarizes the main purpose of the passage. Why was it written? Save lots of time by reading the question and answers before looking at the details in the passage.

STEP 3 Identify the question type, if possible. This is a main purpose question.

STEP 4 Eliminate incorrect answers. Choice (D) is clearly wrong. The main purpose is not about rock collections. You might be able to eliminate more, but you can be sure of this one. If you had to guess, eliminating just this one answer would increase the odds that you will guess correctly.

STEP 5 Scan the details to find the answer. The answer to this question is choice (C) because most of the passage examines that there are thousands of different types of rocks and minerals that have been found on Earth. Choice (A) is incorrect because the passage was not written primarily to discuss that rocks continually change. Choices (B) and (E) are incorrect because each states facts found in the passage that are too detailed to be the main purpose.

13. **(STEP 2)** Read the question and the answers. You have to determine the meaning of a word, perhaps from the context.

(STEP 3) Identify the question type, if possible. This is a vocabulary question.

(STEP 4) Eliminate incorrect answers. Eliminate choice (C) because "accumulate" does not mean "break down."

(STEP 5) Scan the details to find the answer. Choice (D) is the correct answer. If you accumulate something, you gather it. You can actually tell from the context that choice (A) is incorrect because disperse means the opposite of accumulate. It is an antonym. Choice (B) is incorrect because bits of rock do not renew themselves; rather they combine with other bits of rock. Choice (C) was eliminated because break down also means the opposite of accumulate. The rocks broke down before they accumulated. Choice (E) is incorrect because floating is not related to accumulating. Some of the bits of rock may have floated on the surface of a lake when they first landed there, but that had nothing to do with the accumulation.

14. **(STEP 2)** Read the question and the answers. You have to find information in the passage.

(STEP 3) Identify the question type, if possible. This is a supporting details question.

(STEP 4) Eliminate incorrect answers. Eliminate choices (A) and (B) because each of them is just a partial list of the elements from which most rocks are formed. Correctly eliminating two choices means you would have a one-third chance of guessing correctly instead of a one-fifth chance. That is a big difference if you had to guess.

(STEP 5) Scan the details to find the answer. The correct answer is choice (D), because the passage states that elements are combined in a number of ways to form rocks. Choices (A) and (B) were eliminated because they do not list all of the eight elements from the passage. Choice (C) is incorrect because the passage says that rocks are a combination of elements. Choice (E) is incorrect because a rock may have been formed from a coral reef, but that is not the way most rocks near Earth's surface were formed.

15. **(STEP 2)** Read the question and the answers. You have to find the author's purpose for writing something in the passage.

(STEP 3) Identify the question type, if possible. This is a purpose question.

(STEP 4) Eliminate incorrect answers. Eliminate all the choices except for choice (E). If you know that all the other choices are incorrect, then you can be sure choice (E) is correct. Eliminate choice (A) because the author does not mention that all rocks are continually changing, primarily to make the reading more technical. Eliminate choices (B) and (C) because telling the reader that rocks are continually changing does not give him/her a visual or a physical description of rocks. Eliminate choice (D) because the statement that rocks are continually changing does not give the reader a clearer understanding about the formation of rocks.

(STEP 5) Scan the details to find the answer. Choice (E) is the correct answer. All the other answer choices were eliminated, and the author mentions that rocks are continually changing to explain why rocks look different.

16. (STEP 2) Read the question and the answers. You have to look at the overall structure of the passage to see how it is organized.

(STEP 3) Identify the question type, if possible. This is an organization question.

(STEP 4) Eliminate incorrect answers. Eliminate choice (D) because no significant question is raised in the passage.

(STEP 5) Scan the details to find the answer. Choice (A) is correct. The author writes about how rocks are formed and then discusses rocks formed deep in Earth or from a coral reef. Choice (B) is incorrect because the last sentence mentions Earth's history, but there is no discussion of Earth's history. Choice (C) is incorrect because this is more or less the opposite of the actual structure of the passage. Choice (D) was eliminated because the author never raises a significant question, although some scientists may have questions about the exact dates in the second paragraph. Choice (E) is incorrect because the author never presents a theory and gives no counterexamples.

17. (STEP 2) Read the question and the answers. You have to draw an inference from the passage.

(STEP 3) Identify the question type, if possible. This is an inference question.

(STEP 4) Eliminate incorrect answers. Eliminate choice (C) because there is nothing here to suggest that science is a mixture of fact and fiction.

(STEP 5) Scan the details to find the answer. Choice (B) is correct. In the second paragraph the author presents a theory from other scientists about the age of rocks found on Earth. Choice (A) is incorrect because most of what the author presents can't be personally observed. Choice (C) was eliminated because there is nothing to indicate that the author has presented or believes that science includes both fact and fiction. Choice (D) is incorrect because the author presents information about the age of rocks and the age of Earth but nothing about how the planet was formed. Choice (E) is incorrect because there is no evidence that the author has any advanced degree.

18. (STEP 2) Read the question and the answers. You have to identify the statement that is most likely an opinion.

(STEP 3) Identify the question type, if possible. This is an evaluate supporting details question.

(STEP 4) Eliminate incorrect answers. The main idea is "examining the many types of rocks and minerals found on Earth." Eliminate choices (B) and (C). Neither rocks in the Guadalupe Mountains nor wind and water wear address the main idea. Further eliminate choices (D) and (E). The Earth's age and rock collections are similarly unrelated to the main idea.

(STEP 5) Scan the details to find the answer. That leaves choice (A), which discusses the many types of rocks found on Earth. Choice (A) is the best answer among the choices given.

19. (STEP 2) Read the question and the answers. You have to look for several elements in the passage that will lead to a conclusion.

(STEP 3) Identify the question type, if possible. This is a conclusion question.

STEP 4 Eliminate incorrect answers. Eliminate choice (D) because the passage says learners will be exposed to "perspectives beyond their teacher's own view."

STEP 5 Scan the details to find the answer. Choice (C) is the correct answer. The first five lines of the passage mention both technical ability and familiarity as the reasons cable television in the classroom has not been accepted. We use those two bits of information to draw the conclusion. Choice (A) is incorrect because the beginning of the passage says the opposite—that acceptance of cable television in the classroom is eclipsed by the number of educational practitioners who do not use it. Choice (B) is incorrect because the passage mentions other reasons beyond strategies as why cable television in the classroom has not been accepted. Choice (D) was eliminated because the passage mentions that cable television in the classroom will be exposed to views other than the teacher's view. Choice (E) is incorrect because the passage says the opposite of this. "Cable television access in the classroom allows learners to make informed judgments about the content under study."

20. **STEP 2** Read the question and the answers. You have to decide how to use the information from the passage to predict an outcome in a different setting.

STEP 3 Identify the question type, if possible. This is an inference question.

STEP 4 Eliminate incorrect answers. Eliminate everything but choice (E). The main point of the passage is that teachers do not use cable television in the classroom because they do not know about it and do not know how to use it. One part of that message, to infer the success of introducing a new type of vacuum cleaner, is that you have to get the word out. One way to do that is through advertising. You can eliminate all the other choices, which would be important after the new vacuum cleaner is introduced.

STEP 5 Scan the details to find the answer. Choice (E) is the best answer. Advertising is the only choice from among those given that is supported by this passage.

This targeted test is designed to help you further practice the strategies presented in this chapter. Do not identify the question types. (Answers on page 48.)

Directions: Mark your choice, and then check your answers.

USE THIS PASSAGE TO ANSWER QUESTIONS 1 AND 2.

While becoming a teacher, I spent most of my time with books. I read books about the subjects I would teach in school and books that explained how to teach the subjects. As a new teacher, I relied on books to help my students learn. But I learned, and now the basis for my teaching is to help students apply what they have learned to the real world.

1. We can predict that which of the following would most likely be the next line of this passage?

   Ⓐ The world is a dangerous and intimidating place; be wary of it.
   Ⓑ Children should be taught to seek whatever the world has to offer.
   Ⓒ A teacher has to be in the world, not just study about the world.
   Ⓓ But you can't forget about books.
   Ⓔ Teaching is like learning.

2. Which of the following is best inferred from this passage?

   Ⓐ Teaching art is very rewarding.
   Ⓑ Children learn a lot from field trips.
   Ⓒ There is much to be said for teachers who think of their students' experiences first.
   Ⓓ Firsthand experiences are important for a teacher's development.
   Ⓔ You never know what you will end up teaching.

USE THIS PASSAGE TO ANSWER QUESTIONS 3–5.

The American alligator is found in Florida and Georgia, and has also been reported in other states, including North and South Carolina. Weighing in at more than 400 pounds, the length of an adult alligator is twice that of its tail. Adult alligators eat fish and small mammals while young alligators prefer insects, shrimp, and frogs.

An untrained person may mistake a crocodile for an alligator. Crocodiles are found in the same areas as alligators and both have prominent snouts with many teeth. The crocodile has a long thin snout with teeth in both jaws. The alligator's snout is wider with teeth only in the upper jaw.

3. Which of the following would be a good title for this passage?

   Ⓐ Large Reptiles
   Ⓑ Eating Habits of Alligators
   Ⓒ The American Alligator
   Ⓓ How Alligators and Crocodiles Differ
   Ⓔ American Alligator: Endangered Species

4. Which of the following would be a way to distinguish an alligator from a crocodile?

   Ⓐ Number of teeth
   Ⓑ Shape of snout
   Ⓒ Habitat
   Ⓓ Diet
   Ⓔ Mating rituals

5. Which of the following best describes the purpose of the passage?

   Ⓐ All animals are noteworthy.
   Ⓑ Reptiles are interesting animals.
   Ⓒ To educate readers about differences in similar animals
   Ⓓ To describe the life cycle of wetland creatures
   Ⓔ To provide information about the American alligator

Remove the jack from the trunk. Set the jack under the car. Use the jack to raise the car. Remove the lug nuts. Remove the tire and replace it with the doughnut. Reset the lug nuts loosely and use the jack to lower the chassis to the ground. Tighten the lug nuts once the tire is touching the ground.

6. Which of the following is the main idea of this passage?

   Ⓐ Using a jack
   Ⓑ Changing a tire on a car
   Ⓒ Maintaining a car
   Ⓓ Following directions
   Ⓔ Caring for a car

USE THIS PASSAGE TO ANSWER QUESTIONS 7 AND 8.

Farmers and animals are fighting over rain forests. The farmers are clearing the forests and driving out the animals to make room for crops. If this battle continues, the rain forest will disappear. Both the farmers and the animals will lose, and the soil in the cleared forest will form a hard crust.

Of course, there are global implications as well. Clearing the forests increases the amount of carbon dioxide in the atmosphere. The most promising solution to the problems caused by clearing the rain forests is the education of the local farmers.

7. Which information below is not provided in the passage?

Ⓐ Reasons the animals are being run out
Ⓑ Reasons the farmers need more land
Ⓒ Effects of lost rain forests
Ⓓ Ways that people can help globally
Ⓔ Ways that people can help locally

8. What most likely would the attitude of the author be about wildlife conservation?

Ⓐ All animals must fend for themselves.
Ⓑ Damage to Earth affects both people and animals.
Ⓒ Our greatest resource is education.
Ⓓ Testing products on animals is a practice that should be outlawed.
Ⓔ Animals and people should have equal rights.

I love gingerbread cookies, which are flavored with ginger and molasses. I can remember cold winter days when my brother and I huddled around the fire eating gingerbread cookies and sipping warm apple cider. In those days, gingerbread cookies came in many shapes and sizes. When you eat a gingerbread cookie today, you have to bite a "person's" head off.

9. Why did the author of the passage above put quotes around the word *person*?

Ⓐ To emphasize the difference between gingerbread cookies that appear as people rather than windmills
Ⓑ Because gingerbread cookies often don't look like people
Ⓒ To emphasize the most popular current shape of gingerbread cookies
Ⓓ To emphasize this word has a figurative meaning
Ⓔ To emphasize how our culture now puts more importance on people than on things

The Frogs Who Wanted a King

The frogs lived a happy life in the pond. They jumped from lily pad to lily pad and sunned themselves without a care. But a few of the frogs were not satisfied with this relaxed and enjoyable life. These frogs thought that they needed a king to rule them. So they sent a note to the god Jupiter requesting that he appoint a king.

Jupiter was amused by this request. In a good-natured response, Jupiter threw a log into the pond, which landed with a big splash. All the frogs jumped to safety. Some time passed and one frog started to approach the log, which lay still in the pond. When nothing happened, the other frogs jumped on the floating giant, treating it with disdain.

The frogs were not satisfied with such a docile king. They sent another note to Jupiter asking for a strong king to rule over them. Jupiter was not amused by this second request and he was tired of the frogs' complaints.

So Jupiter sent a stork. The stork immediately devoured every frog in sight. The few surviving frogs gave Mercury a message to carry to Jupiter pleading for Jupiter to show them mercy.

Jupiter was very cold. He told Mercury to tell the frogs that they were responsible for their own problems. They had asked for a king to rule them and they would have to make the best of it.

10.   Which of the following morals fits the passage?

    Ⓐ Leave well enough alone.
    Ⓑ Familiarity breeds contempt.
    Ⓒ Slow and steady wins the race.
    Ⓓ Liberty is too high a price to pay for revenge.
    Ⓔ Misery loves company.

11.   Why did the frogs treat the log with contempt?

    Ⓐ The log was sent by Jupiter.
    Ⓑ The log floated in the pond.
    Ⓒ The log was not alive.
    Ⓓ The log could not speak.
    Ⓔ The log was not assertive.

USE THIS PASSAGE TO ANSWER QUESTIONS 12–14.

You may want to go to a park on a virgin prairie in Minnesota. The park borders Canada and is just west of the Mississippi River. The thousands of acres of park land are home to hundreds of species of birds and mammals. In the evening, a sotto wind sweeps across the prairie, creating wave-like ripples in the tall grasses. This prairie park is just one of the wonders you can see when you visit marvelous Minnesota.

12.   We can infer that this passage is most likely from a

  Ⓐ cookbook.
  Ⓑ travel brochure.
  Ⓒ hunting magazine.
  Ⓓ national parks guide.
  Ⓔ conservation organization mailing.

13.   We can conclude that this part of the United States is in the

  Ⓐ Midwest.
  Ⓑ Northeast.
  Ⓒ Southeast.
  Ⓓ Northwest.
  Ⓔ Southwest.

14.   What does the author mean by "virgin prairie"?

  Ⓐ Desolate taiga
  Ⓑ Untouched grasslands
  Ⓒ Wooded plains
  Ⓓ Indian reservation
  Ⓔ Untainted meadows

USE THIS PASSAGE TO ANSWER QUESTIONS 15–18.

There was a time in the United States when a married woman was expected to take her husband's last name. Most women still follow this practice, but things are changing. In fact, Hawaii is the only state with a law requiring a woman to take her husband's last name when she marries.

Some women may enjoy the bond it establishes with their husband, or want to be identified with their husband's professional status. Other women want to keep their own last name. They may prefer their original last name, or want to maintain their professional identity.

Some women resolve this problem by choosing a last name that hyphenates their surname and their husband's surname. This practice of adopting elements of both surnames is common in other cultures.

15. What would be the best title for this passage?

   Ⓐ Women Have Rights
   Ⓑ Determining a Woman's Name After Marriage
   Ⓒ Determining a Woman's Name After Divorce
   Ⓓ Legal Aspects of Surname Changing
   Ⓔ Hawaii's Domestic Laws

16. What can we infer about the author's position on women's rights?

   Ⓐ For women but against men
   Ⓑ For women and against equality
   Ⓒ For women and for men
   Ⓓ Against women but for men
   Ⓔ Against women and against men

17. This passage would LEAST likely be found in a

   Ⓐ online magazine.
   Ⓑ woman's corporate magazine.
   Ⓒ teen magazine aimed at girls.
   Ⓓ fitness magazine.
   Ⓔ bridal magazine.

18. What is the main idea of this passage?

   Ⓐ Women are at the mercy of the law.
   Ⓑ Women in Hawaii have no options.
   Ⓒ Women today have many options related to surnames.
   Ⓓ Children should have the same name as their mother.
   Ⓔ Men have stopped demanding that women change their names.

USE THIS PASSAGE TO ANSWER QUESTIONS 19 AND 20.

In recent years, cooperative learning, which involves students in small group activities, has gained popularity as an instructional approach. Cooperative learning provides students with an opportunity to work on projects presented by the teacher. This type of learning emphasizes group goals, cooperative learning, and shared responsibility. All students must contribute in order for the group to be successful.

19. What is the main idea of this passage?

   Ⓐ To show different learning styles
   Ⓑ To examine the best way to teach
   Ⓒ To explain why cooperative learning is the best method for eliminating classrooms
   Ⓓ To illustrate the method of cooperative learning
   Ⓔ To show the role of the teacher in a cooperative learning environment

20. According to this passage, what would be a good definition of cooperative learning?

Ⓐ An instructional arrangement in which children work in small groups in a manner that promotes student responsibility

Ⓑ An instructional arrangement in which the teacher pairs two students in a tutor–tutee relationship to promote learning of academic skills or subject content

Ⓒ An instructional arrangement consisting of three to seven students that represents a major format for teaching academic skills

Ⓓ An instructional arrangement that is appropriate for numerous classroom activities such as show and tell, discussing interesting events, taking a field trip, or watching a movie

Ⓔ An instructional arrangement in which the teaching responsibilities are shared

---

USE THESE PASSAGES TO ANSWER QUESTIONS 21 AND 22.

I

Extraterrestrial life means life on or from a planet other than Earth. Life can be as simple as bacteria. Scientists believe that bacteria are the ancestors of the first forms of life on Earth beginning about 3.5 billion years ago. Bacteria are microscopic, and for the first 3 billion years or so the first life on Earth were microscopic.

Most scientists agree that the universe has been around three or four times longer than Earth. Humans as we know them have been around for 100,000 years or so. That means similar life could have developed in the universe billions of years ago. When you consider this very low threshold for the presence of life, and scientists' estimate that there may be billions of earth-like planets, it's just hard to believe that life does not exist elsewhere.

II

I've been reading a lot about how likely it is that life exists on other planets. Scientists use probability to arrive at the small percentage chance that life exists elsewhere. The problem is that the same probability calculations could be used to prove life elsewhere is unlikely. So, as nice as it would be, I am unconvinced.

Think of it this way. You arrive at the probability of something by multiplying. I begin with the probability that extraterrestrial life has actually been discovered. That's zero. And no matter what you multiply the result will always be zero.

I know that Earth is a young planet by galactic standards. But to argue Earth's life processes are replicated elsewhere has to be assumed as false until it is proven true. So I'll know there is life beyond Earth when I see it. I'm not holding my breath.

21. Which of the following best describes the relationship of the passages?

Ⓐ Both support the possibility of the existence of extraterrestrial life.

Ⓑ Passage 2 indicates there is no extraterrestrial life, while Passage 1 says there is such life.

Ⓒ Passage 1 is less positive about extraterrestrial life than Passage 2.

Ⓓ Passage 2 is more equivocal about extraterrestrial life than Passage 1.

Ⓔ Both use probability to demonstrate the likely existence of extraterrestrial life.

22. Which of the following when added at the end of the first passage would best strengthen the author's position?

    Ⓐ I firmly believe we will discover life on other planets.

    Ⓑ That there is no specific evidence of extraterrestrial life does not mean that it does not exist.

    Ⓒ It may be that life has been discovered but not revealed to us.

    Ⓓ In addition, a recent study discovered a sugar molecule necessary for life on a distant planet.

    Ⓔ I wish that the life I know would be proven to exist elsewhere.

USE THE BELOW INFORMATION TO ANSWER QUESTIONS 23 AND 24.

Mon	Tue	Wed	Thu	Fri	Sat
8:00 A.M. Priority Mail	8:00 A.M. Priority Mail	8:00 A.M. Priority Mail	8:00 A.M. Priority Mail	8:00 A.M. Priority Mail	8:00 A.M. Priority Mail
11:00 A.M. First Class	11:00 A.M. First Class	11:00 A.M. First Class	11:00 A.M. First Class	11:00 A.M. First Class	11:00 A.M. First Class
2:00 P.M. Parcel Post	2:00 P.M. Parcel Post	2:00 P.M. Parcel Post	2:00 P.M. Parcel Post	2:00 A.M. Parcel Post	2:00 A.M. Parcel Post
3:00 P.M. First Class	3:00 P.M. First Class	3:00 P.M. First Class	3:00 P.M. First Class	3:00 P.M. First Class	
4:00 P.M. Overnight Mail	4:00 P.M. Overnight Mail	4:00 P.M. Overnight Mail	4:00 P.M. Overnight Mail	4:00 P.M. Overnight Mail	

This chart shows the times during the week when letters and packages are sent out from the post office to the central sorting facility. The post office opens at 9:00 A.M.

Priority Mail is guaranteed to be delivered in three business days, Monday through Friday, after dropoff to reach its destination. Overnight Mail is guaranteed to be delivered the next day.

23. Which of the following best explains why Quinn would mail a Priority package on Monday when he wanted it to arrive four days later on Friday?

    Ⓐ Quinn wants to guarantee that the package arrives on time.

    Ⓑ The package will not go out until Wednesday.

    Ⓒ The package will go out too late on Monday.

    Ⓓ Overnight Mail is too expensive.

    Ⓔ There is no delivery guarantee for Parcel Post.

24. Which types of mail below, if dropped off on Monday, are sure to arrive by Friday of that week?
Choose all that apply.

    Ⓐ Priority Mail

    Ⓑ First Class Mail

    Ⓒ Overnight Mail

TARGETED READING COMPREHENSION TEST ANSWERS EXPLAINED

1. **(C)** The passage emphasizes the necessary balance of learning from books and learning from experience.

2. **(D)** The passage notes that firsthand experiences are an important part of a teacher's development.

3. **(D)** The passage gives some insight into how these two reptiles are different.

4. **(B)** The passage indicates that the alligator has a wider snout than the crocodile.

5. **(C)** The passage educates readers about differences between these similar animals.

6. **(B)** The passage gives directions for changing a tire on a car.

7. **(D)** The passage mentions global problems, but gives no advice for how people can help on a global scale.

8. **(C)** The author concludes that education of local farmers offers the most promising solution. Choice (B) is incorrect because it is not an opinion about wildlife conservation.

9. **(D)** The quotes indicate that the word *person* is not to be taken literally.

10. **(A)** Things would clearly have been better for the frogs if they had left well enough alone.

11. **(E)** The passage indicates the frogs were not satisfied with such a docile king.

12. **(B)** This passage has all the flowery and positive wording you would find in a travel guide.

13. **(A)** The passage indicates that the park is near the center of the country around the Mississippi River, so Midwest is best among the choices given to describe this area.

14. **(B)** In this context, virgin means pristine or untouched. The *prairie* is grassland.

15. **(B)** The entire passage discusses ways in which a woman can determine her name after marriage.

16. **(C)** The author is objective and takes a balanced view of women and men.

17. **(D)** The passage would be completely out of place in a fitness magazine.

18. **(C)** The passage describes a range of options for choosing a surname (last name).

19. **(D)** The passage describes cooperative learning without evaluating its effectiveness.

20. **(A)** This choice best paraphrases the passage's description of cooperative learning. The other choices include information about cooperative learning that is not found in the passsage.

21. **(D)** In this context, the term *more equivocal* means "more doubtful." The second paragraph is definitely more doubtful about extraterrestrial life than the first. The other choices are obviously incorrect, and you were likely drawn to this choice even if you did not know that *equivocal* meant "doubtful."

22. **(D)** This sentence best strengthens the author's view that "it's just hard to believe that life does not exist elsewhere" because it presents specific information that supports the possible existence of extraterrestrial life.

23. **(A)** Choice (A) is the best answer. Quinn cannot drop the package off on Tuesday because the Priority Mail goes out before the post office opens. His best option is to drop it off on Monday to go out at 8:00 A.M. on Tuesday.

24. **(A)** and **(C)** are the only types of mail with guaranteed delivery times, and each would be guaranteed for delivery by Friday. First Class Mail carries no guarantee, so while it seems certain that it would arrive by Friday of that week, we cannot be sure.

Writing (5722)

4

TEST INFO BOX		
Computer-delivered Core	40 Multiple-Choice Questions	40 minutes
	Usage	about 16–19 Items
	Sentence Correction	about 12–15 Items
	Revision in Context	about 4–8 Items
	Research Skills	about 4–6 Items
	2 Typed Responses	30 minutes each
	Argumentative	
	Informative/Explanatory	
	(Source-Based)	

USING THIS CHAPTER

This chapter prepares you to take the multiple-choice writing section and the constructed response sections of the computer-delivered Core writing test. You may want to find an English professor, teacher, or tutor to help you prepare for the constructed response section. Choose one of these approaches.

- **I WANT ALL THE WRITING HELP I CAN GET.** Skip the English review quiz and read the English review. Then go back and take the English review quiz. Review the answers to the quiz and reread the indicated parts of this chapter. Take the targeted test at the end of the chapter.

- **I WANT WRITING HELP.** Take the English review quiz. Review the answers to the quiz and read the indicated parts of the English review. Take the targeted test at the end of the chapter.

- **I WANT A QUICK WRITING REVIEW.** Take the English review quiz. Review the answers to the quiz. Then take the targeted test at the end of the chapter.

- **I WANT TO PRACTICE A WRITING TEST.** Take the targeted test at the end of the chapter.

The English review quiz assesses your knowledge of the English topics included in the Core writing test. The first part of the quiz consists of sentences to mark or correct. Make your marks or corrections right on the sentences.

This quiz is not like the real test. It will be more difficult than the questions on the actual certification test. The key is to find out what you know. It is not important to answer all these questions correctly, and do not be concerned if you miss many of them.

The answers are found immediately after the quiz. It is to your advantage not to look until you have completed the quiz. Once you have completed and marked this review quiz, use the checklist to decide which sections to study.

Directions: Correct the sentence. Some sentences may not contain errors.

1. Ron and James fathers each sent them to players camp to learn the mysterys of sport.

2. They go to the camp, ridden horses while they were there, and had write letters home.

3. James went to the water and goes skiing.

4. Ron and James called his coach. The operator never answered, and they wondered what happened to her.

5. Bob and Liz went to the store and got some groceries.

6. Dad want me to do my homework. My sisters try their best to help me.

Directions: Underline the subject in each sentence.

7. Chad's project that he showed the teacher improved his final grade.

8. The legs pumped hard, and the racer finished in first place.

9. Through the halls and down the stairs ran the harried student.

10. Where is the dog's leash?

11. Chad was sure correct, the food tastes bad and the singer sang bad but Ryan played really well. Ryan was more happy than Chad who sat closer to the stage than Ryan.

12. The larger table in the restaurant was full.

13. The waiter brought food to the table on a large tray. The waiter wanted a job in the suburbs that paid well.

14. Waiting for the food to come, the complaining began.

15. The food arrived, the eating began. The waiter stood by he was tired.

16. The coach realized that new selection rules to go into effect in May. She also knew what it would take for Ryan to be selected. Ryan winning every game. But the coach and Ryan had a common goal. To see Ryan on the team.

17. Ryan's parents wanted a success rather than see him fail. They knew he stayed in shape by eating right and exercising daily. Ryan was a person who works hard and has talent.

18. Chad was dog tired after soccer practice. He became a coach for the purpose of helping the college to the soccer finals. During the rein of the former coach, the team had miserable seasons. Chad would stay at the job until such time as he could except the first place trophy.

19. Chad was satisfied but the players were grumbling. The players wanted to practice less have more free time. The players didn't like their light blue uniforms! The finals began in May. The first game was scheduled for Tuesday May 9 at 1:00 P.M. The time for the game was here the players were on the field. Chad had the essential materials with him player list score book soccer balls and a cup of hope.

The answers are organized by review sections. Check your answers. If you miss any item in a section, check the box and review that section.

☐ Nouns, page 58

   1. Ron's and James's fathers each sent them to players' camp to learn the mysteries of sport.

☐ Verbs, page 59

   2. They went to the camp, rode horses while they were there, and wrote letters home.

☐ Tense Shift, page 61

   3. James went to the water and went skiing. James goes to the water and goes skiing.

☐ Pronouns, page 62

   4. Ron and James called (Ron's, James's, their) coach. The operator never answered, and they wondered what happened to him or her.

☐ Subject-Verb Agreement, page 65

   5. No error
   6. Dad wants me to do my homework. My sisters try their best to help me.
   7. Chad's project that he showed the teacher improved his final grade.
   8. The legs pumped hard, and the racer finished in first place.
   9. Through the halls and down the stairs ran the harried student.
10. Where is the dog's leash?

☐ Adjectives and Adverbs, page 66

11. Chad was surely correct, the food tastes bad and the singer sang badly but Ryan played really well. Ryan was happier than Chad who sat closer to the stage than Ryan did.

☐ Comparison, page 67

12. The largest table in the restaurant was full.

☐ Misplaced and Dangling Modifiers, page 69

13. The waiter brought food on a large tray to the table. The waiter wanted a well-paying job in the suburbs.
14. Waiting for the food to come, the (patrons, diners) complained. The (patrons, diners) complained about waiting for the food to come.

☐ Comma Splices and Run-on Sentences, page 70

15. The food arrived. The eating began.
The food arrived; the eating began.
The food arrived, and the eating began. The waiter stood by. He was tired.
The waiter stood by; he was tired.
The waiter stood by, and he was tired.

☐ Sentence Fragments, page 71

16. The coach realized that new selection rules <u>would</u> go into effect in May. She also knew what it would take for Ryan to be selected. Ryan <u>would have to win</u> every game. But the coach and Ryan had a common goal. <u>They wanted</u> to see Ryan on the team.

☐ Parallelism, page 72

17. Ryan's parents wanted a success rather than <u>a failure</u> (wanted success rather than failure). They knew he stayed in shape by eating right and <u>by</u> exercising daily. Ryan is a person who works hard and <u>who</u> has talent. (Ryan is hardworking and talented.)

☐ Diction, page 73

18. Chad was [delete "dog"] tired after soccer practice. He became a coach <u>to help</u> the college <u>ascend</u> to the soccer finals. During the <u>reign</u> of the former coach, the team had miserable seasons. Chad would stay at the job until [delete "such time as"] he could <u>accept</u> the first place trophy.

☐ Punctuation, page 76

19. Chad was satisfied<u>,</u> but the players were grumbling. The players wanted to practice less <u>and</u> have more free time. The players didn't like their light blue uniforms. The finals began in May. The first game was scheduled for Tuesday<u>,</u> May 9, at 1:00 P.M. The time for the game was here<u>;</u> the players were on the field. Chad had the essential materials with him<u>:</u> player list<u>,</u> score book, soccer balls<u>,</u> and a cup of hope.

RATING ESSAYS

Each essay is graded holistically by two raters, using two different 6-point scales described on pages 56 and 57. Holistic rating means that the raters base the scores on their informed sense of your essay and the elements it contains, not on a detailed analysis of the essay.

In practice, a rater often assigns an essay to top third, middle third, or bottom third. Then the rater decides which of the two scores in each third to assign to that essay. If the scores assigned to an essay differ by 2 points or more, the essay is resubmitted for further review.

Rating is not an exact science, and it is not unusual for raters to differ by 1 point. That is a bigger difference than you might think because a rating of 3 with a 1-point difference could be a rating of a 2 or 4. That range represents 50 percent of the available scores. This just emphasizes how important it is to focus your efforts on making it easy for a rater to give you a high score.

6 This is the highest score. Essays with some minor errors can still receive a score of 6.

To score a 6 an essay will:

- perceptively present the main issues under discussion, citing both paraphrased and quoted parts of the accompanying position papers
- demonstrate a clear logical development, a variety of sentence types, and effective use of language
- essentially be free of grammatical and usage errors

5 This is an excellent score, just a little short of a score of 6. Essays with some minor errors can still receive a score of 5. The absence of the word *perceptively* is the primary difference between a 6 and a 5, indicating that essays scored 6 provide more insight than essays scored 5.

To score a 5 an essay will:

- present the main issues under discussion, citing both paraphrased and quoted parts of the accompanying position papers
- demonstrate a clear logical development, a variety of sentence types, and effective use of language
- essentially be free of grammatical and usage errors

4 This essay is best characterized as satisfactory.

To score a 4 an essay will:

- satisfactorily present the main issues under discussion, citing both paraphrased and quoted parts of the accompanying position papers
- demonstrate adequate development, a variety of sentence types, and effective use of language
- may have grammatical and usage errors

3 This essay is best characterized as limited.

To score a 3 an essay will:

- partially present the main issues under discussion, citing one, or partially citing two, paraphrased and quoted parts of the accompanying position papers
- have limited development, a limited variety of sentence types, and limited use of language
- have a number of grammatical and usage errors

2 This essay is best characterized as very limited.

To score a 2 an essay will:

- not present the main issues under discussion, citing none, or inadequately mentioning one, or not mentioning any, of the accompanying position papers
- have poor development, a very limited variety of sentence types, and very limited use of language
- have a large number of grammatical and usage errors

1 This essay is best characterized as unacceptable.

To score a 1 an essay will:

- completely lack development and contain repeated and serious errors or be incomprehensible

ARGUMENTATIVE ESSAY RATING SCALE

6 This essay is extremely well written. It is the equivalent of an A on an in-class assignment. The essay addresses the question and provides clear supporting arguments, illustrations, or examples. The paragraphs and sentences are well organized and show a variety of language and syntax. The essay may contain some minor errors.

5 This essay is well written. It is the equivalent of a B+ on an in-class assignment. The essay addresses the question and provides some supporting arguments, illustrations, or examples. The paragraphs and sentences are fairly well organized and show a variety of language and syntax. The essay may contain some minor mechanical or linguistic errors.

4 This essay is fairly well written. It is the equivalent of a B on an in-class assignment. The essay adequately addresses the question and provides some supporting arguments, illustrations, or examples for some points. The paragraphs and sentences are acceptably organized and show a variety of language and syntax. The essay may contain mechanical or linguistic errors but is free from an identifiable pattern of errors.

3 This essay may demonstrate some writing ability, but it contains obvious errors. It is the equivalent of a C or C+ on an in-class assignment. The essay may not clearly address the question and may not give supporting arguments or details. The essay may show problems in diction including inappropriate word choice. The paragraphs and sentences may not be acceptably developed. There will be an identifiable pattern or grouping of errors.

2 This essay shows only the most limited writing ability. It is the equivalent of a C on an in-class assignment. It contains serious errors and flaws. This essay may not address the question, be poorly organized, or provide no supporting arguments or detail. It usually shows serious errors in diction, usage, and mechanics.

1 This essay does not demonstrate even minimal writing ability. It is the equivalent of a D or F on an in-class assignment. This essay may contain serious and continuing errors, or it may not be coherent.

This review section targets the skills and concepts you need to know in order to pass the Core writing test.

NOUNS AND VERBS

Every sentence has a subject and a predicate. Most sentences are statements. The sentence usually names something (subject). Then the sentence describes the subject or tells what that subject is doing (predicate). Sentences that ask questions also have a subject and a predicate. Here are some examples.

Subject	Predicate
The car	moved.
The tree	grew.
The street	was dark.
The forest	teemed with plants of every type and size.

Many subjects are nouns. Every predicate has a verb. A list of the nouns and verbs from the preceding sentences follows.

Noun	Verb
car	moved
tree	grew
street	was
forest, plants	teemed

Nouns

Nouns name a person, place, thing, characteristic, or concept. Nouns give a name to everything that is, has been, or will be. Here are some simple examples.

Person	Place	Thing	Characteristic	Concept (Idea)
Abe Lincoln	Lincoln Memorial	beard	mystery	freedom
judge	courthouse	gavel	fairness	justice
professor	college	chalkboard	intelligence	number

SINGULAR AND PLURAL NOUNS

Singular nouns refer to only one thing. Plural nouns refer to more than one thing. Plurals are usually formed by adding an *s* or dropping a *y* and adding *ies*. Here are some examples.

Singular	Plural
college	colleges
professor	professors
mystery	mysteries

POSSESSIVE NOUNS

Possessive nouns show that the noun possesses a thing or a characteristic. Make a singular noun possessive by adding *'s*. Here are some examples.

The *child's* sled was in the garage ready for use.
The *school's* mascot was loose again.

The rain interfered with *Jane's* vacation.

Ron's and *Doug's* fathers were born in the same year.
Ron and *Doug's* teacher kept them after school.

Make a singular noun ending in *s* possessive by adding *'s* unless the pronunciation is too difficult.

The teacher read *James's* paper several times.
The angler grabbed the *bass'* fin.

Make a plural noun possessive by adding an apostrophe (') only.

The *principals'* meeting was delayed.
The report indicated that *students'* scores had declined.

Practice

Directions: Write the plural of each singular noun.

1. sheaf
2. deer
3. fry
4. lunch
5. knee

6. lady
7. octopus
8. echo
9. foot
10. half

(Answers on page 94.)

Verbs

Some verbs are action verbs. Other verbs are linking verbs that link the subject to words that describe it. Here are some examples.

Action Verbs
Blaire *runs* down the street.
Blaire *told* her story.
The crowd *roared*.
The old ship *rusted*.

Linking Verbs
Blaire *is* tired.
The class *was* bored.
The players *were* inspired.
It *had been* a proud ship.

TENSE

A verb has three principal tenses: present tense, past tense, and future tense. The present tense shows that the action is happening now. The past tense shows that the action happened in the past. The future tense shows that something will happen. Here are some examples.

Present:	I *enjoy* my time off.
Past:	I *enjoyed* my time off.
Future:	I *will enjoy* my time off.
Present:	I *hate* working late.
Past:	I *hated* working late.
Future:	I *will hate* working late.

REGULAR AND IRREGULAR VERBS

Regular verbs follow the consistent pattern noted previously. However, a number of verbs are irregular. Irregular verbs have their own unique forms for each tense. A partial list of irregular verbs follows. The past participle is usually preceded by *had, has,* or *have.*

Some Irregular Verbs

Present Tense	Past Tense	Past Participle
am, is, are	was, were	been
begin	began	begun
break	broke	broken
bring	brought	brought
catch	caught	caught
choose	chose	chosen
come	came	come
do	did	done
eat	ate	eaten
give	gave	given
go	went	gone
grow	grew	grown
know	knew	known
lie	lay	lain
lay	laid	laid
raise	raised	raised
ride	rode	ridden
see	saw	seen
set	set	set
sit	sat	sat
speak	spoke	spoken
take	took	taken
tear	tore	torn
throw	threw	thrown
write	wrote	written

TENSE SHIFT

Verbs in a sentence should reflect time sequence. If the actions represented by the verbs happened at the same time, the verbs should have the same tense.

Incorrect:	Beth sits in the boat while she wore a life jacket.
Correct:	Beth sits in the boat while she wears a life jacket. [Both verbs are present tense.]
Correct:	Beth sat in the boat while she wore a life jacket. [Both verbs are past tense.]
Correct:	Beth wears the life jacket she wore last week. [The verbs show time order.]

Practice

> **Directions:** Correct the tense errors. Some sentences may be correct.

1. Ryan driven to Florida.

2. Refereeing soccer games is not work.

3. Chad ride to the game with his team last week.

4. Why did Mary ran her errands now?

5. I have speak to my teacher about the grade.

6. Carl paddled across the river every Saturday.

7. Blaire thrown out the ball for the players to use.

8. Joann will lost her bag if she leaves it in the store.

9. Bob is standing on a stool next to the green table.

10. Liz begun to grasp the depth of her happiness.

(Answers on page 94.)

Practice

> **Directions:** Correct the tense shifts. Some sentences may be correct.

1. Lisa already went to the North Pole but she is not going there again.

2. Dennis will take his airline tickets with him because he is leaving for his flight.

3. The runner gasped as she crosses the finish line.

4. I like to hear music so I played the clarinet.

5. Chris wanted to be a producer so he puts in long hours every day.

6. Bertha sews five hours a day because she will need her dress by next month.

7. The car turns over and then bounced down the hill.

8. Lois handed over her money because she wants to buy the computer.

9. The captain wandered out on the deck as she calls to her friends on shore.

10. The sun sets in the west as the moon rose in the east.

(Answers on page 95.)

PRONOUNS

Pronouns take the place of nouns or noun phrases and help avoid constant repetition of the noun or phrase. Here is an example.

> *Blaire* is in law school. *She* studies in *her* room every day.
> [The pronouns *she* and *her* refer to the noun *Blaire*.]

Pronoun Cases

Pronouns take three case forms: subjective, objective, and possessive. The personal pronouns *I, he, she, it, we, they, you* refer to an individual or individuals. The relative pronoun *who* refers to these personal pronouns as well as to an individual or individuals. These pronouns change their case form depending on their use in the sentence.

SUBJECTIVE PRONOUNS: I, WE, HE, IT, SHE, THEY, WHO, YOU

Use the subjective form if the pronoun is, or refers to, the subject of a clause or sentence.

> *He* and *I* studied for the Core.

> The proctors for the test were *she* and *I*.
> [*She* and *I* refer to the subject *proctors*.]

> She is the woman *who* answered every question correctly.

> I do not expect to do as well as *she*.
> [*She* is the subject for the understood verb *does*.]

OBJECTIVE PRONOUNS: ME, US, HIM, IT, HER, THEM, WHOM, YOU

Use the objective form if the pronoun is the object of a verb or preposition.

> Cathy helps both *him* and *me*.

> She wanted *them* to pass.

> I do not know *whom* she helped most.

POSSESSIVE PRONOUNS: MY, OUR, HIS, ITS, HER, THEIR, WHOSE, YOUR

Use the objective form if the pronoun shows possession.

> I recommended they reduce the time they study with *their* friends.
>
> He was the person *whose* help they relied on.

Clear Reference

The pronoun must clearly refer to a particular noun or noun phrase. Here are some examples.

Unclear

> Gary and Blaire took turns feeding *her* cat.
> [We can't tell which person *her* refers to. Blaire is involved but we do not know it is her cat.]
>
> Gary gave *it* to Blaire.
> [The pronoun *it* refers to a noun that is not stated.]

Clear

> Gary and Blaire took turns feeding Blaire's cat.
> [A pronoun doesn't work here. Use a noun.]
>
> Gary got the book and gave it to Blaire.
> [The pronoun works once the noun is stated.]

Agreement

Each pronoun must agree in number (singular or plural) and gender (male or female) with the noun it refers to. Here are some examples.

Nonagreement in Number

> The children played all day, and *she* came in exhausted.
> [*Children* is plural, but *she* is singular.]
>
> The child picked up the hat and brought *them* into the house.
> [*Hat* is singular, but *them* is plural.]

Agreement

> The children played all day, and *they* came in exhausted.
> The child picked up the hat and brought *it* into the house.

Nonagreement in Gender

> The lioness picked up *his* cub.
> [*Lioness* is female, and *his* is male.]
>
> A child must bring in a doctor's note before *she* comes to school.
> [The child may be a male or female but *she* is female.]

Agreement

> The lioness picked up *her* cub.
> A child must bring in a doctor's note before *he* or *she* comes to school.

Practice

> **Directions:** Correct the pronoun reference and case and number errors in these sentences. Some sentences may not have errors.

1. His was the best table tennis player.

2. Whom was the worst table tennis player?

3. Where are the table tennis balls?

4. Before the game everyone are going to choose teams.

5. The names of the winning teams are sent to we.

6. Them are the best table tennis team.

7. Ron and Jeff wanted to use his skates.

8. Jeff went to get them.

9. The couch looked different, depending on how they were arranged.

10. Bob won most of his table tennis games.

11. The student waited for their school bus to come.

12. Either of the buses can arrive on time if they do not break down.

13. The book was most interesting near her beginning.

14. She read the book to find her most interesting parts.

15. I am the winner; victory is ours.

16. His friends got out of the car, and he went over to talk to them.

17. The rain clouds moved toward the pool, and the swimmers tried to wish it away.

18. Was Les disappointed that him team did not win?

19. Whom has more experience than Nicky does?

20. You play better after you have experience.

(Answers on page 95.)

SUBJECT-VERB AGREEMENT

Singular and Plural

Singular nouns take singular verbs. Plural nouns take plural verbs. Singular verbs usually end in *s*, and plural verbs usually do not. Here are some examples.

Singular: My father wants me home early.
Plural: My parents want me home early.

Singular: Ryan runs a mile each day.
Plural: Ryan and Chad run a mile each day.

Singular: She tries her best to do a good job.
Plural: Liz and Ann try their best to do a good job.

Correctly Identify Subject and Verb

The subject may not be in front of the verb. In fact, the subject may not be anywhere near the verb. Say the subject and the verb to yourself. If it makes sense, you probably have it right.

Words may come between the subject and the verb.

Chad's final exam score, which he showed to his mother, improved his final grade.

The verb is *improved*. The word *mother* appears just before *improved*.

Is this the subject? Say it to yourself. [Mother improved the grade.]

That cannot be right. *Score* must be the subject. Say it to yourself. [Score improved the grade.] That is right. *Score* is the subject, and *improved* is the verb.

The racer running with a sore arm finished first.

Say it to yourself. [Racer finished first.] *Racer* is the noun, and *finished* is the verb.

It would not make any sense to say the arm finished first.

The verb may come before the subject.

Over the river and through the woods romps the merry leprechaun.

Leprechaun is the subject, and *romps* is the verb. [Think: Leprechaun romps.]

Where are the car keys?

Keys is the subject, and *are* is the verb. [Think: The car keys are where?]

Examples of Subject-Verb Agreement

Words such as *each, neither, everyone, nobody, someone,* and *anyone* are singular pronouns. They always take a singular verb.

Everyone needs a good laugh now and then.
Nobody knows more about computers than Bob.

Words that refer to number such as *one-half, any, most,* and *some* can be singular or plural.

One-fifth of the students were absent. [*Students* is plural.]
One-fifth of the cake was eaten. [There is only one cake.]

Practice

Directions: Correct any subject-verb agreement errors. Some sentences may be correct.

1. The chess set are still on the shelf.

2. The shortest route to the college are shown in the catalog.

3. The golf pro drive a golf cart every day.

4. Derek and Ann walks every morning.

5. The tropical birds in the tree adds a festive air to the occasion.

6. No one, not even Rick or Ronnie, walk to school today.

7. Do you know who they is?

8. Ron prepare a paper for submission to the committee.

9. The 15 employees of the coffee house shows up each day at 6:00 A.M.

10. Each person who takes the 12 steps improve his or her view.

(Answers on page 97.)

ADJECTIVES AND ADVERBS

Adjectives

Adjectives modify nouns and pronouns. Adjectives add detail and clarify nouns and pronouns. Frequently, adjectives come immediately before the nouns or pronouns they are modifying. At other times, the nouns or pronouns come first and are connected directly to the adjectives by linking verbs. Here are some examples.

Direct	**With a Linking Verb**
That is a *large* dog.	That dog is *large*.
He's an *angry* man.	The man seems *angry*.

Adverbs

Adverbs are often formed by adding *ly* to an adjective. However, many adverbs do not end in *ly* (e.g., *always*). Adverbs modify verbs, adjectives, and adverbs. Adverbs can also modify phrases, clauses, and sentences. Here are some examples.

Modify verb:	Ryan *quickly* sought a solution.
Modify adjective:	That is an *exceedingly* large dog.
Modify adverb:	Lisa told her story *quite* truthfully.
Modify sentence:	*Unfortunately*, all good things must end.
Modify phrase:	The instructor arrived *just* in time to start the class.

AVOIDING ADJECTIVE AND ADVERB ERRORS

- Do not use adjectives in place of adverbs.

Correct	**Incorrect**
Lynne read the book quickly.	Lynne read the book quick.
Stan finished his work easily.	Stan finished his work easy.

- Do not confuse the adjectives *good* and *bad* with the adverbs *well* and *badly*.

Correct	**Incorrect**
Adverbs	
She wanted to play the piano well.	She wanted to play the piano good.
Bob sang badly.	Bob sang bad.
Adjectives	
The food tastes good.	The food tastes well.
The food tastes bad.	The food tastes badly.

- Do not confuse the adjectives *real* and *sure* with the adverbs *really* and *surely*.

Correct	**Incorrect**
Chuck played really well.	Chuck played real well.
He was surely correct.	He was sure correct.

Comparison

Adjectives and adverbs can show comparisons. Avoid clumsy modifiers.

Correct	**Incorrect**
Jim is more clingy than Ray.	Jim is clingier than Ray.
Ray is much taller than Jim.	Ray is more taller than Jim.
Jim is more interesting than Ray.	Jim is interesting than Ray.
Ray is happier than Jim.	Ray is more happy than Jim.

Use word comparisons carefully to be sure that the comparison is clear.

Unclear:	Chad lives closer to Ryan than Blaire.
Clear:	Chad lives closer to Ryan than Blaire does.
Clear:	Chad lives closer to Ryan than he does to Blaire.
Unclear:	The bus engines are bigger than cars.
Clear:	The bus engines are bigger than cars' engines.

Practice

> **Directions:** Correct the adjective and adverb errors. Some sentences may contain no errors.

1. The view of the Grand Canyon was real spectacular.

2. The trainer said the dog behaved very good today.

3. Unfortunate, the tickets for the concert were sold out.

4. Things went smooth.

5. The judge took extremely exception to the defendant's actions.

6. The accident was silly, particularly since driving more careful would have avoided the whole thing.

7. But the reviews said the performance was truly horrible.

8. The manager conveniently forgot that she promised the employee a raise.

9. The bonus was a welcome surprise; it was a real large check.

10. I didn't do good, but didn't do bad either.

(Answers on page 98.)

Practice

> **Directions:** Correct the comparison errors. Some sentences may be correct.

1. Leon was the happier chef in the restaurant.

2. But some of the people eating in the restaurant were happier than Leon.

3. The jet was the faster plane at the airport.

4. John was the fastest of the twins.

5. The taller of the apartment buildings is under repair.

6. The lightest of the two weights is missing.

7. Lonnie was among the most creative students in the school.

8. Ron is the least able of the two drivers.

9. His shoe size is the smallest in his class.

10. She was the more capable of the two referees.

(Answers on page 98.)

MISPLACED AND DANGLING MODIFIERS

Modifiers may be words or groups of words. Modifiers change or qualify the meaning of another word or group of words. Modifiers belong near the words they modify.

Misplaced modifiers appear to modify words in a way that does not make sense.

The modifier in the following sentence is *in a large box*. It does not make sense for *in a large box* to modify *house*. Move the modifier near *pizza* where it belongs.

Misplaced:	Les delivered pizza to the house in a large box.
Revised:	Les delivered pizza in a large box to the house.

The modifier in the next sentence is *paid well*. *Paid well* can't modify *city*. Move it next to *the job* where it belongs.

Misplaced:	Gail wanted the job in the city that paid well.
Revised:	Gail wanted the well-paying job in the city.

Dangling modifiers modify words not present in the sentence. The modifier in the following sentence is *waiting for the concert to begin*.

This modifier describes the audience, but audience is not mentioned in the sentence. The modifier is left dangling with nothing to describe.

Dangling:	Waiting for the concert to begin, the chanting started.
Revised:	Waiting for the concert to begin, the audience began chanting.
Revised:	The audience began chanting while waiting for the concert to begin.

The modifier in the next sentence is *after three weeks in the country*. The modifier describes the person, not the license. But the person is not mentioned in the sentence. The modifier is dangling.

Dangling:	After three weeks in the country, the license was revoked.
Revised:	After he was in the country for three weeks, his license was revoked.
Revised:	His license was revoked after he was in the country three weeks.

Practice

Directions: Correct the misplaced modifiers. Some sentences may be correct.

1. Les was reading his book through glasses with dirty lenses.

2. Jim left work early to go to the doctor on the train.

3. The first train car was crowded; which had to go to the next car.

4. Ron's car ran out of gas when on the way to the store.

5. Zena was jogging, when caused her to fall.

6. Derek wrapped the flowers and put them in the delivery van with colorful paper.

7. Which bus stops at the corner where the stop sign is?

8. Fran is going on the plane, which is just pulling up to the gate.

9. Lisa bought a shirt in the store, which was expensive.

10. The car turned around and the headlights shone quickly into the garage.

(Answers on page 99.)

COMMA SPLICES AND RUN-ON SENTENCES

An *independent clause* is a clause that could be a sentence.

Independent clauses should be joined by a semicolon, or by a comma and a conjunction.

A *comma splice* consists of two independent clauses joined by just a comma.

A *run-on* sentence consists of two independent clauses incorrectly joined.

Correct:	The whole family went on vacation; the parents took turns driving. [Two independent clauses are joined by a semicolon.]
	The whole family went on vacation, and the parents took turns driving. [Two independent clauses are joined by a comma and a conjunction.]
Incorrect:	The whole family went on vacation, the parents took turns driving. [Comma splice. Two independent clauses are joined by just a comma.]
	The whole family went on vacation the parents took turns driving. [Run-on sentence. Two independent clauses are incorrectly joined.]

Practice

> **Directions:** Correct the run-on sentences and comma splices. Some sentences may be correct.

1. It will be tomorrow before the sea is calm enough to go out.

2. It started to rain unexpectedly the boaters were soaked.

3. But right now my sneakers are soaking wet the towel is too wet to help me.

4. The Marine Police sounded the siren the boat stopped immediately.

5. I put the sneakers next to the fire to dry, although they started to steam after a while.

6. The Coast Guard monitors boats as they enter the river they use the data to monitor water pollution.

7. I like to use my compass when I go out on the boat.

8. When the boat breaks down, Liz calls Sea Tow.

9. The fire went out the sun came up.

10. Splashing through the waves, the water skier was covered with salt spray.

(Answers on page 100.)

SENTENCE FRAGMENTS

English sentences require a subject and a predicate (see page 58). Fragments are parts of sentences written as though they were sentences. Fragments are writing mistakes that lack a subject, a predicate, or both subject and predicate. Here are some examples.

> Since when.
> To enjoy the summer months.
> Because he isn't working hard.
> If you can fix old cars.
> What the principal wanted to hear.

Include a subject and/or a verb to rewrite a fragment as a sentence.

Fragment	Sentence
Should be coming up the driveway now.	The *car* should be coming up the driveway now.
Both the lawyer and her client.	Both the lawyer and her client *waited* in court.
Which is my favorite subject.	*I took math*, which is my favorite subject.
If you can play.	If you can play, *you'll improve with* practice.

Verbs such as *to be, to go, winning, starring,* etc., need a main verb.

Fragment	Sentence
The new rules to go into effect in April.	The new rules *will* go into effect in April.
The team winning every game.	The team *was* winning every game.

Often, a fragment is related to a complete sentence. Combine the two to make a single sentence.

Fragment:	Reni loved vegetables. *Particularly corn, celery, lettuce, squash, and eggplant.*
Revised:	Reni loved vegetables, particularly corn, celery, lettuce, squash, and eggplant.
Fragment:	*To see people standing on Mars.* This could happen in the twenty-first century.
Revised:	To see people standing on Mars is one of the things that could happen in the twenty-first century.

Sometimes short fragments can be used for emphasis. However, you should not use fragments in your essay. Here are some examples.

> *Stop!* Do not take one more step toward that apple pie.
> I need some time to myself. *That's why.*

Practice

Directions: Correct the sentence fragments. Some items may be correct.

1. A golf bag, golf clubs, and golf balls. That's what she needed to play.

2. As the rocket prepared for blast-off. Mary saw birds flying in the distance.

3. Jim is mowing the lawn. Then, the mower stopped.

4. The lawn looked lush and green. Like a golf course.

5. The polar bears swept across the ice. Like white ghosts in fur jackets.

6. Jim looked across at the igloo. Like an ice fort, it stood a lonely vigil.

7. Astronauts and their equipment went by. These were the people who would go into space.

8. This was what Joe had been waiting for. To graduate from college.

9. To be finished with this test. That's what I'm waiting for.

10. The test finished and done. The papers graded and good.

(Answers on page 100.)

PARALLELISM

When two or more ideas are connected, use a parallel structure. Parallelism helps the reader follow the passage more clearly. Here are some examples.

Not Parallel:	Toni stayed in shape by eating right and exercising daily.
Parallel:	Toni stayed in shape by eating right and *by* exercising daily.
Not Parallel:	Lisa is a student who works hard and has genuine insight.
Parallel:	Lisa is a student who works hard and *who* has genuine insight.
Not Parallel:	Art had a choice either to clean his room or take out the garbage.
Parallel:	Art had a choice either to clean his room or *to* take out the garbage.
Not Parallel:	Derek wanted a success rather than failing.
Parallel:	Derek wanted a success rather than *a failure*.
Parallel:	Derek wanted *success rather than failure*.

Practice

Directions: Correct any parallel form errors. Some sentences may not have errors.

1. I have to get to work, but first I have to find my way to breakfast.

2. The road was dry; the day was hot and sultry.

3. Jane likes to eat and go shopping when she is at the mall.

4. April chose to be a cameraperson rather than to be a technician who works the sound board.

5. Since I have not heard from you, I decided to write this letter.

6. Although she had driven the road before, Sally proceeded slowly, keeping her eye on the yellow line.

7. The tree withstood the hurricane, but the branches on the tree snapped off.

8. His work on the Board of Education revealed his dedication to the community.

9. Cars, taxis, and buses were my transportation to the airport.

10. The subject matter and the preparation for class created an excellent lesson.

(Answers on page 101.)

DICTION

Diction is choosing and using appropriate words. Good diction conveys a thought clearly without unnecessary words. Good diction develops fully over a number of years; however, there are some rules and tips you can follow.

Do not use slang, colloquialisms, or other non-standard English.
One person's slang is another person's confusion. Slang is often regional, and slang meanings change rapidly. We do not give examples of slang here for that very reason. Do not use slang words in your formal writing.

Colloquialisms are words used frequently in spoken language. This informal use of terms such as *dog tired*, *kids*, and *hanging around* is not generally accepted in formal writing. Save these informal terms for daily speech and omit or remove them from your writing except as quotations.

Omit any other non-standard English. Always choose standard English terms that accurately reflect the thought to be conveyed.

> ## AVOID WORDY, REDUNDANT, OR PRETENTIOUS WRITING
>
> Good writing is clear and economical.
>
> **Wordy:** I chose my career as a teacher because of its high ideals, the truly self-sacrificing idealism of a career in teaching, and for the purpose of receiving the myriad and cascading recognition that one can receive from the community as a whole and from its constituents.
>
> **Revised:** I chose a career in teaching for its high ideals and for community recognition.

Given below is a partial list of wordy phrases and the replacement word.

Wordy Phrases and Replacements

at the present time	now	because of the fact that	because
for the purpose of	for	in the final analysis	finally
in the event that	if	until such time as	until

HOMONYMS

Homonyms are words that sound alike but do not have the same meaning. These words can be confusing and you may use the incorrect spelling of a word. If words are homonyms, be sure you choose the correct spelling for the meaning you intend.

Homonyms

accept (receive)	lessen (make less)
except (other than)	lesson (learning experience)
affect (to influence)	past (gone before)
effect (a result)	passed (moved by)
ascent (rise)	peace (no war)
assent (agreement)	piece (portion)
board (wood)	rain (precipitation)
bored (uninterested)	reign (rule)
fair (average)	rein (animal strap)
fare (a charge)	their (possessive pronoun)
its (shows possession)	there (location)
it's (it is)	they're (they are)
led (guided)	to (toward)
lead (metal)	too (also)
	two (a number)

IDIOMS

Idioms are expressions with special meanings and often break the rules of grammar. Idioms are acceptable in formal writing, but they must be used carefully. Here are some examples.

Idioms

in accordance with	inferior to
angry with	occupied by (someone)
differ from (someone)	occupied with (something)
differ about (an issue)	prior to
independent of	rewarded with (something)

Practice

Directions: Write the word or phrase that fits best in the blank.

1. Many _____ diseases, including pneumonia and swelling in cuts, are caused by bacteria.

   innocuous   unfortunate   infectious   ill-fated

2. Sigmund Freud's views of sexuality had become _____, and the country entered the sexual revolution.

   well known   all knowing   universal   inculcated

3. After crossing the land bridge near the Bering Strait, groups of Native Americans _____ spread throughout all of North, Central, and South America.

   inclusively   eventually   regardless   remotely

4. During the early 1500s Cortez and Pizarro opened up Central America to the Spanish who began _____ slaves from Africa.

   importing   exporting   imparting   immigrating

5. The Stamp Act requiring every legal paper to carry a tax stamp was vehemently _____ and eventually repealed by England.

   denied   deported   proclaimed   protested

Directions: Circle the underlined portion that is unnecessary in the passage.

6. No goal is more noble—no feat more revealing—than the strikingly brave exploration of space.

7. As many as a ton of bananas may have spoiled when the ship was stuck and delayed in the Panama Canal.

8. He was concerned about crossing the bridge, but the officer said that it was all right to cross and he need not worry.

9. A professional golfer told the novice beginning golfer that professional instruction or more practice improves most golfers' scores.

10. The soccer player's slight strain from the shot on goal that won the game led to a pulled muscle that would keep her from playing the next match.

11. He went to the bird's nest near the river, only too realize he missed its assent.

12. The rider pulled back on the horse's reign before the whether turned rainy.

13. The whether turned rainy as he led the hikers on there ascent.

14. The lessen was clear; it was fare, but not easy to accept.

15. They're board relatives were not fare too her father.

Directions: Correct the idiom errors. Some sentences may not have errors.

16. Her grades had everything to do of her efforts.

17. Joanie expected him to wait to the house until she arrived home.

18. She could spend months absorbed in her studies.

19. The two coaches differ significantly with each other's style.

20. That person is wearing the same coat from you.

(Answers on page 102.)

PUNCTUATION

The Comma (,)

The comma may be the most used punctuation mark. This section details a few of these uses.

A clause is part of a sentence that could be a sentence itself. If a clause begins with a conjunction, use a comma before the conjunction.

Incorrect: I was satisfied with the food but John was grumbling.
Correct: I was satisfied with the food, but John was grumbling.

Incorrect: Larry was going fishing or he was going to paint his house.
Correct: Larry was going fishing, or he was going to paint his house.

A clause or a phrase often introduces a sentence. Introductory phrases or clauses should be set off by a comma. If the introductory element is very short, the comma is optional. Here are some examples.

However, there are other options you may want to consider.
When the deicer hit the plane's wing, the ice began to melt.
To get a driver's license, go to the motor vehicle bureau.
It doesn't matter what you want, you have to take what you get.

Parenthetical expressions interrupt the flow of a sentence. Set off the parenthetical expression with commas. Do not set off expressions that are essential to understanding the sentence. Here are some examples.

Tom, an old friend, showed up at my house the other day.

I was traveling on a train, in car 8200, on my way to Florida.

John and Ron, who are seniors, went on break to Florida.
[Use a comma. The phrase "who are seniors" is extra information.]

All the students who are seniors take an additional course.
[Do not use a comma. The phrase "who are seniors" is essential information.]

Commas are used to set off items in a list or series. Here are some examples.

Jed is interested in computers, surfing, and fishing.
[Notice the comma before the conjunction *and*.]

Mario drives a fast, red car.
[The sentence would make sense with *and* in place of the comma.]

Andy hoped for a bright, sunny, balmy day.
[The sentence would make sense with *and* in place of the commas.]

Lucy had a pale green dress.
[The sentence would not make sense with *and*. The word *pale* modifies *green*. Do not use a comma.]

Randy will go to the movies, pick up some groceries, and then go home.

Practice

Directions: Correct the comma errors. Some sentences may have no comma errors.

1. I had a slow day yesterday, but I worked hard in my junior year.

2. Passing calculus seems a difficult, but achievable, result.

3. After making the sandwich, I looked for some pickles, but the jar was empty.

4. Write an outline first and be sure to leave enough time to write the essay.

5. In the attic I found some old clothes, an old trunk, and a shoe.

6. Chad, Blaire, and Ryan have advanced degrees but they are still children at heart.

7. Using a computer the Core tests reading, writing, and arithmetic.

8. Either walk the dog or wash the dishes.

9. Every pilot, who has flown over 20 missions, receives an award.

10. Each time I ate lunch at home, my mother made liverwurst sandwiches.

(Answers on page 104.)

Semicolon and Colon

THE SEMICOLON (;)

Use the semicolon to connect main clauses not connected by a conjunction. Include a semicolon with very long clauses connected by a conjunction. Here are some examples.

> The puck was dropped; the hockey game began.
>
> The puck was dropped, and the hockey game began.
>
> The general manager of the hockey team was not sure what should be done about the player who was injured during the game; but he did know that the player's contract stipulated that his pay would continue whether he was able to play or not.

THE COLON (:)

Use the colon after a main clause to introduce a list. Here are some examples.

> Liz kept these items in her car: spare tire, jack, flares, and a blanket.
>
> Liz kept a spare tire, jack, flares, and a blanket in her car.

Practice

Directions: Correct any semicolon or colon errors. Some sentences may be correct.

1. Pack these other things for camp; a bathing suit, some socks, and a shirt.

2. In your wallet put: your camp information card and your bus pass.

3. I have one thing left to do; say good-bye.

4. We went to the store; and the parking lot was filled with cars.

5. We fought our way through the crowds, the store was even more crowded than the parking lot.

(Answers on page 104.)

Period, Question Mark, and Exclamation Point

THE PERIOD (.)

Use a period to end every sentence, unless the sentence is a direct question, a strong command, or an interjection.

> You will do well on the Core test.

THE QUESTION MARK (?)

Use a question mark to end every sentence that is a direct question.

> What is the passing score for the Core test?

THE EXCLAMATION POINT (!)

Use an exclamation point to end every sentence that is a strong command or interjection. Do not overuse exclamation points.

> Interjection: Pass that test!
>
> Command: Avalanche, head for cover!

Practice

Directions: Correct any punctuation errors.
---

1. I was so worn out after swimming!

2. Avalanche.

3. Who said that!

4. Warning. The danger signal blared in the background.

5. I can't believe this is the last day of camp?

(Answers on page 105.)

This section shows you how to pass the multiple-choice writing portion of the computer-delivered Core writing test.

Types of Questions

The multiple-choice writing test gives you a chance to show what you know about grammar, sentence structure, and word usage. You should be familiar with the subjects covered in the English Review section.

You may be able to get the correct answer from your sense or feel about the sentence. If you are someone who has an intuitive grasp of English usage, you should rely on your intuition as you complete this section of the tests.

There are four types of questions on the computer-delivered Core. Most are usage and sentence correction questions but some are revision in context questions or research skills questions. Examples of these four question types are found below.

USAGE

You are shown a sentence with four parts underlined and lettered (A), (B), (C), and (D). There is a fifth choice: (E) No error. You choose the letter of the flawed part or (E) if there is no error. You do not have to explain what the error is or what makes the other parts correct. No sentence contains more than one error. You just have to recognize the error or realize that there is no error.

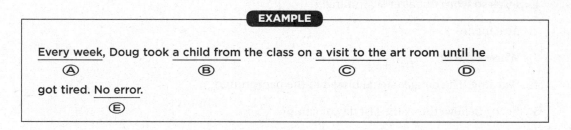

SENTENCE CORRECTION

You are shown a sentence or a passage with one part underlined. Choice (A) repeats the underlined selection exactly. Choices (B) through (E) give suggested changes for the underlined part. You choose the letter of the best choice that does not change the meaning of the original sentence. If the original is best, choose (A). Otherwise, select one of the suggested changes.

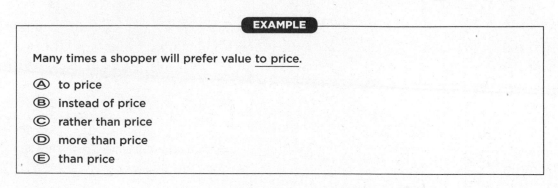

There are fewer revision in context questions and research skills questions.

REVISION IN CONTEXT

These questions ask you to choose the correct revision for a portion of a passage.

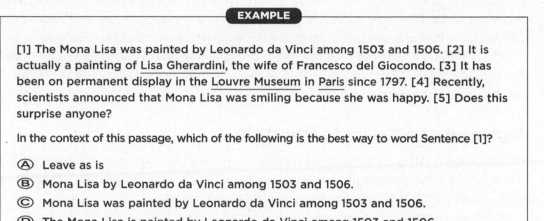

EXAMPLE

[1] The Mona Lisa was painted by Leonardo da Vinci among 1503 and 1506. [2] It is actually a painting of Lisa Gherardini, the wife of Francesco del Giocondo. [3] It has been on permanent display in the Louvre Museum in Paris since 1797. [4] Recently, scientists announced that Mona Lisa was smiling because she was happy. [5] Does this surprise anyone?

In the context of this passage, which of the following is the best way to word Sentence [1]?

Ⓐ Leave as is
Ⓑ Mona Lisa by Leonardo da Vinci among 1503 and 1506.
Ⓒ Mona Lisa was painted by Leonardo da Vinci among 1503 and 1506.
Ⓓ The Mona Lisa is painted by Leonardo da Vinci among 1503 and 1506.
Ⓔ The Mona Lisa was painted by Leonardo da Vinci between 1503 and 1506.

RESEARCH SKILLS

These questions ask you about basic research skills.

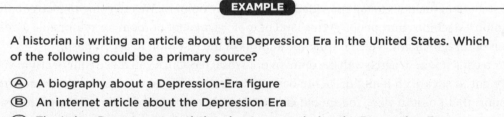

EXAMPLE

A historian is writing an article about the Depression Era in the United States. Which of the following could be a primary source?

Ⓐ A biography about a Depression-Era figure
Ⓑ An internet article about the Depression Era
Ⓒ The Labor Department statistics about wages during the Depression Era
Ⓓ A diary from a Depression-Era family
Ⓔ A film about Depression-Era families

STRATEGIES FOR PASSING THE MULTIPLE-CHOICE WRITING TEST

Read Carefully

In this section, it is often small details that count. Read each sentence carefully. Read the whole sentence and not just the underlined sections. Remember that an underlined section by itself can look fine but be incorrect in the context of the whole sentence or passage. Read each sentence a few times until you get a sense for its rhythm and flow.

This Is a Test of Written English

Evaluate each sentence as written English. Do not apply the more informal rules of spoken English.

Form of the Essays

TIP

Use the rules of grammar as you write your essay. Punctuate as carefully as you can but do not spend an inordinate amount of time on punctuation. Raters will often ignore minor grammatical or spelling errors if the essay is well developed.

You will be given two essay topics, one after the other. One essay is called the Argumentative Essay and the other is called the Informative/Explanatory (Source-Based) Essay. You will have 30 minutes to plan and type each essay. Type the essay in the space provided on the computer screen, below the essay prompt. You may use the scrap paper to write a brief outline.

What follows is a review of each essay type, prompts from these essays, and some strategies to follow. You will write an essay based on these prompts in the Review Test at the end of the chapter and see examples of rated essays.

Argumentative Essay (30 MINUTES)

The first essay is called an Argumentative Essay. You will read an opinion and then discuss the extent to which you agree or disagree with the opinion (with supporting details). There is no right or wrong answer. It is the quality of your essay that counts.

Here is one example of an opinion you may see on the test.

ESSAY OPINION

"Machines hurt people. A machine is just a way of replacing a human in the workplace. Over 30,000 people are killed and hundreds of thousands injured or maimed in accidents involving the machine we call a car."

The main opinion is "machines hurt people." That is clear and unequivocal. The rest of the statement includes details provided to support the opinion. We are going to focus on the opinion "Machines hurt people." This kind of topic gives a lot of room for reasonable agreement or disagreement, which is what the authors of the test want to accomplish.

You can choose to agree with the opinion or to disagree. Once you make your decision you have got to stick with it and make the best argument and be as persuasive as you can, and support that point of view. You should choose the side of the opinion that is easiest for you to argue in your essay.

Remember, there is no right or wrong position, but you must stick to the position you choose. There is no "On the one hand this, but on the other hand that." You have got to write in favor or opposed to the opinion given. Do not write about an opinion not included in the prompt. Well-written but off-topic essays earn the lowest score.

> **STRATEGIES FOR WRITING THE ARGUMENTATIVE ESSAY**
> - Read and understand the topic.
> - Choose your position.
> - Outline your essay.
> - Type the essay.
> - Review and correct the essay.

Informative/Explanatory (Source-Based) Essay (30 MINUTES)

The second essay is called an Informative/Explanatory (Source-Based) Essay. You will read a topic and then read two sources about that topic. Your essay must be based on these sources. There is no right or wrong answer. It is the quality of your essay, how well it discusses the sources' main points, and how well you use and cite the sources that counts.

The Informative/Explanatory (Source-Based) Essay is part reading and part writing. You will read information about a particular topic. Then you are presented with two relatively long position papers on that topic, usually totaling 500 words or more.

You scan these position papers to understand the points of view of each author, which usually present differing opinions about the topic. Use the following steps as you work:

> ### STRATEGIES FOR WRITING AN INFORMATIVE/EXPLANATORY (SOURCE-BASED) ESSAY
>
> - Read and understand the topic and the positions in the two sources.
> - Outline your essay incorporating points from the position papers.
> - Write the essay and include sources and citations.
> - Review and correct the essay.

Your focus for this essay is to identify the important issues raised in the sources and to discuss them using references from the two position papers. You can bring in your own experiences. Your essay will be necessarily shorter than the Argumentative Essay because you have to use part of your 30 minutes to review the position papers. Focus on the points in the position papers and build your essay around them.

You have 30 minutes to read two position papers on a topic and then write an essay based on the topic. The essay will discuss the important points in the two sources.

Read the topic and sources below. Organize your thoughts and plan your essay before you start to write. You MUST write on the given topic and you MUST include references to the sources.

This essay gives you a chance to demonstrate how well you can write and include sources in your writing. That means you should focus on writing well and using examples and references, while being sure to cover the topic presented. While how much you write is not a specific scoring criterion, you will certainly want to write several meaningful paragraphs.

TOPIC

Tracking is a sweeping educational grouping system in which students are assigned to all subjects and classes by academic achievement. Tracking systems are most commonly found in secondary schools where students take each subject class with a different instructor. When the system is used, it is not unusual to find three general tracks—advanced academic, academic, and vocational. Typically, students in one track do not take classes with students from another track. Ability grouping is not the same as tracking. Ability groups are typically found in a single classroom. An assignment to an ability group can change as soon as a change in performance is noted.

SOURCE PASSAGES

Read the following two source passages. Then write an essay that highlights the most important aspects and explain why they are important. Your essay should refer to EACH of the sources and must CITE the sources as you refer to them or you must provide direct quotes. You may also use your own experiences and readings.

Finding a Track to Success . . . Tracking in the Schools, from Robertson (web accessed 10/2/2017)

There is nothing worse than seeing students forced into academic classes that are inappropriate for them. Taking those inappropriate courses seldom prepares students for the real world and they frequently leave school with knowledge they can't use and without the skills and preparation that would enable them to pursue a fruitful career. While no system is perfect, tracking, properly used, helps students prepare for the real world they will live in.

A carefully implemented tracking system enables teachers to structure lessons to the specific needs of students in a class—lessons that challenge students, but challenge them at a level they are capable of achieving. For students in an upper track, it removes the lid placed on instruction for academically talented students that would be present if they were in class with students of lesser ability. At the same time, it ensures that students of lesser ability in a comparable class will also have a chance to achieve at their highest level of potential. Yes, the students most negatively impacted by a nontracked system will be denied the opportunity to achieve at the level expected of them. And look at the students who might be at the lowest educational track. They consist primarily of students who will pursue a career after high school, perhaps in some trade. Those students deserve the opportunities for a track aimed at career preparation. In a world of imperfect solutions, a well-managed tracking system is the best approach.

A Track to Nowhere—the Failure of Tracking,
from Pismenny (web accessed 10/15/2017)

Educators try to dress up student tracking as an approach that benefits all levels of the achievement spectrum. The truth is that tracking only helps more able students from affluent families. In fact, tracking is just a way to assign poor and minority students to the lowest tracks, where one finds the least-qualified teachers. These low-tracked students never have an opportunity to escape the low track and are essentially given a one-way ticket to the same low track of society. Put more simply, tracking is just another form of race and class discrimination. It is more insidious than overt discrimination because it hides behind a cloak of what appears to be a useful educational practice.

Beyond that, even when initial tracks are fairly homogeneous, things change over time. Students learn at different rates and learning impediments decrease in some students. The similarities among students in a track tend to widen or disappear. Accounting for this increasing heterogeneity would require regular reevaluation of students and placement in different tracks when indicated. In practice, the best systems make the reassignment once a year. In most tracking systems it takes an extraordinary event for a student to move from one track to another. If we are talking about a tracking system in a high school, students who stay in one track are more different at the end of high school than they are the same.

In addition to these serious problems, tracking systems often determine a student's peer group. Students in the low track suffer from social stigmatization. Since lower-class and minority students are overrepresented in low tracks with whites and Asians generally dominating high tracks, interaction among these groups can be discouraged by tracking. It is easy to see how for students a tracking system is a track to nowhere.

This targeted test is designed to help you practice the strategies presented in this chapter. For that reason, questions may have a different emphasis than the actual test, and the actual test will certainly be more complete.

Mark your choice, and then check your answers on pages 105–110.

Part A: Usage

> **Directions:** Choose the letter that indicates an error, or choose (E) for no error.

1. Kitty and Harry's anniversary will fall on Father's Day this year. No error.
   Ⓐ   Ⓑ   Ⓒ   Ⓓ   Ⓔ

2. The trees leaves provide a fall festival called "Fall Foliage" in most New England states.
   Ⓐ   Ⓑ   Ⓒ   Ⓓ
   No error.
   Ⓔ

3. Most colleges require a specific number of academic credits for admission.
   Ⓐ   Ⓑ   Ⓒ   Ⓓ
   No error.
   Ⓔ

4. My brother Robert loves to read novels but would enjoy good mystery's more.
   Ⓐ   Ⓑ   Ⓒ   Ⓓ
   No error.
   Ⓔ

5. Louise had lay her mitt on the bench when she got a glass of water. No error.
   Ⓐ   Ⓑ   Ⓒ   Ⓓ   Ⓔ

6. It seems to me that I had spoke to my landlord about the crack in the ceiling
   Ⓐ   Ⓑ   Ⓒ
   about two months ago. No error.
   Ⓓ   Ⓔ

7. The committee on fund-raising gathers in the hall, but Joe went to the room.
   Ⓐ   Ⓑ   Ⓒ   Ⓓ
   No error.
   Ⓔ

8. The administrator wanted all lesson plan books handed in by Friday. No error.
   Ⓐ   Ⓑ   Ⓒ   Ⓓ   Ⓔ

9. Behind the tree, she was reading a book, eating a banana, and she waited for the
    <u>A</u>   <u>B</u>   <u>C</u>   <u>D</u>
   sunset. No error.
           <u>E</u>

10. Is Washington, D. C. closer to Arlington Cemetery than Charleston? No error.
    <u>A</u>   <u>B</u>   <u>C</u>   <u>D</u>   <u>E</u>

11. The student would not do nothing to redeem himself in the eyes of the principal.
        <u>A</u>   <u>B</u>   <u>C</u>   <u>D</u>
   No error.
   <u>E</u>

12. Good teachers are distinguished by their enthusiasm and organization. No error.
        <u>A</u>   <u>B</u>   <u>C</u>   <u>D</u>   <u>E</u>

13. The principle of the middle school wanted to reorganize the lunch schedule. No error.
        <u>A</u>   <u>B</u>   <u>C</u>   <u>D</u>   <u>E</u>

14. Grandmother's shopping list consisted of mustard, green beans, buttermilk, and
        <u>A</u>   <u>B</u>   <u>C</u>
   included some eggs. No error.
        <u>D</u>   <u>E</u>

15. Unless you arm yourself with insect repellent, you will get a bight. No error.
            <u>A</u>   <u>B</u>   <u>C</u>   <u>D</u>   <u>E</u>

16. Graduation exercises will be held on ___ Friday ___ June 19th, at 7:00 P.M. No error.
                <u>A</u>   <u>B</u>   <u>C</u>   <u>D</u>   <u>E</u>

17. With a quick glance the noisy room was silenced. No error.
    <u>A</u>   <u>B</u>   <u>C</u>   <u>D</u>   <u>E</u>

18. Without even trying, the sprinter passed the world record by five tenths of a second.
            <u>A</u>   <u>B</u>   <u>C</u>   <u>D</u>
   No error.
   <u>E</u>

19. Prior to the passage of PL 94-142, special education students
    <u>A</u>   <u>B</u>   <u>C</u>
   were not unrepresented legally. No error.
                <u>D</u>   <u>E</u>

20. Combine the sugar, waters, cornstarch, and eggs. No error.
        <u>A</u>   <u>B</u>   <u>C</u>   <u>D</u>   <u>E</u>

Part B: Sentence Correction

> **Directions:** Choose the letter of the best choice for the underlined section, without changing the meaning of the sentence. If the original is best, choose (A). Otherwise, select one of the suggested changes.

21. Postman's talents were missed <u>not any more</u> as a student but also in his extracurricular activities on campus.

    (A) not any more
    (B) not
    (C) not only
    (D) never any
    (E) any

22. <u>Piled on the table, the students started sorting through their projects.</u>

    (A) Piled on the table, the students started sorting through their projects.
    (B) The students started sorting through their projects, which were piled on the table.
    (C) Piled on the table, the students sorted through their projects.
    (D) The students sorted through their projects as they piled on the table.
    (E) Students started sorting through the table piled with projects.

23. All the soccer players, <u>who are injured,</u> must not play the game.

    (A) , who are injured,
    (B) , who are injured
    (C) who are injured,
    (D) who are injured
    (E) (who are injured)

24. The plumber kept these tools in his <u>truck; plunger, snake, washers and faucets.</u>

    (A) truck; plunger, snake, washers and faucets.
    (B) truck (plunger, snake, washers and faucets).
    (C) truck: plunger; snake; washers and faucets.
    (D) truck; plunger, snake, washers, and faucets.
    (E) truck: plunger, snake, washers, and faucets.

25. The two <u>attorneys meet</u> and agreed on an out-of-court settlement.

    (A) attorneys meet
    (B) attorney's meet
    (C) attorney's met
    (D) attorneys met
    (E) attorney meets

Part C: Revision in Context

Directions: Choose the correct revision for the underlined sentence.

Little Big Horn

(1) In 1875 the United States ordered all nomadic Lakota and Cheyenne to return to the Great Sioux Reservation, established by the Treaty of 1868, or be considered hostile. (2) The immediate issues leading to the conflict, which became known as the Great Sioux War, were the Black Hills Expedition of 1874 and the invasion of the Black Hills by gold miners. (3) The U.S. attempted to acquire the Black Hills by purchase but had been rebuffed by the Lakota. (4) The Grant administration then unilaterally declared the Black Hills outside of the control of the Great Sioux Reservation.

(5) In the early morning hours of June 25, 1876, the large village of the Lakota and Cheyenne was observed from a high promontory in the Wolf Mountains. (6) George Custer's regiment went into the "Battle of the Little Big Horn" piecemeal. (7) It became apparent that the assumptions of the early morning observations, that of a village escaping, were incorrect.

(8) The village was largely intact and from accounts had been surprised by the approaching cavalry contingents. (9) Fortunately, the warrior fighting force was able to concentrate overwhelming numbers against a now divided regiment and defeat it in detail. (10) Approximately 380 members of the 7th Cavalry survived the battle after Major Marcus Reno and Captain Frederick Benteen reunited and developed a strong defensive position on high ground. (11) Custer and the 209 men in his immediate command were killed to a person because they had advanced to a position beyond the ability of the surviving parts of the regiment to support them.

26. In context of this passage, which of the choices below is the best suggestion to place at the beginning of sentence 4, which is reproduced below?

    The Grant administration then unilaterally declared the Black Hills outside of the control of the Great Sioux Reservation.

    Ⓐ Regrettably,
    Ⓑ In retaliation,
    Ⓒ Against his better intentions,
    Ⓓ After 7 years,
    Ⓔ At the Lakota's request,

27. In the context of this passage, which is the best way to reword the underlined portion of sentence 11, which is reproduced below?

    killed to a person because they had advanced to a position beyond the ability of the surviving parts

    Ⓐ Leave as is
    Ⓑ killed in advance of their ability to reach the surviving parts
    Ⓒ all killed because they were too far from reinforcements
    Ⓓ all killed because they were outnumbered
    Ⓔ killed because they had advanced to a position that was within the reach of the surviving elements

Part D: Research Skills

Directions: Choose the best answer.

28. Pismenny, Aaron R. "The First 'R' of Teaching." *Best Teaching Approaches* 215 (2014): pp. 286–387.

    The citation above is from which of the following types of sources?

    (A) A periodical
    (B) A textbook
    (C) An article from a newspaper
    (D) An Internet source
    (E) A textbook chapter

29. You are writing a paper on the role of social media in advertising. Which of the following selections is NOT directly relevant to your paper?

    (A) Social media actually account for a fairly high percentage of contacts that lead to lasting relationships.
    (B) Twitter advertisements can be easily accessed on handheld devices, such as cell phones.
    (C) Facebook can target specific subscribers to receive pictures and messages.
    (D) Opinions vary about the relative merits of social media ads or ads generated by Internet searches.
    (E) The use of social media is still a relatively recent form of communication, and many still think that social media is a fad that will fade with time.

Part E: Essays

The Core Writing test has two essays.

You have 30 minutes to complete each essay.

Rated essay examples are found on pages 106–110.

Argumentative Essay

Directions: Use a computer, but not the spell check or the grammar check features, to type your essay.

ESSAY OPINION

"Machines hurt people. A machine is just a way of replacing a human in the workplace. Over 30,000 people are killed and hundreds of thousands injured or maimed in accidents involving the machine we call a car."

Use this space to write a brief outline before you write your essay:

Informative/Explanatory (Source-Based) Essay

> **Directions:** Use a computer, but not the spell check or the grammar check features, to type your essay.

TOPIC

Tracking is a sweeping educational grouping system in which students are assigned to all subjects and classes by academic achievement. Tracking systems are most commonly found in secondary schools where students take each subject class with a different instructor. When the system is used, it is not unusual to find three general tracks—advanced academic, academic, and vocational. Typically, students in one track do not take classes with students from another track. Ability grouping is not the same as tracking. Ability groups are typically found in a single classroom. An assignment to an ability group can change as soon as a change in performance is noted.

Read the following two source passages. Then write an essay that highlights the most important aspects of them and explain why they are important. Your essay should refer to EACH of the sources and must CITE the sources as you refer to them or you must provide direct quotes. You may also use your own experiences and readings.

Source Passages

Finding a Track to Success . . . Tracking in the Schools,
from Robertson (web accessed 10/2/2017)

There is nothing worse than seeing students forced into academic classes that are inappropriate for them. Taking those inappropriate courses seldom prepares students for the real world and they frequently leave school with knowledge they can't use and without the skills and preparation that would enable them to pursue a fruitful career. While no system is perfect, tracking, properly used, helps students prepare for the real world they will live in.

A carefully implemented tracking system enables teachers to structure lessons to the specific needs of students in a class—lessons that challenge students, but challenge them at a level they are capable of achieving. For students in an upper track, it removes the lid placed on instruction for academically talented students that would be present if they were in class with students of lesser ability. At the same time, it ensures that students of lesser ability in a comparable class will also have a chance to achieve at their highest level of potential. Yes, the students most negatively impacted by a nontracked system will be denied the opportunity to achieve at the level expected of them. And look at the students who might be at the lowest educational track. They consist primarily of students who will pursue a career after high school, perhaps in some trade. Those students deserve the opportunities for a track aimed at career preparation. In a world of imperfect solutions, a well-managed tracking system is the best approach.

A Track to Nowhere—the Failure of Tracking, from Pismenny (web accessed 10/15/2017)

Educators try to dress up student tracking as an approach that benefits all levels of the achievement spectrum. The truth is that tracking only helps more able students from affluent families. In fact, tracking is just a way to assign poor and minority students to the lowest tracks, where one finds the least-qualified teachers. These low-tracked students never have an opportunity to escape the low track and are essentially given a one-way ticket to the same low track of society. Put more simply, tracking is just another form of race and class discrimination. It is more insidious than overt discrimination because it hides behind a cloak of what appears to be a useful educational practice.

Beyond that, even when initial tracks are fairly homogeneous, things change over time. Students learn at different rates and learning impediments decrease in some students. The similarities among students in a track tend to widen or disappear. Accounting for this increasing heterogeneity would require regular reevaluation of students and placement in different tracks when indicated. In practice, the best systems make the reassignment once a year. In most tracking systems it takes an extraordinary event for a student to move from one track to another.

If we are talking about a tracking system in a high school, students who stay in one track are more different at the end of high school than they are the same.

In addition to these serious problems, tracking systems often determine a student's peer group. Students in the low track suffer from social stigmatization. Since lower-class and minority students are overrepresented in low tracks with whites and Asians generally dominating high tracks, interaction among these groups can be discouraged by tracking. It is easy to see how for students a tracking system is a track to nowhere.

Use this space to write a brief outline before you write your essay:

ANSWERS FOR ENGLISH PRACTICE

Nouns, page 59

1. sheaves
2. deer
3. fries
4. lunches
5. knees
6. ladies
7. octopi
8. echoes
9. feet
10. halves

Tense Errors, page 61

drove
1. Ryan ~~driven~~ to Florida.

2. Refereeing soccer games is not work.
   [No tense errors.]

rode
3. Chad ~~ride~~ to the game with his team last week.
   [The words *last week* indicate that the verb must be past tense.]

run
4. Why did Mary ~~ran~~ her errands now?

spoken
5. I have ~~speak~~ to my teacher about the grade.

paddles
6. Carl ~~paddled~~ across the river every Saturday.
   [Use the present tense because it is a regular event.]

had thrown
7. Blaire ~~thrown~~ out the ball for the players to use.

lose
8. Joann will ~~lost~~ her bag if she leaves it in the store.

9. Bob is standing on a stool next to the green table.
   [No tense errors.]

began
10. Liz ~~begun~~ to grasp the depth of her happiness.

Tense Shift, page 61

1. Lisa already went to the North Pole but she is not going there again.
   [No tense shift errors.]

2. Dennis ~~will take~~ **took** his airline tickets with him because he is leaving for his flight.

3. The runner gasped as she crosses the finish line.

   The runner gasped as she crossed the finish line.
   The runner gasps as she crosses the finish line.

4. I like to hear music so I ~~played~~ **play** the clarinet.
   I ~~like~~ **liked** to hear music, so I played the clarinet.

5. Chris ~~wanted~~ **wants** to be a producer so he puts in long hours every day.

6. Bertha sews five hours a day because she will need her dress by next month.
   [No tense shift errors.]

7. The car turns over and then bounced down the hill.

   The car turned over and then bounced down the hill.
   The car turns over and then bounces down the hill.

8. Lois handed over her money because she wants to buy the computer.

   Lois hands over her money because she wants to buy the computer.
   Lois handed over her money because she wanted to buy the computer.

9. The captain wandered out on the deck as she calls to her friends on shore.

   The captain wandered out on the deck as she called to her friends on shore.
   The captain wanders out on the deck as she calls to her friends on shore.

10. The sun sets in the west as the moon rose in the east.

    The sun set in the west as the moon rose in the east.
    The sun sets in the west as the moon rises in the east.

Pronouns, page 64

1. ~~His~~ **He** was the best table tennis player.

2. ~~Whom~~ **Who** was the worst table tennis player?

3. Where are the table tennis balls?
   [No errors.]

                  is
4. Before the game everyone ~~are~~ going to choose teams.

                   us
5. The names of the winning teams are sent to ~~we~~.

They
6. ~~Them~~ are the best table tennis team.

             Ron's
7. Ron and Jeff wanted to use ~~his~~ skates.
   [Jeff's, or any other name, could be used in place of Ron's.]

       the skates
8. Jeff went to get ~~them~~.
   [Other nouns that make sense in this context could be used in place of skates.]

             the pillows
9. The couch looked different, depending on how ~~they~~ were arranged.

10. Bob won most of his table tennis games.
    [No errors.]

          her or his
11. The student waited for ~~their~~ school bus to come.

              it doesn't
12. Either of the buses can arrive on time if ~~they do not~~ break down.

              its
13. The book was most interesting near ~~her~~ beginning.

             the
14. She read the book to find ~~her~~ most interesting parts.
    [There are other possible substitutes for *her*.]

15. I am the winner; victory is ours.

    I am the winner; victory is mine.
    We are the winners; victory is ours.

16. His friends got out of the car, and he went over to talk to them.
    [No errors.]

17. The rain clouds moved toward the pool, and the swimmers tried to wish it away.

    The rain cloud moved toward the pool, and the swimmers tried to wish it away.
    The rain clouds moved toward the pool, and the swimmers tried to wish them away.

              his
18. Was Les disappointed that ~~him~~ team did not win?

    Who
19. ~~Whom~~ has more experience than Nicky does?

20. You play better after you have experience.
    [No errors.]

Subject-Verb Agreement, page 66

      is
1. The chess set ~~are~~ still on the shelf.

           is
2. The shortest route to the college ~~are~~ shown in the catalog.

     drives
3. The golf pro ~~drive~~ a golf cart every day.

       walk
4. Derek and Ann ~~walks~~ every morning.

         add
5. The tropical birds in the tree ~~adds~~ a festive air to the occasion.

          walks
6. No one, not even Rick or Ronnie, ~~walk~~ to school today.

       are
7. Do you know who they ~~is~~?

    prepares
8. Ron ~~prepare~~ a paper for submission to the committee.

           show
9. The 15 employees of the coffee house ~~shows~~ up each day at 6:00 A.M.

         improves
10. Each person who takes the 12 steps ~~improve~~ his or her view.

Adjectives and Adverbs, page 67

               really

1. The view of the Grand Canyon was ~~real~~ spectacular.

               well

2. The trainer said the dog behaved very ~~good~~ today.

    Unfortunately

3. ~~Unfortunate~~, the tickets for the concert were sold out.

          smoothly

4. Things went ~~smooth~~.

            extreme

5. The judge took ~~extremely~~ exception to the defendant's actions.

                     carefully

6. The accident was silly, particularly since driving more ~~careful~~ would have avoided the whole thing.

7. But the reviews said the performance was truly horrible.
   [No adjective or adverb errors.]

8. The manager conveniently forgot that she promised the employee a raise.
   [No adjective or adverb errors.]

                  really

9. The bonus was a welcome surprise; it was a ~~real~~ large check.

       well   **badly**

10. I didn't do ~~good~~, but didn't do ~~bad~~ either.

Comparison, page 68

       happiest

1. Leon was the ~~happieer~~ chef in the restaurant.

2. But some of the people eating in the restaurant were happier than Leon.
   [No error.]

       fastest

3. The jet was the ~~faster~~ plane at the airport.

       faster

4. John was the ~~fastest~~ of the twins.

tallest

5. The ~~taller~~ of the apartment buildings is under repair.

lighter

6. The ~~lightest~~ of the two weights is missing.

7. Lonnie was among the most creative students in the school.
   [No error.]

less

8. Ron is the ~~least~~ able of the two drivers.

9. His shoe size is the smallest in his class.
   [No error.]

10. She was the more capable of the two referees.
    [No error.]

Misplaced and Dangling Modifiers, page 69

1. Les was reading his book through glasses with dirty lenses.
   [No modifier errors.]

2. Jim left work early to go to the doctor on the train.

   Jim left work early to go on a train to the doctor.

3. The first train car was crowded; which had to go to the next car.

   The first train car was crowded; someone (he) (she) had to go to the next car.

4. Ron's car ran out of gas when on the way to the store.

   Ron's car ran out of gas when he was on the way to the store.
   [Many other substitutions are possible for *he was.*]

5. Zena was jogging, when caused her to fall.

   Zena was jogging, when a hole caused her to fall.
   [Many other substitutions are possible for *a hole.*]

6. Derek wrapped the flowers and put them in the delivery van with colorful paper.

   Derek wrapped the flowers with colorful paper and put them in the delivery van.

7. Which bus stops at the corner where the stop sign is?
   [No modifier errors.]

8. Fran is going on the plane, which is just pulling up to the gate.
   [No modifier errors.]

9. Lisa bought a shirt in the store, which was expensive.

   Lisa bought an expensive shirt in the store.
   Lisa bought a shirt in an expensive store.
   Lisa bought an expensive shirt in an expensive store.

10. The car turned around and the headlights shone quickly into the garage.

    The car turned around quickly and the headlights shone into the garage.

Comma Splices and Run-On Sentences, page 70

There are three ways to remedy run-on sentence errors and comma splice errors. You can create two sentences, put a comma and a conjunction between the clauses, or put a semicolon between the two clauses. Only one of these options is shown in the answers.

1. It will be tomorrow before the sea is calm enough to go out.
   [No errors.]

2. It started to rain unexpectedly; the boaters were soaked.

3. But right now my sneakers are soaking wet; the towel is too wet to help me.

4. The Marine Police sounded the siren; the boat stopped immediately.

5. I put the sneakers next to the fire to dry, although they started to steam after a while.
   [No errors.]

6. The Coast Guard monitors boats as they enter the river; they use the data to monitor water pollution.

7. I like to use my compass when I go out on the boat.
   [No errors.]

8. When the boat breaks down, Liz calls Sea Tow.
   [No errors.]

9. The fire went out; the sun came up.

10. Splashing through the waves, the water skier was covered with salt spray.
    [No errors.]

Sentence Fragments, page 72

1. A golf bag, golf clubs, and golf balls. That's what she needed to play.

   A golf bag, golf clubs, and golf balls were what she needed to play.

2. As the rocket prepared for blast-off. Mary saw birds flying in the distance.

The rocket prepared for blast-off. Mary saw birds flying in the distance.
As the rocket prepared for blast-off, Mary saw birds flying in the distance.

3. Jim is mowing the lawn. Then, the mower stopped.
[No sentence fragment errors.]

4. The lawn looked lush and green. Like a golf course.

The lawn looked lush and green, like a golf course.

5. The polar bears swept across the ice. Like white ghosts in fur jackets.

The polar bears swept across the ice, like white ghosts in fur jackets.

6. Jim looked across at the igloo. Like an ice fort, it stood a lonely vigil.
[No sentence fragment errors.]

7. Astronauts and their equipment went by. These were the people who would go into space.
[No sentence fragment errors.]

8. This was what Joe had been waiting for. To graduate from college.

This was what Joe had been waiting for, to graduate from college.

9. To be finished with this test. That's what I'm waiting for.

To be finished with this test is what I'm waiting for.

10. The test finished and done. The papers graded and good.

The tests were finished and done.
The papers were graded and good.

Parallelism, page 73

1. I have to get to work, but first I have to ~~find my way~~ to breakfast.
   get

2. The road was dry; the day was hot and sultry.
[No parallel form errors.]

3. Jane likes to eat and go shopping when she is at the mall.
[No parallel form errors.]

4. April chose to be a cameraperson rather than to be a ~~technician who works the sound board.~~
   sound technician

5. Since I have not heard from you, I decided to write this letter.
[No parallel form errors. The conjunction *since* shows subordination.]

6. Although she had driven the road before, Sally proceeded slowly, keeping her eye on the yellow line.
   [No parallel form errors. The conjunction *although* shows subordination.]

tree branches

7. The tree withstood the hurricane, but ~~the branches on the tree~~ snapped off.

8. His work on the Board of Education revealed his dedication to the community.
   [No parallel form errors.]

9. Cars, taxis, and buses were my transportation to the airport.
   [No parallel form errors.]

class preparation

10. The subject matter and the ~~preparation for class~~ created an excellent lesson.

Diction, page 75

1. Many <u>infectious</u> diseases, including pneumonia and swelling in cuts, are caused by bacteria.
   Infectious means a disease caused by bacteria. While the disease may be unfortunate, the context of the sentence calls for a word that means *caused by bacteria*.

2. Sigmund Freud's views of sexuality had become <u>well known</u>, and the country entered the sexual revolution.
   Well known means known by many people. *Universal* means known everywhere, which does not fit the context of this sentence.

3. After crossing the land bridge near the Bering Strait, groups of Native Americans <u>eventually</u> spread throughout all of North, Central, and South America.
   Eventually means over a period of time. The other words do not make sense in this context.

4. During the early 1500s Cortez and Pizarro opened up Central America to the Spanish who began <u>importing</u> slaves from Africa.
   Importing means to bring in. Exporting means to send out, which does not fit the context of the sentence.

5. The Stamp Act requiring every legal paper to carry a tax stamp was vehemently <u>protested</u> and eventually repealed by England.
   The act could only be *protested* in this context. It was not *denied*, and it does not make sense to say it was *vehemently* denied.

The circled phrases make the sentence too wordy.

6. No goal is more noble—no feat more revealing—than the (strikingly) brave exploration of space.

7. As many as a ton of bananas may have spoiled when the ship was stuck (and delayed) in the Panama Canal.

8. He was concerned about crossing the bridge, but the officer said that it was all right to cross (and he need not worry.)

9. A professional golfer told the (novice) beginning golfer that professional instruction or more practice improves most golfers' scores.

10. The soccer player's slight strain from the shot on goal (that won the game) led to a pulled muscle that would keep her from playing the next match.

The circled words are homonym errors.

11. He went to the bird's nest near the river, only (too) realize he missed its (assent.)

12. The rider pulled back on the horse's (reign) before the (whether) turned rainy.

13. The (whether) turned rainy as he led the hikers on (there) ascent.

14. The (lessen) was clear; it was (fare,) but not easy to accept.

15. (They're) (board) relatives were not (fare,) (too) her father.

Refer to page 74 for a list of idioms.

with
16. Her grades had everything to do of her efforts.

at
17. Joanie expected him to wait to the house until she arrived home.

18. She could spend months absorbed in her studies.
    [No idiom error.]

from
19. The two coaches differ significantly with each other's style.

as
20. That person is wearing the same coat from you.

Commas, page 77

1. I had a slow day yesterday, but I worked hard in my junior year.
   [No comma errors.]

2. Passing calculus seems a difficult, but achievable, result.
   [No comma errors.]

3. After making the sandwich, I looked for some pickles, but the jar was empty.
   [No comma errors.]

4. Write an outline first, and be sure to leave enough time to write the essay.
   [Add a comma before the conjunction to separate the two clauses.]

5. In the attic I found some old clothes, an old trunk, and a shoe.
   [No comma errors.]

6. Chad, Blaire, and Ryan have advanced degrees, but they are still children at heart.
   [Add a comma to separate the clauses.]

7. Using a computer, the Core tests reading, writing, and arithmetic.
   [Add a comma to set off the introductory phrase.]

8. Either walk the dog or wash the dishes.
   [No comma errors.]

9. Every pilot who has flown over 20 missions receives an award.
   [Remove the commas.]

10. Each time I ate lunch at home my mother made liverwurst sandwiches.
    [Remove the comma.]

Semicolons and Colons, page 78

1. Pack these other things for camp: a bathing suit, some socks, and a shirt.
   [Replace the semicolon with a colon.]

2. In your wallet put your camp information card and your bus pass.
   [Remove the colon.]

3. I have one thing left to do: say good-bye.
   [Replace the semicolon with a colon.]

4. We went to the store, and the parking lot was filled with cars.
   [Replace the semicolon with a comma.]

5. We fought our way through the crowds; the store was even more crowded than the parking lot.
   [Replace the comma with a semicolon.]

Period, Question Mark, and Exclamation Point, page 79

1. I was so worn out after swimming.
   [Change the exclamation point to a period.]

2. Avalanche!
   [Change the period to an exclamation point.]

3. Who said that?
   [Change the exclamation point to a question mark.]

4. Warning! The danger signal blared in the background.
   [Change the period to an exclamation point.]

5. I can't believe this is the last day of camp.
   [Change the question mark to a period.]

TARGETED WRITING TEST ANSWERS EXPLAINED

Part A: Usage, page 86

1. **(E)** The underlined sections are all correct.

2. **(A)** Replace the word *trees* with the possessive *trees'*.

3. **(E)** The underlined sections are all correct.

4. **(D)** Replace the word *mystery's* with the plural *mysteries*.

5. **(A)** Replace the words *had lay* with *laid* to show the past tense.

6. **(B)** Replace the words *had spoke* with *spoke* or *had spoken* to show the past tense.

7. **(C)** Replace *gathers* with *gathered* to show past tense and agree with the plural *committee*.

8. **(E)** The underlined sections are all correct.

9. **(D)** Replace the phrase with *and waiting* to maintain the parallel form.

10. **(D)** Replace the phrase with *than to Charleston* to maintain the parallel form.

11. **(B)** Replace the phrase with *would do nothing*, or similar phrases to eliminate the double negative.

12. **(E)** The underlined sections are all correct.

13. **(A)** Replace the word *principle* with the correct spelling *principal*.

14. **(D)** Replace the phrase with *eggs* to maintain the parallel form.

15. **(D)** Replace the phrase with *bitten* to show the future tense.

16. **(C)** Replace the blank space with a comma.

17. **(E)** The underlined sections are all correct.

18. **(D)** Replace *five tenths* with the hyphenated *five-tenths*.

19. **(D)** Replace *unrepresented* with *represented* to eliminate the double negative.

20. **(C)** Replace the word *waters* with the singular *water*.

Part B: Sentence Correction, page 88

21. **(C)** The conjunction pair *not only . . . but also* is the correct coordination for this sentence.

22. **(B)** This wording conveys the meaning of students sorting through projects, which are piled on the table.

23. **(D)** The phrase *who are injured* is essential to the sentence, and it is not set off by commas.

24. **(E)** This choice shows the correct combination of punctuation, a colon, and three commas.

25. **(D)** This choice shows the correct combination of a plural noun and a past tense verb.

Part C: Revision in Context, page 89

26. **(C)** The Grant administration was reacting against the Lakota's rebuff of Grant's attempts to purchase the land, and his decision to just take the land was in clear retaliation for the Lakota's acts.

27. **(C)** This choice clearly and accurately restates the sentence's meaning and is less wordy than the original sentence. Choice (D) is incorrect because, while the troops may have been outnumbered, this choice changes the meaning of the sentence.

Part D: Research Skills, page 90

28. **(A)** The volume number, 215, is the best clue that this citation refers to a periodical, a publication such as a magazine published on a regular schedule. The second clue is that we see a specific name for an article, "The First 'R' of Teaching," together with the name of the publication, *Best Teaching Approaches*. These clues, together with the absence of a name for a newspaper, establish the publication as a periodical.

29. **(E)** This choice gives no insight into the use of social media for advertising. You might have been drawn to choice A, but personal contacts are a form of advertising and give some insight into the role social media plays in advertising.

Part E: Essays, page 91

Compare your essay to these sample essays. Refer to the rating scale on pages 56–57.

RATED ESSAYS

Rated Argumentative essays and Informative/Explanatory (Source-Based) essays are given below.

There are literally many thousands of different approaches and essays that would earn high scores.

RATED ARGUMENTATIVE ESSAYS EXAMPLES

TIP

Take a few minutes to write an outline like the one to the left.

This essay would likely receive a rating of 5 or 6.

It is hard to disagree with the point made in the prompt about automobile fatalities. It is a serious problem in this country. There are still impaired drivers behind the wheels of cars who are too disoriented to make good decisions. Lately, many drivers are distracted by cell phones and tablets, which has increasingly become a cause of accidents. In this day there are still some people who do not wear seatbelts. Most automobile accidents are caused by drivers themselves and through education and laws we need to address these problems and reduce the number of automobile accidents.

However I completely disagree with the notion that a problem with car safety means that, as a general rule, machines harm people. I have one particular example in mind that has to do with my mother. Several years ago she had to undergo serious heart surgery. I didn't know anything about it, but I quickly learned that she would not be breathing on her own nor would her heart be beating on its own during the surgery. It was a very scary proposition.

I learned that my mother would be connected to a heart lung machine during the surgery. For the purposes of this essay—the word "machine" is very important. As I read the opinion for this essay I thought that someone may not have thought of this lifesaving machine—a machine that made such a positive difference in my life. I learned that doctors would be operating inside the heart and that the flow of blood through the heart would actually have to be stopped. I learned that the heart lung machine was a wonderful machine that makes open heart surgery possible by pumping and cleaning blood. Without the heart lung machine this type of surgery would not be as successful, and my mother may have died. Fortunately, the surgeons were good, the machine was available, and my mother is fine.

Whenever I think of a machine I think of the heart lung machine that probably saved my mother's life. And I think of some of the other machines used in the hospital to keep her breathing and to keep her alive during recovery. There may be some machines that hurt people, but there are more that do not. When I think machine, I think good.

Discussion

This essay clearly establishes that the writer does not agree with the main proposition. The details to support her position come from a very personal experience with a machine that probably saved her mother's life. The essay is well developed with a minimum of grammatical errors. The force of the writer's experiences and the conclusions make this a particularly compelling essay.

This essay would likely receive a rating of 4 or 3.

I disagree with the opinion that machines hurt people. It is such a sweeping statement that you just need one counterexample to show that it is not true. Personally, I can think of lots of machines that help people. I could not live without my smartphone. People undergoing open heart surgery could not live without a heart-lung machine or a respirator.

I guess what bothers me is that the statement is so silly. How can you make a general statement that machines hurt people. It just does not make any sense. The list of machines that help people is practically endless. Even the automobile casualties cited in the opinion are most often caused by human error, and it is certainly clear that ambulances, a car of sorts, are extremely helpful and certainly save more lives than those lost in automobile accidents.

An opinion as sweeping and general as the one found on this test can be proven false through many examples including the one described here in detail, and the few others alluded to. It just takes one true counterexample to prove the statement untrue and to conclusively support position that the statement "machines hurt people" is simply not true.

Discussion

This essay clearly states the author's position about the opinion that "machines hurt people." It provides some logic-based arguments that a sweeping statement can be proven false with a single counterexample, and offers several counterexamples to bolster that point. The essay lacks the development and detail necessary to place it in the upper third of essays.

This essay would likely receive a rating of 2.

The general statement that machines hurt people is simply not true. I just think of the heart lung machine. It is a machine and it does not hurt people. Really, what more is there to say. That counterexample proves the statement is false. You do not need more than that.

But there are other examples. You do not even have to talk about a hospital and saving lives. I have clothes that need to be washed. I'd rather not do that by hand so I use a washing machine—I use that "machine." I can absolutely tell you that a washing machine helps me. So there are two examples and there are plenty more of why I disagree with the opinion.

Discussion

There is nothing wrong with this very brief essay, and it makes the point. The intent of this essay is not to prove you can make a point, but that you can write a well-developed essay. This essay lacks the development, detail, and length to receive a rating above 2.

RATED INFORMATIVE/EXPLANATORY (SOURCE-BASED) ESSAYS EXAMPLES

> # Outline
> Robertson—little wrong with tracking; Pismenny—tracking is discriminatory
> Locked in track? Rob—no comment; Pis—students usually locked
> Support tracking? Rob—yes; Pis—no

Here is an essay that would receive a rating of 5 or 6.

The primary concerns about school tracking are its effectiveness as an instructional structure, its unfairness to minority students, and the potential for locking students into a plan of study after they show growth. Both authors seem to agree that tracking helps more able students, but the reasons for that view are quite different. Robertson points to the beneficial impact of tracking, while Pismenny finds tracking discriminatory, writing that "tracking only helps more able students from affluent families."

The differences grow as we move to the next point. The first position paper (Robertson) finds little wrong with tracking, even finding vocational benefits for students in the lowest track when the author points out that "students deserve the opportunities for a track aimed at a career." (Robertson) Pismenny is having none of that and labels tracking programs as discriminatory and goes on to point out that tracking is "insidious" (Pismenny) because it presents itself as an effective educational practice.

Robertson is completely silent on the issue of locking students into a plan of study, while Pismenny highlights that point in a "Track to Nowhere," which condemns tracking because it can take an "extraordinary event" for a students to move up to the next track.

A fair summary seems to be that tracking is a system that seems to work well for more able students from more affluent families. Each position paper makes that point. The main difference appears when Robertson, who supports tracking, finds the advantages of a lower track, while Pismenny opposes tracking and sees it as a discriminatory system that locks in students.

Discussion

This essay does what every high-scoring essay does. It identifies the three main issues. The essay addresses the three issues in turn, bringing information in from both sources into a discussion of each issue, and clearly associates the information presented with the source. It clearly shows the points of agreement and disagreement in the position. The essay is free of meaningful errors, uses an array of sentence types, and shows a notable language structure. The 269 words in this essay will make raters comfortable about placing the essay in the upper third. The difference between a rating of 5 and 6 will hinge on the raters' perception that the analysis was sophisticated enough to receive a rating of 6.

This essay would likely receive a rating of 3 or 4.

There seem to be a range of positive things and negative things about tracking. The first paper by Robertson focuses mainly on the positive with an emphasis on benefits to higher achieving learners. Pismenny's essay focuses on the faults, primarily noting that tracking is just one form of discrimination.

It is obvious that Pismenny does not support tracking. It's the discriminatory nature of tracking that seems to cause this author the most trouble. It just seems to Pismenny that there are more potential problems to make the tracking thing worthwhile. That point is really hammered home when we read "It (tracking) is more insidious than overt discrimination because it hides behind a cloak of what appears to be a useful educational practice." (Pismenny) That is powerful language. Another point Pismenny make is that students are forever stuck in the track they start with at the beginning of high school. They can never escape. It is obvious that tracking is one type of approach with many problems. After reading Pismenny's position I am left wonder just whether there is enough there alone to say that tracking is bad.

Robertson's essay supports tracking as much as we see Pismenny's paper saying that it is bad. Robertson really like how much tracking helps better students. That position is really hammered home by the quote, "For students in an upper track, it removes the lid placed on instruction for academically talented students that would be present if they were in class with students of lesser ability." (Robertson) Robertson also. The system for low track students by saying that it will help these students prepare for careers. In this age when jobs are not really available, I guess that can be a strong argument. Robertson really seems to be saying that tracking is great for all students, but really great for more affluent students. I guess if you are a better students you'll agree with Robertson's position. Some people would say that's the way it is supposed to be. Students who can do the work should be in the top classes.

Robertson says that tracking is the best choice of imperfect choices. If you look at it another way Pismenny says it's just a bad idea all around. I guess every school uses some kind of tracking. The high school I went to had Advanced Placement courses for better students. Since most schools have one I guess it can't be a terrible idea.

Discussion

This essay does a fairly good job discussing the main positions of each position paper, and brings in the writer's own experiences. However, it does not clearly identify the main issues. It discusses one writer's position and then the other's instead of synthesizing them. There is fairly effective use of grammar, mechanics, and usage but with some errors including grammar, sentence fragments (Robertson also. The system . . .), and repetition. The referenced explanation and language usage likely earn this essay a rating of 3 or 4.

This essay would receive a rating of 2.

These two writers seem to have two completely different opinions of tracking. One likes it and the other do not. "In a world of imperfect solutions, a well-managed tracking system is the best approach." It is an imperfect world and I guess that is why these two positions are very different.

Just the whole idea of tracking gets so complicated. You have all these students assigned to classes and if one of those students does better in the middle of this year how can it be so easy to make a change. Besides tracking means different things to different people. "It is easy to see how for students a tracking system is a track to nowhere." That seems hard to disagree with too.

To draw a conclusion you could say that if you like tracking then you do, but there could be very good reasons for not liking tracking. I guess it is up to each person.

Discussion

This essay suffers from two problems. It mentions material from the sources, if inadequately, but it does not reference those sources. The essay also suffers from poor and inadequate development. Either one of these shortcomings would lead to a rating of 2 for this essay.

Additional Sample Responses

You will find additional examples of rated constructed responses on pages 29–40 at *www.ets.org/s/praxis/pdf/5722.pdf*.

Mathematics (5732)

5

USING THIS CHAPTER

This chapter prepares you to take the Core mathematics test. Choose one of the following approaches.

I want all the Mathematics review I can get.

- Skip the Mathematics review quiz and complete the entire mathematics review section starting on page 118.
- Take the Mathematics review quiz starting on page 112.
- Review the answers to the Mathematics review quiz and reread the indicated parts of the Mathematics review section.
- Go over the Strategies for Passing the Mathematics Test on pages 181–182.
- Complete the Targeted Mathematics Test on page 183.

I want a thorough Mathematics review.

- Take the Mathematics review quiz starting on page 112.
- Review the answers to the Mathematics review quiz and reread the indicated parts of the Mathematics review section.
- Go over the Strategies for Passing the Mathematics Test on pages 181–182.
- Complete the Targeted Mathematics Test on page 183.

I want a quick Mathematics review.

- Take and review the answers to the Mathematics review quiz starting on page 112.
- Go over the Strategies for Passing the Mathematics Test on pages 181–182.
- Complete the Targeted Mathematics Test on page 183.

SAMPLE MATHEMATICS ITEMS

Most mathematics multiple-choice items look like this, with just one oval to select.

If $x = \dfrac{5}{6}$, which of the following inequalities is correct?

Ⓐ $\dfrac{5}{9} < x < \dfrac{7}{9}$

Ⓑ $\dfrac{5}{8} < x < \dfrac{3}{4}$

Ⓒ $\dfrac{3}{4} < x < \dfrac{7}{8}$

Ⓓ $\dfrac{7}{8} < x < \dfrac{5}{16}$

Ⓔ $\dfrac{5}{6} < x < \dfrac{6}{5}$

Some items look like this, with one or more boxes to select.

You know the equation of a line 1 is $y = \dfrac{-3x}{4} + 2$.

Which of the following is an equation of a line parallel to line 1?

Select all that apply.

☐A $y = \dfrac{3x}{4} + 2$

☐B $y = \dfrac{-3x}{4} - 2$

☐C $y = \dfrac{-3x}{4} + 4$

☐D $y = \dfrac{3x}{3} + 2$

☐E $y = \dfrac{3x}{4} - 2$

A numeric-entry item like this appears infrequently.

$(3x - 7) + 3 = 4(x - 2)$

What is the value of x?

☐

MATHEMATICS REVIEW QUIZ

This quiz uses a short-answer format to help you find out what you know about the mathematics topics reviewed in this chapter. The quiz results direct you to the portions of the chapter you should review. You do not have to take the quiz in one sitting.

This quiz will also help focus your thinking about mathematics, and these questions and answers are a good review in themselves. It is not important to answer all these questions correctly, and do not be concerned if you miss many of them.

The answers are found immediately after the quiz. It is to your advantage NOT to look at them until you have completed the quiz. Once you have completed and reviewed the answers to this quiz, use the study checklist to decide which sections of the review to study.

It is to your advantage to not use a calculator for this review quiz.

Directions: Write the answers in the space provided.

1. Which number is missing from this sequence?

   6 _____ 12

Questions 2–4: Use symbols for less than, greater than, and equal to, and compare these numbers:

2. 23 _____ 32

3. 18 _____ 4 + 14

4. 9 _____ 10 _____ 11

5. Write the place value of the digit 7 in the numeral 476,891,202,593.

6. Write this number in words: 600,000,000,000.

7. $2^2 \times 2^3 =$

8. $6^9 \div 6^7 =$ _____

9. $3^2 \times 2^3 =$ _____

10. Write 8,342 in scientific notation.

   _____

11. Write the place value of the digit 4 in the numeral 529.354.

   _____

Questions 12–13: Use symbols for less than, greater than, and equal to, and compare these numbers:

12. 9,879 _____ 12,021

13. 98.1589 _____ 98.162

Questions 14–15: Round 234,489.0754 to the:

14. thousands place _____

15. hundredths place _____

16. Is 0.333 . . . a rational or irrational number?

   _____

17. Write these fractions from least to greatest.

   $$\frac{7}{8}, \frac{11}{12}, \frac{17}{20}$$

   _____, _____, _____

18. Which integer is one smaller than –6?

   _____

19. $5 + 7 \times 3^2$ _____

20. $5 \times 8 - (15 - 7 \times 2)$ _____

21. Is 4 a factor of 1,528? Why?

   _____

22. Write the GCF and LCM of 6 and 14.

   _____

23. $426 \div 16 =$ _____

24. Write the property illustrated by:

   $$x(x + 2) = x^2 + 2x$$

   _____

25. $30.916 - 8.72$ _____

26. 3.4×0.0021 _____

27. $0.576 \div 0.32$ _____

28. $1\frac{2}{3} \times 3\frac{3}{4}$ _____

29. $1\frac{2}{3} \div \frac{3}{8}$ _____

30. $1\frac{4}{9} + \frac{5}{6}$ _____

31. $4\frac{5}{6} - 2\frac{3}{5}$ _____

32. Simplify this square root

   $\sqrt{98}$ = _____

33. Complete the following ratio so that it is equivalent to 4 : 5

    28 : _____

34. Use a proportion and solve this problem. Bob uses jelly and peanut butter in a ratio of 5 : 2. He uses 10 teaspoons of jelly. How many teaspoons of peanut butter will he use?

    _____

Questions 35–40: Change among decimals, percents, and fractions to complete the table.

Decimal	Percent	Fraction
0.56	35. _____	36. _____
37. _____	15.2%	38. _____
39. _____	40. _____	$\frac{3}{8}$

41. What is 35 percent of 50?

42. What percent of 120 is 40?

43. A $25 item is on sale for $23.50. What percent of decrease is that?

44. What is the probability of rolling one die and getting a 7? _____

45. You flip a fair coin five times in a row and it comes up heads each time. What is the probability that it will come up tails on the next flip?

    _____

46. You pick one card from a deck. Then you pick another one without replacing the first. Are these dependent or independent events? Explain.

    _____

47. Anna has four pictures. How many different pairs can she make?

Questions 48–49: Find the median and mode of this set of data.

    10, 5, 2, 1, 8, 5, 3, 0

48. Median _____

49. Mode _____

50. What type of correlation does this scatter plot show?

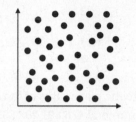

    _____

51. A recreation center is going to be built. The builders randomly poll people in town of various ages, male and female, to find out what is wanted in the recreation center. Is this an appropriate or inappropriate form of sampling?

    _____

52. The graph below represents the percentage of money that is given to each department at Ryan's college. If there is $3,000,000 in available funds, how much does the mathematics department get?

    _____

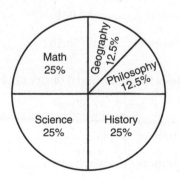

53. $+85 + -103 =$

54. $-12 - +7 =$ _____

55. $-72 - -28 =$ _____

56. $-12 \times -6 =$ _____

57. $-28 \div +7 =$ _____

58. $-72 \div -9 =$ _____

59. Add $(3x^2 + 4xy^2 - 2xy - 3) + (4x^2y - 2y)$

_____

60. Find the area of a triangle with a base of 3 and a height of 2.

_____

61. Find the area of a square with a side of 5.

_____

62. Find the area of a circle with a radius of 6.

_____

Write the value of the variable.

63. $x - 35 = 26$ _____

64. $x + 81 = 7$ _____

65. $y \div 8 < 3$ _____

66. $3z \geq 54$ _____

67. $4y - 9 = 19$ _____

Questions 68–71: Draw a model of:

68. an acute angle

69. complementary angles

70. an isosceles triangle

71. a rectangle

72. Triangle *PQR* and triangle *LMN* are similar. What is the length of side *LN*?

_____

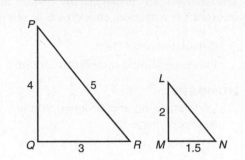

73. Use this coordinate grid and plot these points: A (3, 2), B (–4, –2), C (2, 0). Connect the points to form a triangle.

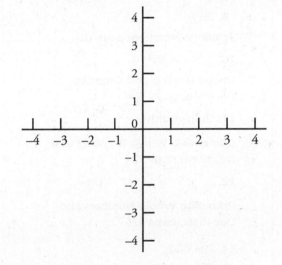

74. The figure in the preceding diagram is shifted up 3 units. What is the coordinate of point B?

75. The figure in the preceding diagram is shifted left 2 units. What is the coordinate of point C?

The answers are organized by review sections. Check your answers. If you miss any questions in a section, check the box and review that section.

☐ Calculator page 118
Everyone should review this section.

NUMBERS

☐ Understanding and Ordering Whole Numbers, page 121

1. 9   **3.** =

2. <   **4.** <, <

☐ Place Value, page 121

5. 10 billion
6. six hundred billion

☐ Positive Exponents, page 122

7. 32   **9.** 72
8. 36

☐ Scientific Notation, page 123

10. 8.342×10^3

☐ Understanding and Ordering Decimals, page 124

11. thousandths

☐ Comparing Whole Numbers and Decimals, page 124

12. <   **13.** <

☐ Rounding Whole Numbers and Decimals, page 125

14. 234,000
15. 234,489.08
16. Rational $0.333 \ldots = \dfrac{1}{3}$

☐ Rational and Irrational Numbers and Fractions, page 125

17. $\dfrac{17}{20}, \dfrac{7}{8}, \dfrac{11}{12}$

☐ Integers, page 129

18. −7

☐ How and When to Add, Subtract, Multiply, and Divide, page 129

19. 68
20. 39

☐ Common Factors and Multiples, page 131

21. Yes, $1,528 \div 4 = 382$. There is no remainder.
22. GCF is 2. LCM is 42.

☐ Whole Number Computation, page 132

23. 26 R 10

☐ Properties of Operations, page 134

24. Distributive

☐ Add, Subtract, Multiply, and Divide Decimals, page 135

25. 22.196
26. 0.00714
27. 1.8

☐ Multiply, Divide, Add, and Subtract Fractions and Mixed Numbers, page 137

28. $6\dfrac{1}{4}$ **30.** $2\dfrac{5}{18}$

29. $4\dfrac{4}{9}$ **31.** $2\dfrac{7}{30}$

☐ Square Roots, page 138

32. $7\sqrt{2}$

☐ Ratio and Proportion, page 139

33. 35
34. 4

☐ Percent, page 140

Decimal	Percent	Fraction
0.56	**35.** 56%	**36.** $\dfrac{14}{25}$
37. 0.152	15.2%	**38.** $\dfrac{19}{125}$
39. 0.375	**40.** 37.5%	$\dfrac{3}{8}$

☐ Three Types of Percent Problems, page 141

41. 17.5   **42.** $33\dfrac{1}{3}$ %

☐ Percent of Increase and Decrease, page 142

43. 6%

PROBABILITY AND STATISTICS

☐ **Probability, page 144**

44. Zero

45. $\frac{1}{2}$

☐ **Independent and Dependent Events, page 145**

46. Dependent. The outcome of one event affects the probability of the other event.

☐ **Permutations, Combinations, and the Fundamental Counting Principle, page 145**

47. 6

☐ **Statistics and Scatter Plots, page 146**

48. 4

49. 5

50. There is no correlation.

51. Appropriate

52. $750,000

ALGEBRA AND FUNCTIONS

☐ **Add and Subtract Integers, page 150**

53. −18

54. −19

55. −44

☐ **Multiply and Divide Integers, page 151**

56. +72

57. −4

58. +8

☐ **Polynomials, page 151**

59. $3x^2 + 4xy^2 + 4x^2y - 2xy - 2y - 3$

☐ **Formulas, page 153**

60. 3

61. 25

62. about 113 (113.097...)

☐ **Equations and Inequalities, page 156**

63. 61

64. −74

65. $y < 24$

66. $z \geq 18$

67. 7

GEOMETRY AND MEASUREMENT

☐ **Two-Dimensional Geometry, page 159**

68. Acute angle

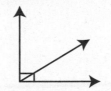

69. Complementary angles

70. Isosceles triangle

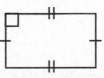

71. Rectangle

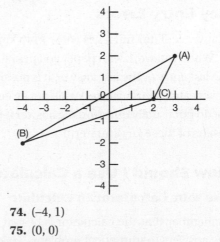

☐ **Similar Triangles, page 163**

72. 2.5

☐ **Coordinate Grid and Translations, page 165**

73.

74. (−4, 1)

75. (0, 0)

☐ **Problem Solving, page 168**

Everyone should review this section.

This review section targets the skills and concepts you need to know to pass the mathematics test of the Core Academic Skills for Educators (Core).

USING THE ON-SCREEN CALCULATOR

This calculator will always be available on the screen to use during the mathematics test. You can use it, when appropriate. For numeric-entry items, press Transfer Display to transfer an answer from the calculator directly to an answer box.

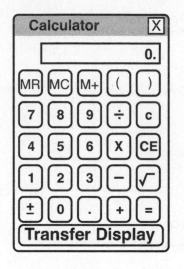

It is a good idea to get a very simple calculator like this one to prepare for the test. The TI-108 is an example of an inexpensive calculator. The TI-108 has the same keys as the on-screen calculator, except for the parentheses keys. Also the TI-108 keys are arranged a little differently. Although there are other basic calculators available, DO NOT use a calculator with more capabilities than the on-screen calculator.

Key Entry Errors

Many calculator mistakes come from key entry errors. Avoid that at all costs.

When you work with paper and pencil, you see all your work. On this calculator, you see only the last entry or the last answer. It is possible to make a key entry error and, in a flurry of entries, never catch your mistake. We all put an enormous amount of trust in the calculator answer, and we do not usually question the answer it produces. This makes us particularly vulnerable to the results of these key entry errors.

How Should I Use a Calculator?

Use Your Calculator to Calculate

Remember that the calculator is best at helping you find answers quickly. Use it to calculate the answers to numerical problems. Use it to try out answers quickly to find which is correct. Whenever you come across a problem involving calculation, you can use the calculator to do or check your work.

Estimate Before You Calculate

Earlier we mentioned that many calculator errors are caused by key entry mistakes. You think you put in one number, but you really put in another. One way to avoid this type of error is to estimate before you calculate. Then compare the estimate to your answer. If they are not close, then either your estimate or your calculation is off.

Recognize When Your Calculator Will Be Helpful

Think of problems in three categories. The calculator can be a big help, some help, or no help. The idea is to use your calculator on the first two types of problems and not to use it when it will not help.

BIG HELP

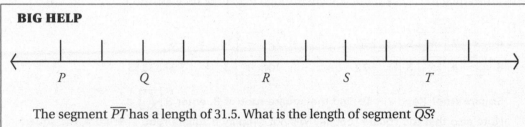

The segment $\overline{PT}$ has a length of 31.5. What is the length of segment $\overline{QS}$?

A calculator is a big help here. There are 9 units from P to T. So divide 31.5 by $9 = 3.5$ to find the length of each unit. Multiply 3.5 by $5 = 17.5$ to find the length of $\overline{QS}$.

SOME HELP

A rectangle has length 3 and width 5. What is the area?

You can do this computation in your head. A calculator could help you check the answer, but you do not absolutely need it. The area is $(3)(5) = 15$.

NO HELP

Calculators are no help with problems involving equations or nonnumerical solutions. Using a calculator when it will not help will cause trouble and waste time.

Order of Operations

There is a difficulty with the TI-108 that you'll have to work around during the test. The TI-108 does not use order of operations, and it does not include keys with parentheses. The TI-108 just does the calculations in the order you press the keys.

You will have to be sure you follow this order of operations.

1. Parentheses (Operations in parentheses are done first.)
2. Exponents
3. Multiplication
4. Division
5. Addition
6. Subtraction

Find the answer: $4 + 6 \times 5$

Using order of operations: $4 + 6 \times 5 = 4 + 30 = 34$

That is because you multiply first and then add.

But press $4 + 6 \times 5$ on a TI-108 and the answer is 50. That's wrong!

That is because the TI-108 just completes the calculation in the order you press the keys.

You have to press the TI-108 calculator keys as shown below to find the correct answer.
$6 \times 5 + 4 =$

How Are Calculator Keys Used?

Press the numeral keys and the decimal point to represent numbers.

Press the $\boxed{+}$, $\boxed{-}$, $\boxed{\times}$, and $\boxed{\div}$ keys to add, subtract, multiply, and divide.

Press the equal $\boxed{=}$ key when you are through to get the final answer.

4 $\boxed{\times}$ 7 $\boxed{+}$ 9 $\boxed{=}$ 37   12 $\boxed{-}$ 18 $\boxed{=}$ -6

6 $\boxed{\times}$ 4 $\boxed{\times}$ 3 $\boxed{=}$ 72   10 $\boxed{\div}$ 3 $\boxed{=}$ 3.3333333

Square Root Key. $\boxed{\sqrt{}}$ To find the square root of 8, enter 8 $\boxed{\sqrt{}}$ =.

Note also that the square root key will not simplify a square root. Therefore, the square root shows up as 2.8284, not $2\sqrt{2}$.

Integer Key. $\boxed{+/-}$ The subtraction key on the calculator cannot be used to represent negative integers. Use the $\boxed{+/-}$ key on the calculator after a number to change the sign. For example, to subtract –62 – +25, enter 62 $\boxed{+/-}$ $\boxed{-}$ 25 $\boxed{=}$. To multiply –8 × –6, enter 8 $\boxed{+/-}$ $\boxed{\times}$ 6 $\boxed{+/-}$ $\boxed{=}$.

Percent Key $\boxed{\%}$

Use the percent key to find percent of increase or percent of decrease, such as the price after a sales tax is added or the price after a percent discount.

Find the cost of an item sold for $16 after a 7% sales tax.
Use these key strokes.

16 $\boxed{+}$ 7 $\boxed{\%}$ 17.12 [Do not press the equal sign.]

The cost with sales tax is $17.12.

Find the price of a $15.50 item sold at a 20% discount.
Use these key strokes.

15.50 $\boxed{-}$ 20 $\boxed{\%}$ 12.40 [Do not press the equal sign.]

The cost after the discount is $12.40.

Memory Keys $\boxed{M+}$ $\boxed{M-}$ $\boxed{MRC}$

The memory can be a handy place to store a number. The keys let you add and subtract values in memory, recall the value from memory, and erase that number.

13 $\boxed{\text{M+}}$ places the 13 in memory.

5 $\boxed{\text{M--}}$ subtracts 5 from memory.

32.5 $\boxed{\text{M+}}$ adds 32 to the memory.

Press $\boxed{\text{MRC}}$ after this series of key strokes and the display shows 40.5, the value stored in memory.

Press the $\boxed{\text{MRC}}$ a second time and the value in memory is erased.

$\boxed{\text{ON/C}}$

This key turns the calculator on. Press the key once after the calculator is on to erase the display. Press the key a second time to erase all the work you have done. Pressing this key does not erase the memory.

NUMBERS

Understanding and Ordering Whole Numbers

Whole numbers are the numbers you use to tell how many. They include 0, 1, 2, 3, 4, 5, 6 . . . . The dots tell us that these numbers keep going on forever. There are an infinite number of whole numbers, which means you will never reach the last one.

Cardinal numbers such as 1, 9, and 18 tell how many. There are 9 players on the field in a baseball game. Ordinal numbers such as 1st, 2nd, 9th, and 18th tell about order. For example, Lynne batted 1st this inning.

You can visualize whole numbers evenly spaced on a number line.

You can use the number line to compare numbers. Numbers get smaller as you go to the left and larger as you go to the right. The terms *equal to* (=), *less than* (<), *greater than* (>), and *between* are used to compare numbers.

12 equals 10 + 2	2 is less than 5	9 is greater than 4	6 is between 5 and 7
12 = 10 + 2	2 < 5	9 > 4	5 < 6 < 7

Place Value

We use ten digits, 0–9, to write out numerals. We also use a place value system of numeration. The value of a digit depends on the place it occupies. Look at the following place value chart.

millions	hundred thousands	ten thousands	thousands	hundreds	tens	ones
3	5	7	9	4	1	0

The value of the 9 is 9,000. The 9 is in the thousands place. The value of the 5 is 500,000. The 5 is in the hundred thousands place. Read the number three million, five hundred seventy-nine thousand, four hundred ten.

Some whole numbers are very large. The distance from Earth to Pluto is about six trillion (6,000,000,000,000) yards. The distance from Earth to the nearest star is about 40 quadrillion (40,000,000,000,000,000) yards.

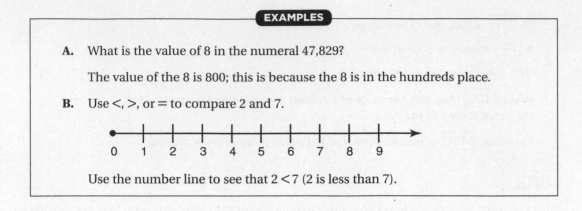

A. What is the value of 8 in the numeral 47,829?

The value of the 8 is 800; this is because the 8 is in the hundreds place.

B. Use <, >, or = to compare 2 and 7.

Use the number line to see that 2 < 7 (2 is less than 7).

Practice

Fill in the space with =, <, or > to make each statement true.

1. 2 _____ 3

2. 4 _____ 1

3. 8 _____ 9

4. 1 _____ 1

5. 7 _____ 6

6. Write a numeral in which the value of 7 is seven, the value of 9 is nine thousand, the value of 3 is thirty, and the 0 is in the hundreds place.

7. Write a numeral in which the value of 5 is fifty, the value of 2 is two thousand, the value of 1 is one, and the value of 8 is eight hundred.

8. What place values in the numeral 65,747 contain the same digit?

9. Write the whole numbers between 0 and 15.

10. How many whole numbers are there between 0 and 50?

(Answers on page 199.)

Positive Exponents

You can show repeated multiplication as an exponent. The exponent shows how many times the factor appears.

$$\text{Base} \rightarrow 3^{\overset{\text{[Exponent]}}{5}} = \underbrace{3 \times 3 \times 3 \times 3 \times 3}_{\text{[Factors]}} = 243$$

RULES FOR EXPONENTS

Use these rules to multiply and divide exponents with the *same base*.

$$7^8 \times 7^5 = 7^{13} \qquad\qquad a^n \times a^m = a^{m+n}$$
$$7^8 \div 7^5 = 7^3 \qquad\qquad a^n \div a^m = a^{n-m}$$

A. $4^3 + 6^2$ $= 4 \times 4 \times 4 + 6 \times 6$ $= 64 + 36$ $= 100$

B. $(2^3)(4^2)$ $= (2 \times 2 \times 2) \times (4 \times 4)$ $= 8 \times 16$ $= 128$

C. $(3^2)^2$ $= 3^4$ $= 3 \times 3 \times 3 \times 3$ $= 81$

D. $(10 - 9)^2$ $= 1^2$ $= 1$

Practice

1. $5^2 + 6^3 =$
2. $(3^2)^3 =$
3. $(8 - 6)^3 =$
4. $(5^2)(6^2) =$
5. $3^3 + 2^3 =$
6. $10^2 - 7^2 =$
7. $(4^3)^2 =$
8. $(2^1)^5 =$
9. $6^2 + 2^3 =$
10. $(25 - 15)^3 =$
11. $(4^2)^2 =$
12. $(2^3)(3^2) =$

(Answers on page 199.)

Scientific Notation

Scientific notation uses powers of 10. The power shows how many zeros to use.

$10^0 = 1$	$10^1 = 10$	$10^2 = 100$	$10^3 = 1,000$	$10^4 = 10,000$
	$10^{-1} = 0.1$	$10^{-2} = 0.01$	$10^{-3} = 0.001$	$10^{-4} = 0.0001$

$$10^5 = 100,000$$
$$10^{-5} = 0.00001$$

Write whole numbers and decimals in scientific notation. Use a decimal with one numeral to the left of the decimal point.

$2,345 \quad = \quad 2.345 \times 10^3$ The decimal point moved three places to the left.
Use 10^3.

$176.8 \quad = \quad 1.768 \times 10^2$ The decimal point moved two places to the left.
Use 10^2.

$0.0034 \quad = \quad 3.4 \times 10^{-3}$ The decimal point moved three places to the right.
Use 10^{-3}.

$2.0735 \quad = \quad 2.0735 \times 10^0$ The decimal is in the correct form.
Use 10^0 to stand for 1.

EXAMPLES

A. Write 7,952 in scientific notation.

Move the decimal point three places to the left and write
$7,952 = 7.952 \times 10^3$.

B. Write 0.03254 in scientific notation.

Move the decimal point two places to the right and write
3.254×10^{-2}.

Practice

Rewrite using scientific notation.

1. 0.0564
2. 0.00897
3. 0.06501
4. 0.000354
5. 545
6. 7,790
7. 289,705
8. 1,801,319

(Answers on page 199.)

Understanding and Ordering Decimals

Decimals are used to represent numbers between 0 and 1. Decimals can also be written on a number line.

We also use ten digits 0–9 and a place value system of numeration to write decimals. The value of a digit depends on the place it occupies. Look at the following place value chart.

ones	tenths	hundredths	thousandths	ten thousandths	hundred thousandths	millionths	ten millionths	hundred millionths	billionths
0 .	3	6	8	7					

The value of 3 is three tenths. The 3 is in the tenths place. The value of 8 is eight thousandths. The 8 is in the thousandths place.

Comparing Whole Numbers and Decimals

To compare two numbers, line up the place values. Start at the left and keep going until the digits in the same place are different.

Compare	9,879 and 16,459	23,801 and 23,798	58.1289 and 58.132
Line up the	9,879	23,801	58.1289
place values	16,459	23,798	58.132
	$9,879 < 16,459$	$23,801 > 23,798$	$58.1289 < 58.132$
	Less than	Greater than	Less than

EXAMPLES

A. What is the value of the digit 2 in the decimal 35.6829?

The 2 is in the thousandths place. $2 \times 0.001 = 0.002$.
The value of the 2 is 0.002 or 2 thousandths.

B. Use $<$, $>$, or $=$ to compare 1248.9234 and 1248.9229.

1248.9234 ◯ 1248.9229. The digits in the numerals are the same until you reach the thousandths place where $3 > 2$. Since $3 > 2$, then $1248.9234 > 1248.9229$.

Practice

Use $<$, $>$, or $=$ to compare.

1. 0.02 _____ 0.003

2. 4.6 _____ 1.98

3. 0.0008 _____ 0.00009

4. 1.0 _____ 1

5. 7.6274 _____ 7.6269

Write the answer.

6. Write a numeral in which the value of 5 is five tenths, the value of 2 is two, the value of 6 is six thousandths, and the value of 8 is eight hundredths.

7. Write a numeral in which the value of 4 is in the ten thousandths place, the value of 3 is three hundred, the 7 is in the hundredths place, the 1 is in the tens place, the 9 is in the ten thousands place, and the rest of the digits are zeros.

8. In the numeral 6.238935, which place values contain the same digit?

9. Using only the tenths place, write all the decimals from 0 to 1.

10. If you used only the tenths and hundredths places, how many decimals are between 0 and 1?

(Answers on page 199.)

Rounding Whole Numbers and Decimals

Follow these steps to round a number to a place.

- Look at the digit to the right of the number.
- If the digit to the right is 5 or more, round up. If the digit is less than 5, leave the numeral to be rounded as written.

EXAMPLES

A. *Round 859,465 to the thousands place.*
Underline the thousands place.
Look to the right. The digit 4 is less than 5 so leave as written.
859,465 rounded to the thousands place is 859,000.
859,465 rounded to the ten-thousands place is 860,000.

B. *Round 8.647 to the hundredths place.*
Underline the hundredths place.
Look to the right. The digit 7 is 5 or more so you round up.
8.647 rounded to the *hundredths* place is 8.65.
8.647 rounded to the *tenths* place is 8.6.

Practice

1. Round 23,465 to the hundreds place.

2. Round 74.1508 to the thousandths place.

3. Round 975,540 to the ten thousands place.

4. Round 302.787 to the tenths place.

5. Round 495,244 to the tens place.

6. Round 1508.75 to the hundreds place.

7. Round 13.097 to the hundredths place.

8. Round 198,704 to the hundred thousands place.

9. Round 51.8985 to the ones place.

10. Round 23,457 to the hundreds place.

(Answers on page 199.)

Rational and Irrational Numbers and Fractions

Most numbers can be written as a fraction or a ratio, with an integer in the numerator and in the denominator. These are called rational numbers.

Some numbers cannot be written as fractions with an integer in the numerator and in the denominator. These are called irrational numbers.

Never write 0 in the denominator. These numbers are undefined.

Look at these examples.

9 is rational because it can be written as the ratio 9/1 (or 18/2 and so on).

0.25 is rational because it can be written as the ratio 1/4.

0.4 is rational because it can be written as the ratio 4/10 (2/5 in simplest form).

0.666 . . . (6 continues to repeat) is rational because it can be written as the ratio 2/3.

Rational numbers can be written as decimals that terminate or repeat.

0.25 and 0.4 are examples of decimals that terminate.

$\frac{1}{3}$ = 0.333 . . . and $\frac{1}{7}$ = 0.14285714285 . . . (the "142857" repeats) are examples of decimals that repeat.

Every fraction can be represented by a decimal that terminates or repeats.

IRRATIONAL NUMBERS

Irrational numbers cannot be written as a fraction.

The most famous irrational number is π.

You could try forever and never find a fraction or a terminating or repeating decimal that equals π.

π = 3.141592653 . . .

The calculator for this test does not have a π key, so you will have to use rational numbers to approximate π. Use 3.14, 3.1416 or 22/7 (= 3.14285). The test item will indicate which approximation to use or the answer will be so obvious that you will not need that specific information.

Square Root of 2

Another famous irrational number is the square root of $2(\sqrt{2})$. If you draw a diagonal in a square with sides equal to 1, the Pythagorean theorem tells you that the length of that diagonal is $\sqrt{2}$.

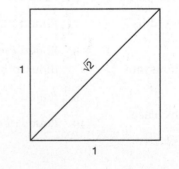

$$a^2 + b^2 = c^2 = 1^2 + 1^2 \qquad c^2 = 1 + 1 = 2: c = \sqrt{2}$$

$\sqrt{2}$ = 1.41421356 . . .

You can use 99/70 ($\approx$ 1.41429) to approximate $\sqrt{2}$. You can see that this approximation is very close to the decimal value of the number.

The test calculator has a square root key so you could approximate the square root of 2. Most often just leave it as is and write the answer in radical form, such as $3\sqrt{2}$.

Practice

Write these fractions as terminating or repeating decimals. You can use a calculator.

1. $\dfrac{2}{3}$ 2. $\dfrac{9}{12}$ 3. $\dfrac{5}{9}$ 4. $\dfrac{7}{12}$

5. What is a reasonable approximation of 7π?

6. What is a reasonable approximation of $105\sqrt{2}$?

(Answers on page 199.)

Understanding and Ordering Fractions

A fraction names a part of a whole or of a group. A fraction has two parts: a numerator and a denominator. The denominator tells how many parts in all. The numerator tells how many parts are identified.

$$\dfrac{3 \quad \text{Numerator}}{4 \quad \text{Denominator}}$$

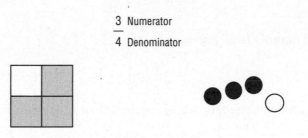

EQUIVALENT FRACTIONS

Two fractions that stand for the same number are called equivalent fractions. Multiply or divide the numerator and the denominator by the same number to find an equivalent fraction.

$$\frac{2\times3}{5\times3}=\frac{6}{15} \qquad \frac{6\div3}{9\div3}=\frac{2}{3} \qquad \frac{6\times4}{8\times4}=\frac{24}{32} \qquad \frac{8\div2}{10\div2}=\frac{4}{5}$$

Fractions can also be written and ordered on a number line. You can use the number line to compare fractions. Fractions get smaller as you go to the left and larger as you go to the right. Use the terms equivalent to (=), less than (<), greater than (>), and between to compare fractions.

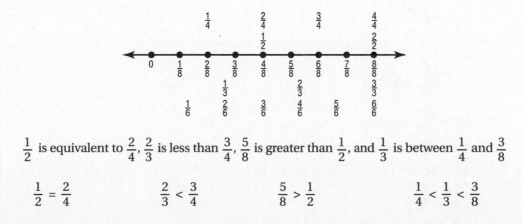

$\dfrac{1}{2}$ is equivalent to $\dfrac{2}{4}$, $\dfrac{2}{3}$ is less than $\dfrac{3}{4}$, $\dfrac{5}{8}$ is greater than $\dfrac{1}{2}$, and $\dfrac{1}{3}$ is between $\dfrac{1}{4}$ and $\dfrac{3}{8}$

$$\frac{1}{2}=\frac{2}{4} \qquad\qquad \frac{2}{3}<\frac{3}{4} \qquad\qquad \frac{5}{8}>\frac{1}{2} \qquad\qquad \frac{1}{4}<\frac{1}{3}<\frac{3}{8}$$

COMPARE TWO FRACTIONS

Use this method to compare two fractions. For example, compare $\frac{13}{18}$ and $\frac{5}{7}$. First write the two fractions and cross multiply as shown. The larger cross product appears next to the larger fraction. If cross products are equal, then the fractions are equivalent.

$$91 = \qquad = 90$$

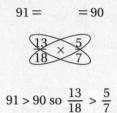

$$91 > 90 \text{ so } \frac{13}{18} > \frac{5}{7}$$

MIXED NUMBERS AND IMPROPER FRACTIONS

Change an improper fraction to a mixed number:

$$\frac{23}{8} = 8\overline{)23} = 2\frac{7}{8}$$

Change a mixed number to an improper fraction:

$$3\frac{2}{5} = \frac{17}{5}$$

Multiply the denominator and the whole number. Then add the numerator.

$$\frac{(3\times5)+2}{5} = \frac{15+2}{5} = \frac{17}{5}$$

EXAMPLES

A. Compare $\frac{5}{7}$ and $\frac{18}{19}$.

Use cross multiplication.

$\frac{5}{7} \times \frac{18}{19}$, $5 \times 19 = 95$ and $7 \times 18 = 126$, therefore $\frac{5}{7} < \frac{18}{19}$.

B. Write $\frac{27}{7}$ as a mixed number.

$$\begin{array}{r} 3 \text{ R6} \\ 7\overline{)27} \\ \underline{-21} \\ 6 \end{array}$$

$$\frac{27}{7} = 3\frac{6}{7}$$

C. Write $6\frac{5}{8}$ as a fraction.

Multiply the denominator and the whole number. $6 \times 8 = 48$.

Add the numerator to the product. $48 + 5 = 53$.

$$6\frac{5}{8} = \frac{53}{8}$$

Practice

Write the improper fraction as a mixed number.

1. $\dfrac{5}{3}$　　　　　　　2. $\dfrac{15}{7}$　　　　　　　3. $\dfrac{24}{9}$

Write the mixed number as an improper fraction.

4. $8\dfrac{1}{5}$　　　　　　　5. $6\dfrac{7}{8}$　　　　　　　6. $9\dfrac{5}{7}$

Use >, <, or = to compare the fractions.

7. $\dfrac{3}{7}\bigcirc\dfrac{4}{9}$　　　　　　　8. $\dfrac{5}{6}\bigcirc\dfrac{25}{30}$　　　　　　　9. $\dfrac{4}{5}\bigcirc\dfrac{7}{8}$

(Answers on page 199.)

Integers

The number line can also show negative numbers. There is a negative whole number for every positive whole number. Zero is neither positive nor negative. The negative whole numbers, the positive whole numbers, and zero, together, are called integers. Integers are smaller as you go left on the number line and larger as you go to the right.

$$^-10 < {}^-1 \qquad ^-8 < {}^-3 \qquad ^+1 > {}^-9 \qquad ^+6 > {}^+4$$

How and When to Add, Subtract, Multiply, and Divide

ORDER OF OPERATIONS

Use this phrase to remember the order of operations:

Please Excuse My Dear Aunt Sally

(1) **P**arentheses (2) **E**xponents (3) **M**ultiplication or **D**ivision (4) **A**ddition or **S**ubtraction

For example,

$$4 + 3 \times 7^2 \quad = \quad 4 + 3 \times 49 \quad = \quad 4 + 147 \quad = \quad 151$$
$$(4 + 3) \times 7^2 \quad = \quad 7 \times 7^2 \quad = \quad 7 \times 49 \quad = \quad 343$$
$$(6 - 10 \div 5) + 6 \times 3 = (6 - 2) + 6 \times 3 = 4 + 6 \times 3 = 4 + 18 = 22$$

EXAMPLES

$$7 + 3 \times 6 + 4^2 - (8 + 4) \quad = \quad 7 + 3 \times 6 + 4^2 - \underline{12} \quad =$$
$$7 + 3 \times 6 + \underline{16} - 12 \quad = \quad 7 + \underline{18} + 16 - 12 \quad = 29$$

DECIDE WHETHER TO ADD, SUBTRACT, MULTIPLY, OR DIVIDE

Before you can solve a problem, you should know which operation to use. You can use key words to decide which operation to use or you can use a problem-solving strategy called choosing the operation.

Key Words

Addition	sum, and, more, increased by
Subtraction	less, difference, decreased by
Multiplication	of, product, times
Division	per, quotient, shared, ratio
Equals	is, equals

You cannot just use these key words without thinking. You must check to be sure that the operation makes sense when it replaces the key word. See the examples below.

EXAMPLES

19 and 23 is 42   16 is 4 more than 12   What percent of 19 is 5.7

$19 + 23 = 42$ $16 = 4 + 12$ $\rule{2cm}{0.4pt}\% \times 19 = 5.7$

Practice

Find the answer.

1. $4 \times 5 + 4 \div 2 =$

2. $(5 + 7 - 9) \times 8^2 + 2 =$

3. $((7 + 4) - (1 + 4)) \times 6 =$

4. $6^2 + 3(9 - 5 + 7)^2 =$

5. $(12 + 5) \times 3 - 6^2 =$

6. $8 \times 5 + 4 - 8 \div 2 =$

7. $100 - 30 \times 5 + 7 =$

8. $((5 + 2)^2 + 16) \times 8 =$

(Answers on page 200.)

CHOOSING THE OPERATION

To use the choosing-the-operation strategy, you think of each situation in this way. What do I know? What am I trying to find? The answers to these questions lead you directly to the correct operation.

You Know	You Want to Find
Add	
1. How many in two or more groups	How many in all
2. How many in one group How many join it	The total amount
3. How many in one group How many more in the second group	How many in the second group
Subtract	
4. How many in one group Number taken away	How many are left
5. How many in each of two groups	How much larger one group is than the other
6. How many in one group How many in part of that group	How many in the rest of the group

You Know	You Want to Find

Multiply

7. How many in each group

    There is the same number in each group   How many in all

    How many groups

Divide

8. Same number in each group   How many groups

    How many in all

    How many in each group

9. Same number in each group   How many in each group

    How many in all

    How many groups

Common Factors and Multiples

FACTORS

The factors of a number evenly divide the number with no remainder. For example, 2 is a factor of 6, but 2 is not a factor of 5.

Here are the factors for the numbers 1–10.

The number 1 is a factor of every number. Each number is a factor of itself.

1	The only factor is 1	6	1, 2, 3, 6
2	1, 2	7	1, 7
3	1, 3	8	1, 2, 4, 8
4	1, 2, 4	9	1, 3, 9
5	1, 5	10	1, 2, 5, 10

LEAST COMMON MULTIPLE (LCM), GREATEST COMMON FACTOR (GCF)

Multiples

The multiples of a number are all the numbers you get when you count by that number. Here are some examples.

Multiples of 1: 1, 2, 3, 4, 5, . . .

Multiples of 2: 2, 4, 6, 8, 10, . . .

Multiples of 3: 3, 6, 9, 12, 15, . . .

Multiples of 4: 4, 8, 12, 16, 20, . . .

Multiples of 5: 5, 10, 15, 20, 25, . . .

Least Common Multiple

The least common multiple is the smallest multiple shared by two numbers.

The least common multiple of 6 and 8 is 24.

List the multiples of 6 and 8. Notice that 24 is the smallest multiple common to both numbers.

Multiples of 6: 6, 12, 18, **24**, 30, 36

Multiples of 8: 8, 16, **24**, 32, 40

Greatest Common Factor

The greatest common factor is the largest factor shared by two numbers.

The greatest common factor of 28 and 36 is 4.

List the factors of 28 and 36.

Factors of 28: 1, 2, **4**, 7, 14, 28
Factors of 36: 1, 2, 3, **4**, 9, 12, 18, 36

EXAMPLES

A. Find the factors of 24.

The factors are 1, 2, 3, 4, 6, 8, 12, and 24.
These are the only numbers that divide 24 with no remainder.

B. Find the GCF of 14 and 22.

Write out the factors of each number.
14: 1, 2, 7, 14
22: 1, 2, 11, 22
The greatest common factor is 2.

C. Find the LCM of 6 and 9.

List some of the multiples of each number.
6: 6, 12, 18, 24, . . .
9: 9, 18, 27, . . .
The least common multiple is 18.

Practice

Write the factors of each number.

1. 13   2. 26   3. 40   4. 23

Find the LCM of the two numbers.

5. 4 and 6   6. 5 and 12   7. 7 and 35   8. 4 and 14

Find the GCF of the two numbers.

9. 24 and 30   10. 15 and 40   11. 32 and 64   12. 56 and 84

(Answers on page 200.)

Whole Number Computation

You have a calculator, but it may help to review these steps.

Follow these steps to add, subtract, multiply, and divide whole numbers.
Estimate first and then check to be sure your answer is reasonable.

Add

24,262 + 8,921.

Estimate first.

24,262 rounded to the nearest ten thousand is 24,000.

8,921 rounded to the nearest thousand is 9,000.

24,000 + 9,000 = 33,000. The answer should be close to 33,000.

Add.

```
                          1 1
    2 4 2 6 2          2 4 2 6 2
  +   8 9 2 1        +   8 9 2 1
  -----------        -----------
                      3 3 1 8 3
```

Align digits.   Add.

33,183 is close to 33,000, so the answer is reasonable.

Subtract

20,274 − 17,235.

Estimate first.

20,274 rounded to the nearest thousand is 20,000.

17,235 rounded to the nearest thousand is 17,000.

20,000 − 17,000 = 3,000.

The answer should be close to 3,000.

Subtract.

```
                     1 10     6 14
    2 0 2 7 4        2  0  2  7  4
  − 1 7 2 3 5      − 1  7  2  3  5
  -----------      --------------
                         3  0  3  9
```

Align digits.   Subtract.

3,039 is close to 3,000, so the answer seems reasonable.

Multiply

32 × 181.

Estimate first.

Multiplication answers may look correct but may be wrong by a multiple of 10.

32 rounded to the nearest ten is 30.

181 rounded to the nearest hundred is 200.

30 × 200 = 6,000.

The answer should be near 6,000.

Multiply.

```
      181              181
  ×    32          ×    32
  -------          -------
     362              362
    5430           +5430
  -------          -------
                     5792
```

Find the partial products.   Add the partial products.

The answer is close to 6,000.

The answer seems reasonable.

Divide

$927 \div 43$.

Estimate first.

You may make a division error if you misalign digits.

927 rounded to the nearest hundred is 900.

43 is close to 45.

$900 \div 45 = 20$

The answer should be somewhere near 20.

Divide.

$$43\overline{)927}$$

$$
\begin{array}{r}
21 \text{ R}24 \\
43\overline{)927} \\
-86\downarrow \\
\hline
67 \\
-43 \\
\hline
24
\end{array}
$$

Divide.

Find the quotient and the remainder.

The answer is close to 20.

The answer seems reasonable.

Practice

Find the answer.

1. $\begin{array}{r} 97,218 \\ + 1,187 \end{array}$
2. $\begin{array}{r} 23,045 \\ + 4,034 \end{array}$
3. $\begin{array}{r} 67,914 \\ +27,895 \end{array}$
4. $\begin{array}{r} 48,549 \\ +17,635 \end{array}$

5. $\begin{array}{r} 20,591 \\ - 4,578 \end{array}$
6. $\begin{array}{r} 34,504 \\ - \ \ 405 \end{array}$
7. $\begin{array}{r} 57,895 \\ - 23,207 \end{array}$
8. $\begin{array}{r} 84,403 \\ -42,194 \end{array}$

9. $\begin{array}{r} 240 \\ \times \ 57 \end{array}$
10. $\begin{array}{r} 302 \\ \times \ 91 \end{array}$
11. $\begin{array}{r} 725 \\ \times \ 41 \end{array}$
12. $\begin{array}{r} 146 \\ \times \ 36 \end{array}$

13. $328 \div 41 =$
14. $240 \div 59 =$
15. $754 \div 26 =$
16. $2,370 \div 74 =$

(Answers on page 200.)

Properties of Operations

Subtraction and division are not commutative or associative.

Commutative $a + b = b + a$ $a \times b = b \times a$

$3 + 5 = 5 + 3$ $3 \times 5 = 5 \times 3$

Associative $(a + b) + c = a + (b + c)$ $(a \times b) \times c = a \times (b \times c)$

$(3 + 4) + 5 = 3 + (4 + 5)$ $(3 \times 4) \times 5 = 3 \times (4 \times 5)$

Identity	$a + 0 = a$	$a \times 1 = a$
	$5 + 0 = 5$	$5 \times 1 = 5$

Inverse	$a + (-a) = 0$	$a \times \dfrac{1}{a} = 1$
	$5 + (-5) = 0$	$5 \times \dfrac{1}{5} = 1 \ (a \neq 0)$

Distributive property of
multiplication over addition

$a(b + c) = (a \times b) + (a \times c)$
$3(4 + 5) = (3 \times 4) + (3 \times 5)$

EXAMPLES

A. Use a property of operations to write an expression equivalent to $8y - 4x$.
These items ask you to identify equivalent statements produced by the properties.
The distributive property creates the equivalent expressions
$4(2y - x)$ or $2(4y - 2x)$.

B. What property is illustrated by $7^2 + 8^3 = 8^3 + 7^2$?
This statement demonstrates the commutative property.

Practice

1. Use a property to write an expression equivalent to $\dfrac{6}{8} \times \dfrac{7}{9}$.

2. What property is illustrated by $(2 + 3) + 4 = 2 + (3 + 4)$?

3. What property is illustrated by $3x(x + 2y) = 3x^2 + 6xy$?

4. Write an expression equivalent to $a(6) + a(3)$.

5. What property is illustrated by $3a + 3b = 3b + 3a$?

6. Choose a statement that is *not* true for all real numbers.

   Ⓐ $A(1/A) = 0$ for $A \neq 0$.
   Ⓑ $x^2(y^2) = (xy)^2$
   Ⓒ $(3x + y)(x - y) = (x - y)(3x + y)$
   Ⓓ $10^2 + 12 = 12 + 10^2$

(Answers on page 200.)

Add, Subtract, Multiply, and Divide Decimals

ADD AND SUBTRACT DECIMALS

Line up the decimal points and add or subtract.

Add: $14.9 + 3.108 + 0.16$ Subtract: $14.234 - 7.14$

$$
\begin{array}{r}
14.9 \\
3.108 \\
+\,0.16 \\
\hline
18.168
\end{array}
\qquad
\begin{array}{r}
14.234 \\
-\,7.14 \\
\hline
7.094
\end{array}
$$

MULTIPLY DECIMALS

Multiply as with whole numbers. Count the total number of decimal places in the factors. Put that many decimal places in the product. You may have to write leading zeros.

Multiply: 17.4×1.3 Multiply: 0.016×1.7

```
    17.4                    0.016
  × 1.3                   × 1.7
    522                     112
  +174                    +16
  2 2 6 2 = 22.62         0 2 7 2 = 0.0272
```

DIVIDE DECIMALS

Make the divisor a whole number. Match the movement in the dividend and then divide.

$0.16\overline{)1.328}$ $0.16\overline{)1.32.8}$

```
        8.3
  16)132.8
    −128
      48
     −48
       0
```

Practice

1. 12.79
    8.1
    + 5.2

2. 40.267
    23.2
    + 9.15

3. 940.17
    36.15
    + 12.07

4. 5290.3
    167.81
    + 15.09

5. 37.9
    − 29.7

6. 136.804
    − 65.7944

7. 513.72
    − 59.75

8. 2451.06
    − 683.19

9. 0.249
    × 2.5

10. 46.7
    × 3.5

11. 56.2
    × 65.49

12. 93.57
    × 40.2

13. $10.32 \div 2.15$ 14. $16.8 \div 1.75$ 15. $250.32 \div 7.45$ 16. $659.5575 \div 5.25$

(Answers on page 200.)

Multiply, Divide, Add, and Subtract Fractions and Mixed Numbers

MULTIPLY FRACTIONS AND MIXED NUMBERS

Write any mixed number as an improper fraction. Multiply numerator and denominator. Write the product in simplest form. For example, multiply $\frac{3}{4}$ and $\frac{1}{6}$.

$$\frac{3}{4} \times \frac{1}{6} = \frac{3}{24} = \frac{1}{8}$$

Now, multiply $3\frac{1}{3}$ times $\frac{3}{5}$.

$$3\frac{1}{3} \times \frac{3}{5} = \frac{10}{3} \times \frac{3}{5} = \frac{30}{15} = 2$$

DIVIDE FRACTIONS AND MIXED NUMBERS

To divide $1\frac{4}{5}$ by $\frac{3}{8}$:

$$1\frac{4}{5} \div \frac{3}{8} = \frac{9}{5} \div \frac{3}{8} = \frac{9}{5} \times \frac{8}{3} = \frac{72}{15} = 4\frac{12}{15} = 4\frac{4}{5}$$

Write any mixed numbers as improper fractions   Invert the divisor and multiply   Write the product   Write in simplest form

ADD FRACTIONS AND MIXED NUMBERS

Write fractions with common denominators. Add and then write in simplest form.

Add: $\frac{3}{8} + \frac{1}{4}$

$$\frac{3}{8} = \frac{3}{8}$$
$$+\frac{1}{4} = \frac{2}{8}$$
$$\frac{5}{8}$$

Add: $\frac{7}{8} + \frac{5}{12}$

$$\frac{7}{8} = \frac{21}{24}$$
$$+\frac{5}{12} = \frac{10}{24}$$
$$\frac{31}{24} = 1\frac{7}{24}$$

Add: $2\frac{1}{3} + \frac{5}{7}$

$$2\frac{1}{3} = 2\frac{7}{21}$$
$$+\frac{5}{7} = \frac{15}{21}$$
$$2\frac{22}{21} = 3\frac{1}{21}$$

SUBTRACT FRACTIONS AND MIXED NUMBERS

Write fractions with common denominators. Subtract and then write in simplest form.

Subtract: $\frac{5}{6} - \frac{1}{3}$

$$\frac{5}{6} = \frac{5}{6}$$
$$-\frac{1}{3} = \frac{2}{6}$$
$$\frac{3}{6} = \frac{1}{2}$$

Subtract: $\frac{3}{8} - \frac{1}{5}$

$$\frac{3}{8} = \frac{15}{40}$$
$$-\frac{1}{5} = \frac{8}{40}$$
$$\frac{7}{40}$$

Subtract: $3\frac{1}{6} - 1\frac{1}{3}$

$$3\frac{1}{6} = 3\frac{1}{6} = 2\frac{7}{6}$$
$$-1\frac{1}{3} = 1\frac{2}{6} = 1\frac{2}{6}$$
$$1\frac{5}{6}$$

Practice

1. $\frac{1}{3} \times \frac{5}{9} =$

5. $\frac{3}{4} \div \frac{7}{8} =$

9. $\frac{5}{9} + \frac{2}{3} =$

13. $\frac{2}{7} - \frac{5}{21} =$

2. $\frac{2}{3} \times \frac{1}{4} =$

6. $\frac{2}{5} \div \frac{7}{9} =$

10. $\frac{7}{10} + \frac{2}{4} =$

14. $\frac{2}{5} - \frac{3}{8} =$

3. $3\frac{3}{8} \times 4\frac{1}{8} =$

7. $9\frac{5}{7} \div 4\frac{1}{3} =$

11. $1\frac{6}{7} + 2\frac{3}{14} =$

15. $3\frac{4}{5} - 3\frac{2}{15} =$

4. $3\frac{1}{5} \times 2\frac{4}{7} =$

8. $2\frac{4}{5} \div 7\frac{3}{5} =$

12. $5\frac{2}{3} + 6\frac{5}{6} =$

16. $8\frac{1}{7} - 4\frac{2}{9} =$

(Answers on page 200.)

Square Roots

The square root of a given number, when multiplied by itself, equals the given number. This symbol means the square root of 25: $\sqrt{25}$. The square root of 25 is 5. $5 \times 5 = 25$.

SOME SQUARE ROOTS ARE WHOLE NUMBERS

The numbers with whole-number square roots are called perfect squares.

$$\sqrt{1} = 1 \quad \sqrt{4} = 2 \quad \sqrt{9} = 3 \quad \sqrt{16} = 4 \quad \sqrt{25} = 5 \quad \sqrt{36} = 6$$

$$\sqrt{49} = 7 \quad \sqrt{64} = 8 \quad \sqrt{81} = 9 \quad \sqrt{100} = 10 \quad \sqrt{121} = 11 \quad \sqrt{144} = 12$$

The fractional exponent $a^{\frac{1}{2}}$ is another way to write square root.

$$16^{\frac{1}{2}} = \sqrt{16} = 4 \quad 324^{\frac{1}{2}} = \sqrt{324} = 18$$

USE THIS RULE TO WRITE A SQUARE ROOT IN ITS SIMPLEST FORM

$$\sqrt{a \times b} = \sqrt{a} \times \sqrt{b} \quad \sqrt{5 \times 3} = \sqrt{5} \times \sqrt{3}$$

$$\sqrt{72} = \sqrt{36 \times 2} = \sqrt{36} \times \sqrt{2} = 6 \times \sqrt{2}$$

EXAMPLES

A. Write the square root of 162 in simplest form.

$$\sqrt{162} = \sqrt{81 \times 2} = \sqrt{81} \times \sqrt{2} = 9\sqrt{2}$$

B. Write the square root of 112 in simplest form.

$$\sqrt{112} = \sqrt{16 \times 7} = \sqrt{16} \times \sqrt{7} = 4\sqrt{7}$$

Practice

Simplify.

1. $\sqrt{256}$

3. $\sqrt{576}$

5. $\sqrt{1225}$

7. $\sqrt{245}$

9. $\sqrt{567}$

2. $\sqrt{400}$

4. $\sqrt{900}$

6. $\sqrt{48}$

8. $\sqrt{396}$

10. $\sqrt{832}$

(Answers on page 200.)

Ratio and Proportion

RATIO

A ratio is a way of comparing two numbers with division. It conveys the same meaning as a fraction. There are three ways to write a ratio.

Using words   3 to 4   As a fraction $\dfrac{3}{4}$ Using a colon   3 : 4

PROPORTION

A proportion shows two ratios that have the same value; that is, the fractions representing the ratios are equivalent. Use cross multiplication. If the cross products are equal, then the two ratios form a proportion.

$\dfrac{3}{8}$ and $\dfrac{27}{72}$ form a proportion. The cross products are equal. $(3 \times 72 = 8 \times 27)$

$\dfrac{3}{8}$ and $\dfrac{24}{56}$ do not form a proportion. The cross products are not equal.

SOLVING A PROPORTION

You may have to write a proportion to solve a problem. For example, the mason mixes cement and sand using a ratio of 2 : 5. Twelve bags of cement will be used. How much sand is needed?

To solve, use the numerator to stand for cement. The denominator will stand for sand.

$$\dfrac{2}{5} = \dfrac{12}{S} \qquad\qquad \dfrac{2}{5} = \dfrac{12}{S}$$

$$2 \times S = 5 \times 12$$
$$2S = 60$$
$$S = 30$$

Write the proportion   Cross multiply to solve

Thirty bags of sand are needed.

EXAMPLE

In a bakery, the ratio of whole wheat bread to rye bread is 3 : 7. If there are 51 loaves of whole wheat bread, how many loaves of rye bread are there?

The problem compares loaves of whole wheat bread with loaves of rye bread. Let the numerators stand for loaves of whole wheat bread. Let the denominators stand for loaves of rye bread.

Ratio of whole wheat to rye: $\dfrac{3}{7}$ Ratio of whole wheat to rye for $\dfrac{51}{R}$
                                              51 loaves of whole wheat:

Write a proportion: $\dfrac{3}{7} = \dfrac{51}{R}$

Solution: $3R = 357$ $R = 119$

There are 119 loaves of rye bread.

Practice

1. A salesperson sells 7 vacuum cleaners for every 140 potential buyers. If there are 280 potential buyers, how many vacuums are sold?

2. There is one teacher for every 8 preschool students. How many teachers are needed if there are 32 preschool students?

3. There are 3 rest stops for every 20 miles of highway. How many rest stops would there be on 140 miles of highway?

4. Does $\frac{7}{9}$ and $\frac{28}{36}$ form a proportion? Explain.

(Answers on page 201.)

Percent

Percent comes from per centum, which means per hundred. Whenever you see a number followed by a percent sign it means that number out of 100.

DECIMALS AND PERCENTS

To write a decimal as a percent, move the decimal point two places to the right and write the percent sign.

$$0.34 = 34\% \qquad 0.297 = 29.7\% \qquad 0.6 = 60\% \qquad 0.001 = 0.1\%$$

To write a percent as a decimal, move the decimal point two places to the left and delete the percent sign.

$$51\% = 0.51 \qquad 34.18\% = 0.3418 \qquad 0.9\% = 0.009$$

FRACTIONS AND PERCENTS

Writing Fractions as Percents

Divide the numerator by the denominator. Write the answer as a percent.

Write $\frac{3}{5}$ as a percent.   Write $\frac{5}{8}$ as a percent.

$$5\overline{)3.0}^{0.6} \qquad 0.6 = 60\% \qquad 8\overline{)5.000}^{0.625} \qquad 0.625 = 62.5\%$$

Write an equivalent fraction with 100 in the denominator. Write the numerator followed by a percent sign.

Write $\frac{13}{25}$ as a percent.

$$\frac{13}{25} = \frac{52}{100} = 52\%$$

Use these equivalencies.

$\frac{1}{4} = 25\%$ $\frac{1}{2} = 50\%$ $\frac{3}{4} = 75\%$ $\frac{4}{4} = 100\%$

$\frac{1}{5} = 20\%$ $\frac{2}{5} = 40\%$ $\frac{3}{5} = 60\%$ $\frac{4}{5} = 80\%$

$\frac{1}{6} = 16\frac{2}{3}\%$ $\frac{1}{3} = 33\frac{1}{3}\%$ $\frac{2}{3} = 66\frac{2}{3}\%$ $\frac{5}{6} = 83\frac{1}{3}\%$

$\frac{1}{8} = 12\frac{1}{2}\%$ $\frac{3}{8} = 37\frac{1}{2}\%$ $\frac{5}{8} = 62\frac{1}{2}\%$ $\frac{7}{8} = 87\frac{1}{2}\%$

Writing Percents as Fractions

Write a fraction with 100 in the denominator and the percent in the numerator. Simplify.

$$18\% = \frac{18}{100} = \frac{9}{50} \qquad\qquad 7.5\% = \frac{7.5}{100} = \frac{75}{1000} = \frac{3}{40}$$

EXAMPLES

A. Write 0.567 as a percent.

Move the decimal two places to the right and write a percent sign; therefore, $0.567 = 56.7\%$.

B. Write $\frac{1}{4}$ as a percent.

Write $\frac{1}{4}$ as a decimal: $(1 \div 4) = 0.25$

Write 0.25 as a percent: $0.25 = 25\%$

C. Write 26% as a fraction.

Place the percent number in the numerator and 100 in the denominator.

$26\% = \frac{26}{100}$. Simplify: $\frac{26}{100} = \frac{13}{50}$

Practice

Write the decimal as a percent.

1. 0.359   2. 0.78   3. 0.215   4. 0.041

Write the fraction as a percent.

5. $\frac{1}{9}$ 6. $\frac{5}{8}$ 7. $\frac{3}{10}$ 8. $\frac{4}{9}$

Write the percents as fractions in simplest form.

9. 58%   10. 79%   11. 85.2%   12. 97.4%

(Answers on page 201.)

Three Types of Percent Problems

FINDING A PERCENT OF A NUMBER

To find a percent of a number, write a number sentence with a decimal for the percent and solve.

$$\text{Find } 40\% \text{ of } 90.$$
$$0.4 \times 90 = 36$$

It may be easier to write a fraction for the percent.

$$\text{Find } 62\frac{1}{2}\% \text{ of } 64.$$

$$\frac{5}{8} \times 64 = 5 \times 8 = 40$$

FINDING WHAT PERCENT ONE NUMBER IS OF ANOTHER

To find what percent one number is of another, write a number sentence and solve to find the percent.

What percent of 5 is 3?

$$n \times 5 = 3$$
$$n = \frac{3}{5} = 0.6 = 60\%$$

FINDING A NUMBER WHEN A PERCENT OF IT IS KNOWN

To find a number when a percent of it is known, write a number sentence with a decimal or a fraction for the percent and solve to find the number.

5% of what number is 2?

$$0.05 \times n = 2$$
$$n = 2 \div 0.05$$
$$n = 40$$

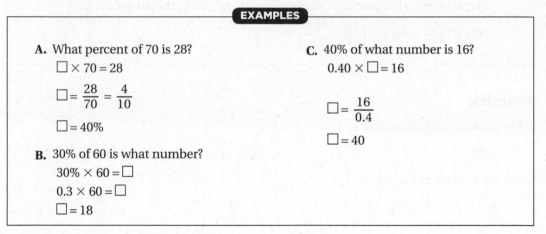

EXAMPLES

A. What percent of 70 is 28?

$\square \times 70 = 28$

$\square = \dfrac{28}{70} = \dfrac{4}{10}$

$\square = 40\%$

B. 30% of 60 is what number?

$30\% \times 60 = \square$

$0.3 \times 60 = \square$

$\square = 18$

C. 40% of what number is 16?

$0.40 \times \square = 16$

$\square = \dfrac{16}{0.4}$

$\square = 40$

Practice

1. 120 is what percent of 240?

2. 15% of 70 is what number?

3. 60% of 300 is what number?

4. What percent of 60 is 42?

5. What percent of 25 is 2.5?

6. 40% of what number is 22?

7. 70% of what number is 85?

8. 25% of 38 is what number?

9. 35% of what number is 24?

10. 24 is what percent of 80?

(Answers on page 201.)

Percent of Increase and Decrease

PERCENT OF INCREASE

A price increases from $50 to $65. What is the percent of increase?

Subtract to find the amount of increase. $65 - $50 = $15

$15 is the amount of increase

Write a fraction. The amount of increase is the numerator. The original amount is the denominator.

$15   Amount of increase
──────────────────────
$50   Original amount

Write the fraction as a percent. The percent of increase is 30%.

$$\begin{array}{r} 0.3 \\ 50\overline{)15.00} \end{array} \qquad 0.3 = 30\%$$

PERCENT OF DECREASE

A price decreases from $35 to $28. What is the percent of decrease?

Subtract to find the amount of decrease.

$35 − $28 = $7
$7 is the amount of decrease

Write a fraction. The amount of decrease is the numerator. The original amount is the denominator.

$7   Amount of decrease
──────────────────────
$35   Original amount

Write the fraction as a percent. The percent of decrease is 20%.

$$\frac{7}{35} = \frac{1}{5} = 20\%$$

EXAMPLES

A. The price increased from $30 to $36. What is the percent of increase?

$36 − $30 = $6

$$\frac{6}{30} = \frac{1}{5} = 20\%$$

B. An $80 item goes on sale for 25% off. What is the sale price?

$80 × 25% = $80 × 0.25 = $20

$80 − $20 = $60. $60 is the sale price.

Practice

1. The price increased from $25 to $35. What is the percent of increase?

2. A sale marks down a $100 item 25%. What is the sale price?

3. The price decreases from $80 by 15%. What is the new price?

4. The price increased from $120 to $150. What is the percent of increase?

5. A sale marks down a $75 item 10%. What is the sale price?

6. The price decreases from $18 to $6. What is the percent of decrease?

7. A sale marks down a $225 item to $180. What is the percent of decrease?

8. A sale price of $150 was 25% off the original price. What was the original price?

(Answers on page 201.)

PROBABILITY AND STATISTICS

Probability

The probability of an occurrence is the likelihood that it will happen. Most often, you write probability as a fraction.

Flip a fair coin and the probability that it will come up heads is $\frac{1}{2}$. The same is true for tails. Write the probability this way.

$$P(H) = \frac{1}{2} \qquad P(T) = \frac{1}{2}$$

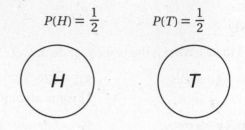

If something will never occur, the probability is 0. For example, if you toss a single die, $P(7) = 0$. If something will always occur, the probability is 1. Therefore, if you flip a fair coin, $P(H \text{ or } T) = 1$.

Write the letters A, B, C, D, and E on pieces of paper. Pick them randomly without looking. The probability of picking any letter is $\frac{1}{5}$.

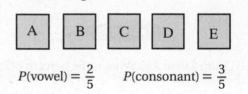

$$P(\text{vowel}) = \frac{2}{5} \qquad P(\text{consonant}) = \frac{3}{5}$$

RULES FOR COMPUTING PROBABILITY

$$P(A \text{ or } B) = P(A) + P(B) = \frac{1}{5} + \frac{1}{5} = \frac{2}{5}$$

when A and B have no common elements

$$P(A \text{ and } B) = P(A) \times P(B) = \frac{1}{5} \times \frac{1}{5} = \frac{1}{25}$$

$$P(\text{not } C) = 1 - P(C) = 1 - \frac{1}{5} = \frac{4}{5}$$

EXAMPLE

In one high school, 40% of the students go on to college. Two graduates of the high school are chosen at random. What is the probability that they both went to college?

Write the probabilities you know.

$$P(\text{college}) = \frac{40}{100} = \frac{2}{5}$$

Solve the problem.

$P(A \text{ and } B)$ probability the two students went to college.

$$P(A \text{ and } B) = P(A) \times P(B) = \frac{2}{5} \times \frac{2}{5} = \frac{4}{25}$$

The probability that they both went to college is $\frac{4}{25}$.

Practice

1. There are 3 black, 2 white, 2 gray, and 3 blue socks in a drawer. What is the probability of drawing a sock that is not black?

2. Six goldfish are in a tank; 4 are female and 2 are male. What is the probability of scooping out a male?

3. A standard deck of 52 playing cards is spread facedown on a table. What is the probability of choosing a card that is a king or a queen?

4. Six names are written on pieces of paper. The names are Aaron, Ben, Carl, Edith, Elizabeth, and Phyllis. One name is picked and replaced. Then another name is picked. What is the probability that the names were Carl and Phyllis?

5. A fair die having six sides is rolled. What is the probability that the side facing up is a prime number?

6. A fair coin is tossed in the air 5 times. What is the probability of getting five tails?

(Answers on page 202.)

Independent and Dependent Events

Events are *independent* when the outcome of one event does not affect the probability of the other event. Each coin flip is an independent event. No matter the outcome of one flip, the probability of the next flip remains the same.

Flip heads 10 times in a row with a fair coin. On the next flip, the $P(H)$ is still 1/2. Coin flips are independent events.

Events are *dependent* where the outcome of one event does affect the probability of the other event. For example, you have a full deck of cards. The probability of picking the Queen of Hearts is 1/52.

You pick one card and it is not the Queen of Hearts. You do not put the card back. The probability of picking the Queen of Hearts is now 1/51. Cards picked without replacement are dependent events.

Permutations, Combinations, and the Fundamental Counting Principle

PERMUTATIONS

A permutation is the way a set of things can be arranged in order. There are 6 permutations of the letters A, B, and C.

ABC   ACB   BAC   BCA   CAB   CBA

Permutation Formula

The formula for the number of permutations of n things is **n! (n factorial)**.

$$6! = 6 \times 5 \times 4 \times 3 \times 2 \times 1 \qquad 4! = 4 \times 3 \times 2 \times 1 \qquad 2! = 2 \times 1$$

There are 120 permutations of 5 things.

$$n! = 5! = 5 \times 4 \times 3 \times 2 \times 1 = 120$$

COMBINATIONS

A combination is the number of ways of choosing a given number of elements from a set. The order of the elements does not matter. There are 3 ways of choosing 2 letters from the letters A, B, and C.

AB AC BC

FUNDAMENTAL COUNTING PRINCIPLE

The fundamental counting principle is used to find the total number of possibilities. Multiply the number of possibilities from each category.

EXAMPLE

An ice cream stand has a sundae with choices of 28 flavors of ice cream, 8 types of syrups, and 5 types of toppings. How many different sundae combinations are available?

$$28 \quad \times \quad 8 \quad \times \quad 5 \quad = \quad 1{,}120$$

flavors   syrups   toppings   sundaes

There are 1,120 possible sundaes.

Practice

1. There are 2 chairs left in the auditorium, but 4 people are without seats. In how many ways could 2 people be chosen to sit in the chairs?

2. The books *Little Women*, *Crime & Punishment*, *Trinity*, *The Great Santini*, *Pygmalion*, *The Scarlet Letter*, and *War and Peace* are on a shelf. In how many different ways can they be arranged?

3. A license plate consists of 2 letters and 2 digits. How many different license plates can be formed?

4. There are four students on line for the bus, but there is only room for three students on this bus. How many different ways can 3 of the 4 students get on the bus?

(Answers on page 202.)

Statistics and Scatter Plots

Descriptive statistics are used to explain or describe a set of numbers. Most often you use the mean, median, or mode to describe these numbers.

MEAN (AVERAGE)

The mean is a position midway between two extremes. To find the mean:

1. Add the items or scores.
2. Divide by the number of items.

For example, find the mean of 24, 17, 42, 51, 36.

$$24 + 17 + 42 + 51 + 36 = 170 \qquad 170 \div 5 = 34$$

The mean or average is 34.

MEDIAN

The median is the middle number. To find the median:

1. Arrange the numbers from least to greatest.
2. If there are an odd number of scores, then find the middle score.
3. If there is an even number of scores, average the two middle scores.

For example, find the median of these numbers.

6, 9, 11, <u>17</u>, <u>21</u>, 33, 45, 71

There are an even number of scores.

$$17 + 21 = 38 \qquad 38 \div 2 = 19$$

The median is 19.

Do not forget to arrange the scores in order before finding the middle score!

MODE

The mode is the number that occurs most often.

For example, find the mode of these numbers.

6, 3, 7, 6, 9, 3, 6, 1, 2, 6, 7, 3

The number 6 occurs most often so 6 is the mode.

Not all sets of numbers have a mode. Some sets of numbers may have more than one mode.

EXAMPLE

What is the mean, median, and mode of 7, 13, 18, 4, 14, 22?

Mean Add the scores and divide by the number of scores.

$7 + 13 + 18 + 4 + 14 + 22 = 78 \div 6 = 13$ The mean is 13.

Median Arrange the scores in order. Find the middle score.

4, 7, 13, 14, 18, 22 $13 + 14 = 27 \div 2 = 13.5$ The median is 13.5.

Mode Find the score that occurs most often.

Each score occurs only once.   There is no mode.

Practice

1. A group of fourth graders received the following scores on a science test.

80, 87, 94, 100, 75, 80, 98, 85, 80, 95, 92

Which score represents the mode?

2. What is the mean of the following set of data?

44, 13, 84, 42, 12, 18

3. What is the median of the following set of data?

8, 9, 10, 10, 8, 10, 7, 6, 9

4. What measure of central tendency does the number 16 represent in the following data?

14, 15, 17, 16, 19, 20, 16, 14, 16

5. What is the mean of the following set of scores?

100, 98, 95, 70, 85, 90, 94, 78, 80, 100

6. What is the mode of the following data?

25, 30, 25, 15, 40, 45, 30, 20, 30

(Answers on page 202.)

Scatter Plots

Scatter plots are an indication about the trend of a set of data. They indicate how the data are correlated. Correlation can be complicated, but test questions will not ask for a sophisticated understanding of scatter plots or correlation.

Look at these examples.

Example A shows a positive correlation. The dots in the plot move generally from lower left to upper right. Example B shows a negative correlation. The dots move generally from upper left to lower right. Example C shows little or no correlation. The dots do not show any organized pattern.

Negative and positive linear correlations are also called negative and positive linear relationships. You may come across this term on the test.

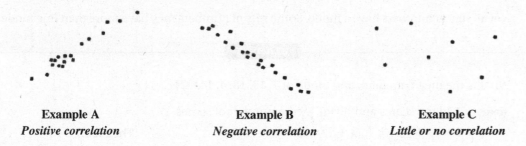

Example A	Example B	Example C
Positive correlation	*Negative correlation*	*Little or no correlation*

Scatter plots are usually based on sets of data.

Practice

Plot this data on the graph that follows. Then answer the other questions.

Students chose a number from 1 to 5 to indicate their preference for school subjects and activities. School subjects and activities students prefer.

Student	Computers	Art
1	5	4
2	3	2
3	1	2
4	5	5
5	2	3
6	1	1
7	5	3
8	3	3
9	4	5
10	2	4

1. Plot the responses to create a scatter plot. The first response of 5 for computers and 4 for art is plotted for you.

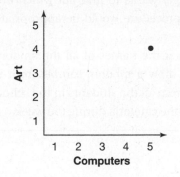

2. Does the scatter plot generally show a positive correlation, a negative correlation, or no correlation? How can you tell?

3. Would the correlation change if the values for art and computers were switched?

(Answers on page 202.)

Choose a Process That Involves Random Selection

Random selection means that the sample is picked by chance. Every person in the larger population has an equal chance of being picked.

Examples of random sampling:

Pick a sample of names by chance out of a container with all the names.

Have a computer use a random selection program to choose the sample.

Partition a group into a male group and a female group, and then choose names at random from each group.

Examples of nonrandom sampling:

Sample the first 100 people you meet.

Choose every sixth person from a list of names.

Rely on voluntary responses.

Choose Your Sample from the Correct Population

The random selection must be from the group you want to study.

Examples of sampling from the wrong population:

Sample college alumni to determine current reactions to the cafeteria.

Sample from one town to determine statewide views.

Sample from 18- to 22-year-old military recruits to determine the views of college students.

The college cafeteria manager wants to find out which new selections students want added to the menu. What procedure would be appropriate for selecting an unbiased sample?

The manager could gather the names of all the students who ate in the cafeteria during the week and then draw a random sample from those names. The manager should not draw a sample from all the students in the school. You should not interview every fifth student entering the cafeteria during the week.

Practice

1. A group is taking a poll to determine working parents' day-care needs. They interview parents at work. Give examples of good and poor sampling techniques.

2. The town architect wants to find out about senior community members' ideas for the new senior center. Give examples of good and poor sampling techniques.

(Answers on page 203.)

ALGEBRA AND FUNCTIONS

Add, Subtract, Multiply, and Divide Integers

ADDITION

When the signs are the same, keep the sign and add.

$$
\begin{array}{rr}
+7 & -3 \\
+\ +8 & +\ -11 \\
\hline
+15 & -14
\end{array}
$$

When the signs are different, disregard the signs, subtract the numbers, and keep the sign of the larger number.

$$
\begin{array}{rr}
+28 & -86 \\
+\ -49 & +\ +135 \\
\hline
-21 & +49
\end{array}
$$

SUBTRACTION

Change the sign of the number being subtracted. Then add using the preceding rules.

$$
\begin{array}{cccc}
+13 & -43 & +29 & -92 \\
-\ -18 & -\ -17 & -\ -49 & -\ +135 \\
\downarrow & \downarrow & \downarrow & \downarrow \\
+13 & -43 & +29 & -92 \\
+\ +18 & +\ +17 & +\ +49 & +\ -135 \\
\hline
+31 & -26 & +78 & -227
\end{array}
$$

MULTIPLY

Multiply as you would whole numbers. The product is *positive* if there are an even number of negative factors. The product is *negative* if there are an odd number of negative factors.

$$-2 \times +4 \times -6 \times +3 = +144 \qquad -2 \times -4 \times +6 \times -3 = -144$$

DIVIDE

Forget the signs and divide. The quotient is *positive* if both integers have the same sign. The quotient is *negative* if the integers have different signs.

$$+24 \div +4 = +6 \quad -24 \div -4 = +6 \quad +24 \div -4 = -6 \quad -24 \div +4 = -6$$

Practice

1. $6 + 9 =$
2. $18 + -17 =$
3. $-24 + -45 =$
4. $-38 + 29 =$

5. $7 - 6 =$
6. $15 - -39 =$
7. $-36 - -58 =$
8. $-27 - 53 =$

9. $9 \times 11 =$
10. $26 \times -25 =$
11. $-31 \times -59 =$
12. $-42 \times 35 =$

13. $120 \div 8 =$
14. $68 \div -4 =$
15. $-352 \div -8 =$
16. $-66 \div 3 =$

(Answers on page 203.)

POLYNOMIALS

Polynomials are made up of constants and variables.

Constant—A constant is a number such as 9, $\frac{1}{2}$, 0.56.

Variable—A variable is represented by a letter (such as x, a, c) to show that we do not know the value.

Polynomials do not have equal signs.

Polynomials are described by the number of terms. Terms are separated by addition or subtraction.

A term can be a constant, a variable, or the product of constants and variables.

In a term with a constant and a variable or variables, the constant is called the coefficient.

In the term $9x$, the coefficient is 9 and the variable is x.

MONOMIALS

A monomial has one term.

There are no addition or subtraction signs in a monomial.

Here are some monomials.

$$7, x, 3x, \frac{6}{27}, y^2, -16$$

BINOMIALS

A binomial has two terms.

Here are some binomials.

$$5x - 6, \qquad 3y^2 + 7, \qquad 13x^2 + 0.5y^2$$

TRINOMIALS

A trinomial has three terms.

Here are some trinomials.

$$6x^2 \ + \ 12y^2 \ + \ 12y, \ \ 13x^6z^5 \ + \ 12y^2 \ + \ 12y$$

SIMPLIFY POLYNOMIALS

Combine similar terms to simplify a polynomial.

Similar terms have the same variable part. The order of the variables is not important. $3x$ is similar to $5x$ and $0.9x$. The variable in each term is x.

$2x^3y$ is similar to $12yx^3$.

$3x^3y$ is not similar to $3y^3x$.

Combine Similar Terms

Add or subtract the coefficient and keep the variable part.

Combine the terms in $5x + 9xy + 2y^3 - 8y + 2x^2 - 8y^3$

Rearrange the terms so that similar terms are next to one another.

The similar terms are $2y^3$ and $8y^3$.

$$5x + 9xy \underline{+ 2y^3 - 8y^3} - 8y + 2x^2$$

$$5x + 9xy \underline{- 6y^3} - 8y + 2x^2$$

ADD AND SUBTRACT POLYNOMIALS

Add Polynomials

Combine similar terms.

Add: $(5x^6 + 7x^3y - y^2 + 9) + (7x^5 - 3x^3y + y^2z)$

Write as a polynomial: $5x^6 + 7x^3y - y^2 + 9 + 7x^5 - 3x^3y + y^2z$

The common terms are $7x^3y$ and $3x^3y$.

Rearrange terms: $5x^6 + \underline{7x^3y - 3x^3y} - y^2 + 9 + 7x^5 + y^2z$

Combine: $5x^6 + 4x^3y - y^2 + 9 + 7x^5 + y^2z$

Subtract Polynomials

Change the signs in the polynomial being subtracted.

Then combine similar terms.

Subtract: $(2x^4 + 15x^2 - y^2 + x) - (x^4 - 8x^3y + y^2z - 3x + 4)$

Change the signs in the polynomial
being subtracted and add: $(2x^4 + 15x^2 - y^2 + x) + (-x^4 + 8x^3y - y^2z + 3x + 4)$

The common terms are $2x^4$ and $-x^4$, x and $3x$.

Rearrange terms: $\underline{2x^4 - x^4} + 15x^2 - y^2 + \underline{x + 3x} + 8x^3y - y^2z + 4$

Combine: $x^4 + 15x^2 - y^2 + 4x + 8x^3y - y^2z + 4$

Practice

Combine terms.

1. $3x^2 + 4y + 3x^2y + 6y$

2. $7x + 3x^2y + 17x + 3yx^2 + 7x^2y^2$

Add.

3. $(3x^5 + 3x^2 - 5x^2y + 6xy^2) + (3x^5 - 2x^2 + 4x^3y - x^2y + 3xy^3 - y^2)$

4. $(x^4 - 4x^3 + 2x^2y^2 - 4xy^2) + (3x^5 - 7x^4 + 3x^3 - 2x^2y^3 + 7xy^2)$

Subtract.

5. $(6x^7 + 9x^4 - 3x^2y + 5xy^3) - (6x^8 - 15x^4 - 3x^3y + x^2y)$

6. $(7x^2 - 9x + 3xy^2 + 3y^3 - 12) - (x^3 - 9x^2 + 2xy^2 - 3y^5 - 18)$

(Answers on page 203.)

Formulas

EVALUATING AN EXPRESSION

Evaluate an expression by replacing the variables with values. Remember to use the correct order of operations. For example, evaluate

$$3x - \frac{y}{z} \text{ for } x = 3, y = 8, \text{ and } z = 4$$

$$3(3) - \frac{8}{4} = 9 - 2 = 7$$

Using Formulas

Using a formula is like evaluating an expression. Just replace the variables with values. Here are some important formulas to know. The area of a figure is the amount of space it occupies in two dimensions. The perimeter of a figure is the distance around the figure. Use 3.14 for π.

FIGURE	FORMULA	DESCRIPTION
Triangle	Area $= \dfrac{1}{2}bh$ Perimeter $= s_1 + s_2 + s_3$	
Square	Area $= s^2$ Perimeter $= 4s$	
Rectangle	Area $= lw$ Perimeter $= 2l + 2w$	
Parallelogram	Area $= bh$ Perimeter $= 2s + 2b$	
Trapezoid	Area $= \dfrac{1}{2}h(b_1 + b_2)$ Perimeter $= b_1 + b_2 + s_1 + s_2$	
Circle	Area $= \pi r^2$ Circumference $= 2\pi r$ or $= \pi d$	

Pythagorean Formula

The Pythagorean formula for right triangles states that the sum of the square of the legs equals the square of the hypotenuse:

$$a^2 + b^2 = c^2$$

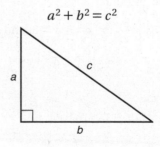

Other Polygons

Pentagon	5 sides	Octagon	8 sides
Hexagon	6 sides	Nonagon	9 sides
Heptagon	7 sides	Decagon	10 sides

Regular Polygon—All sides are the same length.

DISTANCE AND AREA

Solve the distance and area problems.

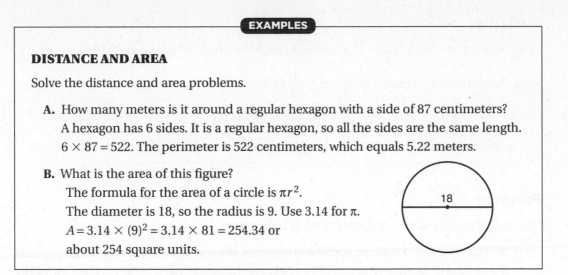

A. How many meters is it around a regular hexagon with a side of 87 centimeters?
A hexagon has 6 sides. It is a regular hexagon, so all the sides are the same length.
$6 \times 87 = 522$. The perimeter is 522 centimeters, which equals 5.22 meters.

B. What is the area of this figure?
The formula for the area of a circle is πr^2.
The diameter is 18, so the radius is 9. Use 3.14 for π.
$A = 3.14 \times (9)^2 = 3.14 \times 81 = 254.34$ or
about 254 square units.

Volume

Volume—The amount of space occupied by a three-dimensional figure.
The test will give you the formulas.

FORMULAS FOR VOLUME

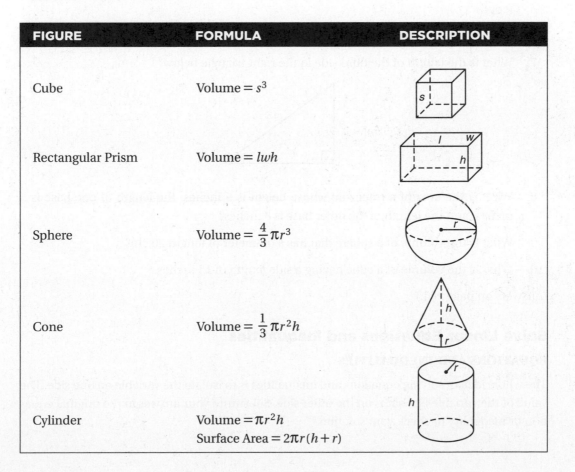

FIGURE	FORMULA	DESCRIPTION
Cube	Volume $= s^3$	
Rectangular Prism	Volume $= lwh$	
Sphere	Volume $= \frac{4}{3}\pi r^3$	
Cone	Volume $= \frac{1}{3}\pi r^2 h$	
Cylinder	Volume $= \pi r^2 h$ Surface Area $= 2\pi r(h+r)$	

EXAMPLES

VOLUME

A circular cone has a radius of 8 cm and a height of 10 cm. What is the volume?

Formula for the volume of a cone $= \frac{1}{3}\pi r^2 h$.

$$V = \left(\frac{1}{3}\right)(3.14)(8^2)(10) = \left(\frac{1}{3}\right)(3.14)(64)(10) = \left(\frac{1}{3}\right)(3.14)(640) = 669.87$$

The volume of the cone is 669.87 cubic centimeters or about 670 cubic centimeters.

Practice

1. A circle has a radius of 9 meters. What is the area?

2. The faces of a pyramid are equilateral triangles. What is the surface area of the pyramid if the sides of the triangles equal 3 inches and the height is 2.6 inches? (The base of the pyramid is also a triangle.)

3. A regular hexagon has one side 5 feet long. What is the distance around its edge?

4. What is the surface area of the side of a cylinder (not top and bottom) with a height of 10 cm and a diameter of 2.5 cm?

5. A rectangle has a width x and a length $(x + 5)$. If the perimeter is 90 feet, what is the length?

6. The perimeter of one face of a cube is 20 cm. What is the surface area?

7. What is the length of the third side in the right triangle below?

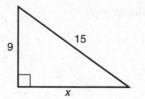

8. What is the area of a trapezoid whose height is 5 inches, the length of one base is 5 inches, and the length of the other base is 8 inches?

9. What is the volume of a sphere that has a diameter of length 20 cm?

10. What is the volume of a cube having a side length of 15 inches.

(Answers on page 203.)

Solve Linear Equations and Inequalities

EQUATIONS AND INEQUALITIES

The whole idea of solving equations and inequalities is to isolate the variable on one side. The value of the variable is what is on the other side. Substitute your answer in the original equation or inequality to check your solution.

Solving Equations and Inequalities by Adding or Subtracting

$$\text{Solve: } y + 19 = 23$$

$$\text{Subtract 19} \quad y + 19 - 19 = 23 - 19$$

$$y = 4$$

Check: Does $4 + 19 = 23$? Yes. It checks.

$$\text{Solve: } x - 23 \leq 51$$

$$\text{Add 23} \quad x - 23 + 23 \leq 51 + 23$$

$$x \leq 74$$

Check: Is $74 - 23 \leq 51$. Yes. It checks.

Solving Equations and Inequalities by Multiplying or Dividing

$$\text{Solve: } \frac{z}{7} \geq 6$$

$$\text{Multiply by 7} \quad \frac{x}{7} \times 7 \geq 6 \times 7$$

$$z \geq 42$$

Check: Is $\frac{42}{7} \geq 6$? Yes. It checks.

$$\text{Solve: } 21 = -3x$$

$$\text{Divide by -3} \quad \frac{21}{-3} = \frac{-3x}{-3}$$

$$-7 = x$$

Check: Does $21 = (-3)(-7)$? Yes. It checks.

EXAMPLES

A. Solve for x $x - 7 = 4$

Add 7 $\underline{+7 \ +7}$

$x = \ 11$

B. Solve for n $5n > 2$

Divide by 5 $\dfrac{5n}{5} > \dfrac{2}{5}$

Simplify $n > \dfrac{2}{5}$

Practice

1. Solve for x: $x + \dfrac{2}{5} = 17$

2. Solve for y: $6y > -32$

3. Solve for x: $15 < 4x$

4. Solve for y: $22 = -2y$

(Answers on page 204.)

GEOMETRY AND MEASUREMENT
Symmetry

Symmetric objects, figures, and designs have a pleasing, balanced appearance.

There are three primary types of symmetry—line (reflection), rotational, and translational.

LINE OR REFLECTIVE SYMMETRY

A figure with line symmetry can be folded in half so that one half exactly matches the other half.

This letter M has line symmetry.

Fold the M in half at the line and one half exactly matches the other half.

Flip the M over the line and it looks the same.

Place a mirror on that line and half the M and the reflection will form the entire M.

The line is called the line of symmetry.

ROTATIONAL SYMMETRY

A figure has rotational symmetry if it can be turned less than a full turn and look exactly as it did before it was turned.

This letter N has rotational symmetry.

Turn the Z half a turn and it looks exactly as it did before the turn.

TRANSLATIONAL SYMMETRY

A design has translational symmetry if it repeats a pattern.

Many wallpaper patterns have translational symmetry.

This simple pattern has translational symmetry because it shows a repeating pattern.

A   B   C   A   B   C

EXAMPLES

A. Which of these letters has line symmetry?

B. Which of these letters has rotational symmetry?

A   B   C   D   E   F   G   H   I

These letters have both line and rotational symmetry: H, I

These letters have only line symmetry: A, B, C, D, E

None of the letters has only rotational symmetry.

These letters have neither type of symmetry: F, G

Practice

1. Which of these numerals has rotational or line symmetry?

   1   2   3   4   5   6   7   8   9   0

2. Complete this pattern so that the final pattern has translational symmetry.

   2   3   4

(Answers on page 204.)

Two-Dimensional Geometry

Geometry has two or three dimensions. A two-dimensional model is this page. A three-dimensional model is the room where you will take the test.

DEFINITION	MODEL	SYMBOL
Point—a location	. A	A
Plane—a flat surface that extends infinitely in all directions		plane ABC
Line—a set of points in a straight path that extends infinitely in two directions		$\overleftrightarrow{AB}$
Line segment—part of a line with two endpoints		$\overline{AB}$
Ray—part of a line with one endpoint		$\overrightarrow{AB}$
Parallel lines—lines that stay the same distance apart and never touch		$\overline{AB} \parallel \overline{DF}$
Perpendicular lines—lines that meet at right angles		$\overline{AB} \perp \overline{CD}$

DEFINITION	MODEL	SYMBOL

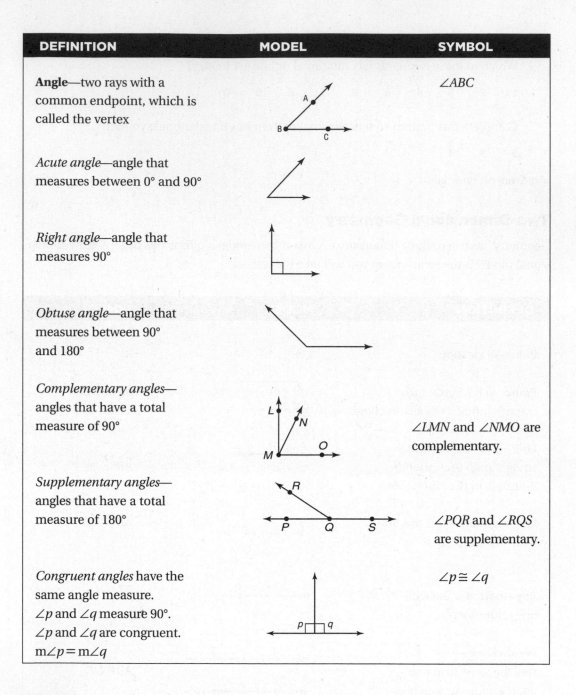

Angle—two rays with a common endpoint, which is called the vertex

∠ABC

Acute angle—angle that measures between 0° and 90°

Right angle—angle that measures 90°

Obtuse angle—angle that measures between 90° and 180°

Complementary angles—angles that have a total measure of 90°

∠LMN and ∠NMO are complementary.

Supplementary angles—angles that have a total measure of 180°

∠PQR and ∠RQS are supplementary.

Congruent angles have the same angle measure.
∠p and ∠q measure 90°.
∠p and ∠q are congruent.
m∠p = m∠q

∠p ≅ ∠q

CIRCLES

A circle is a shape with all points the same distance from its center. A circle is named by its center. The distance around the circle is called the circumference.

The region inside a circle is not part of the circle. It is called the area of a circle.

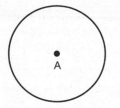

The diameter of a circle is a line segment across a circle through the center.

The radius of a circle is a line segment from the center of the circle to any point on the circle. Two radii lined up end-to-end form a diameter. The diameter and radius each has a length, and the length of the diameter is twice the length of the radius.

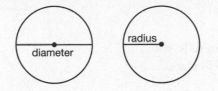

A chord is a line segment with endpoints on a circle. A diameter is the longest chord of a circle. Every diameter is a chord but not every chord is a diameter.

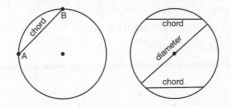

Practice

1. Can a circle have more than one diameter?

2. Can part of a chord not be on the circle?

3. Do two radii always form a diameter?

4. Can two separate chords form a diameter?

(Answers on page 204.)

Polygons

A closed figure made up of line segments; if all sides are the same length, the figure is a regular polygon.

Pentagon	*Hexagon*	*Octagon*
	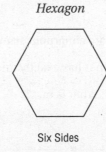	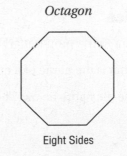
Five Sides	Six Sides	Eight Sides

TRIANGLES

A polygon with three sides and three angles; the sum of the angles is always 180°.

Equilateral triangle—all the sides are the same length; all the angles are the same size, 60°.

Isosceles triangle—two sides the
same length; two angles the same size.

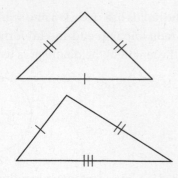

Scalene triangle—all sides different
lengths; all angles different sizes.

Congruent triangle—Two triangles are congruent
if the lengths of each corresponding pair of sides
are equal and the measures of each corresponding
pair of angles are equal. That means one triangle
fits exactly on top of the other triangle.

QUADRILATERALS

A polygon with four sides

| Square | Rectangle | Parallelogram | Rhombus | Trapezoid |

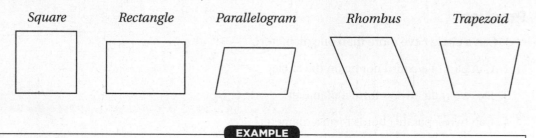

EXAMPLE

Which types of quadrilaterals can be constructed using four congruent line segments
AB, BC, CD, and *DA*?

You can create a square and a rhombus.

Practice

Be certain to use proper markings to indicate congruent segments and congruent angles.

1. What is the name of a quadrilateral that has exactly one pair of parallel sides?

2. Use the figure below. The m∠1 = 45°. What is m∠2?

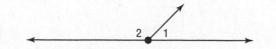

3. In the triangle below, *AB = AC* and m∠*BAC* = 80°.

    What are the measures of ∠*ABC* and ∠*ACB*?

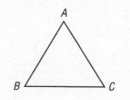

4. Draw a diagram of an equilateral triangle.

5. Which has more sides, an octagon or a hexagon?
   What is the difference in the number of sides for these figures?

6. What type of angle with a measure less than 180° is neither obtuse nor acute?

7. Draw a diagram in which ray (*AB*) intersects ray (*AC*) at point *A*, and name the new figure that is formed.

8. Draw a diagram of line *AB* intersecting line segment *CD* at point *E*.

9. Draw a diagram of two parallel lines perpendicular to a third line.

10. Given a triangle *ABC*, describe the relationship among the measures of the three angles.

(Answers on page 204.)

SIMILAR TRIANGLES

In similar triangles, corresponding angles are congruent. The ratio of the lengths of corresponding sides are equal.

These triangles are similar.

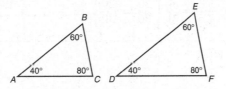

Corresponding angles of the two triangles are congruent.

$\angle A$ and $\angle D$ $\angle B$ and $\angle E$ $\angle C$ and $\angle F$

That means the measures of congruent angles are equal.

measure of $\angle A$ = measure of $\angle D$ = 40°
measure of $\angle B$ = measure of $\angle E$ = 60°
measure of $\angle C$ = measure of $\angle F$ = 80°

Corresponding sides (Corresponding sides are opposite corresponding angles)

$\overline{BC}$ and $\overline{EF}$ $\overline{AC}$ and $\overline{DF}$ $\overline{AB}$ and $\overline{DE}$

The ratios of the lengths of corresponding sides are equal.

$$\frac{BC}{EF} = \frac{AC}{DF} = \frac{AB}{DE}$$

Are these triangles similar?

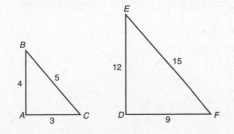

Corresponding sides: $\overline{AB}$ and $\overline{DE}$, $\overline{BC}$ and $\overline{EF}$, $\overline{AC}$ and $\overline{DF}$.

Does $\dfrac{AB}{DE} = \dfrac{BC}{EF}$? $\dfrac{AB}{DE} = \dfrac{4}{12}$; $\dfrac{BC}{EF} = \dfrac{5}{15}$; $\dfrac{4}{12} = \dfrac{1}{3}$; $\dfrac{5}{15} = \dfrac{1}{3}$

These triangles are similar. Ratios of corresponding sides of the two triangles are equal.

EXAMPLE

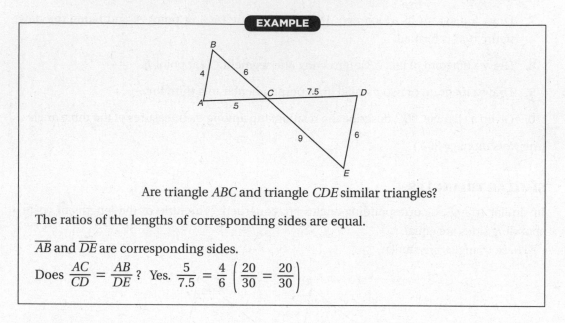

Are triangle *ABC* and triangle *CDE* similar triangles?

The ratios of the lengths of corresponding sides are equal.

$\overline{AB}$ and $\overline{DE}$ are corresponding sides.

Does $\dfrac{AC}{CD} = \dfrac{AB}{DE}$? Yes. $\dfrac{5}{7.5} = \dfrac{4}{6}$ $\left(\dfrac{20}{30} = \dfrac{20}{30} \right)$

Practice

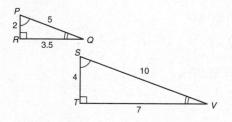

1. Are $\triangle PQR$ and $\triangle SVT$ similar?

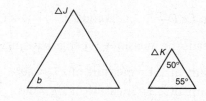

2. The triangles above are similar. What is the measure of $\angle b$?

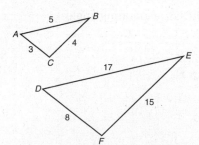

3. Which of these statements is true for the triangles above?

    Ⓐ $\angle C$ is congruent to $\angle F$

    Ⓑ $\angle B$ is congruent to $\angle E$

    Ⓒ $\dfrac{AB}{DE} = \dfrac{CB}{FE}$

    Ⓓ $\triangle ABC$ and $\triangle DEF$ are congruent

(Answers on page 204.)

Coordinate Grid and Translations

You can plot ordered pairs of numbers on a coordinate grid.

The *x*-axis goes horizontally from left to right. The first number in the pair tells how far to move left or right from the origin. A minus sign means move left. A plus sign means move right.

The *y*-axis goes vertically up and down. The second number in the pair tells how far to move up or down from the origin. A minus sign means move down. A plus sign means move up.

Pairs of numbers show the *x*-coordinate first and the *y*-coordinate second (*x*, *y*). The origin is point (0, 0) where the *x*-axis and the *y*-axis meet.

Plot these pairs of numbers on the grid.

A (+3, −7) B (+5, +3) C (−6, +2) D (−3, −6)

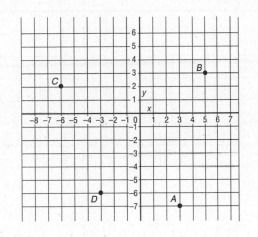

Practice

The following grid is for questions 1 and 2.

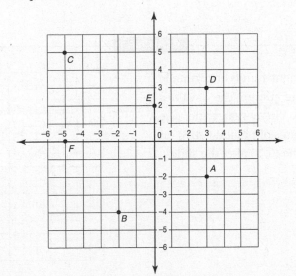

1. Write the coordinates of the points on the grid provided.

   A _____ B _____ C _____ D _____ E _____ F _____

2. Plot these points on the grid provided.

   G (3, −1) H (2, −3) I (5, 6) J (−4, 0) K (−5, −2) L (−1, 6) M (0, 3) N (−5, 2)

3. Plot these points on the grid below and connect them in alphabetical order.

$Z\,(-5, 5)$ $Y\,(-2, 0)$ $X\,(2, -6)$ $W\,(3, 5)$ $V\,(-6, -2)$ $U\,(2, 0)$ $T\,(6, 1)$

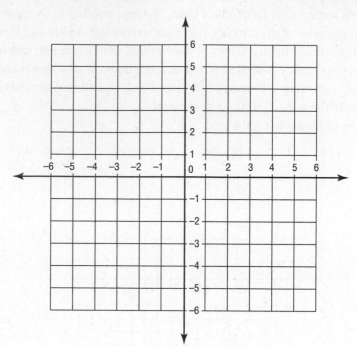

(Answers on page 205.)

TRANSLATIONS ON A COORDINATE GRID

You can slide or translate points and geometric shapes on the coordinate grid. You can describe the translations by what happens to the positions of the vertices. Look at these simple examples:

EXAMPLE 1

This triangle slid right 4 units horizontally on the coordinate plane. The *y*-values remain the same. The *x*-values increase by 4. The coordinates of point $A\,(-4, 3)$ on the triangle became $(0, 3)$ after the slide.

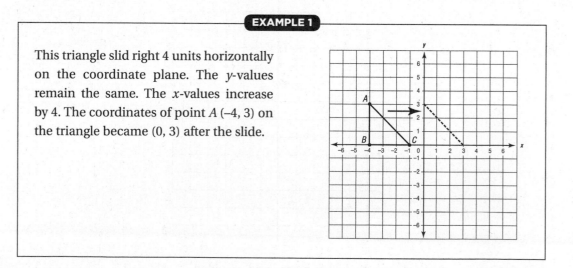

EXAMPLE 2

This triangle slid down five units vertically. The *x*-values remain the same. The *y*-values decrease by 3. The coordinate of point *Q* (4, 3) became (4, –2) after the slide.

EXAMPLE 3

This triangle slid right 6 units and up 3 units. The *x*-values increased by 6 and the *y*-values increased by 5. The coordinate of point *M* (–2, –2) became (4, 1) after the slide.

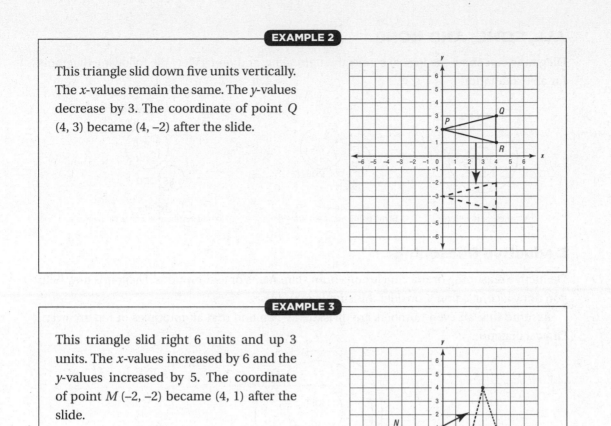

Practice

1. In Example 1, what is the coordinate of point *C* if the triangle moved down 4 units and left 3 units?

2. In Example 3, what are the coordinates of point *M* if point *L* slid up and over to the coordinate (0, 0)?

3. A triangle slid right 3 units and down 4 units. What is the new coordinate of a point that started at (–7, 2) before the slide?

4. Point *B* is at the right angle of a right triangle. Point *A* is at coordinates (–2, 3). The triangle is shifted up 2 units and right 3 units. What can you tell about the other vertices of the triangle?

(Answers on page 205.)

ALL, SOME, AND NONE

Diagrams can show the logical connectives *all, some,* and *none.* View the following diagrams for an explanation.

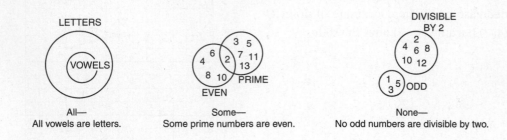

All—
All vowels are letters.

Some—
Some prime numbers are even.

None—
No odd numbers are divisible by two.

Deductive Reasoning

Deductive reasoning draws conclusions from statements or assumptions. Diagrams may help you draw a conclusion. Consider this simple example.

Assume that all even numbers are divisible by two and that all multiples of ten are even. Draw a diagram:

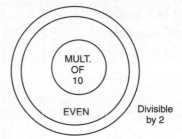

The multiple of ten circle is entirely within the divisible by two circle. Conclusion: All multiples of ten are divisible by two.

Practice

Write whether the statement is true or false. Explain your answer.

1. A ball is used in all sports.

2. Some numbers divisible by 5 are also divisible by 7.

3. There are no even numbers divisible by 3.

4. Some prime numbers are divisible by 2.

(Answers on page 205.)

PROBLEM SOLVING

The problem-solving strategies of choosing a reasonable answer, estimating, choosing the operation, writing a number sentence, and identifying extra or needed information were discussed earlier in the review. This section shows you how to use more problem-solving strategies.

Estimate to Be Sure Your Answer Is Reasonable

You can use estimation and common sense to be sure that the answer is reasonable. You may make a multiplication error or misalign decimal points. You may be so engrossed in a problem that you miss the big picture because of the details. These difficulties can be headed off by making sure your answer is reasonable.

A few examples follow.

A question involves dividing or multiplying. Multiply: 28×72.

Estimate first: $30 \times 70 = 2{,}100$. Your answer should be close to 2,100. If not, then your answer is not reasonable. A mistake was probably made in multiplication.

A question involves subtracting or adding. Add: $12.9 + 0.63 + 10.29 + 4.3$.

Estimate first: $13 + 1 + 10 + 4 = 28$. Your answer should be close to 28. If not, then your answer is not reasonable. The decimal points may not have been aligned.

A question asks you to compare fractions to $\frac{11}{10}$.

Think: $\frac{11}{10}$ is more than 1. Any number 1 or less will be less than $\frac{11}{10}$. Any number larger than $1\frac{1}{10}$ will be more than $\frac{11}{10}$. You have to look closely only at numbers from 1 to $1\frac{1}{10}$.

A question asks you to multiply two fractions or decimals.

The fractions or decimals are less than 1. The product of two fractions or decimals less than one is less than either of the two fractions or decimals. If not, you know that your answer is not reasonable.

Stand back for a second after you answer each question and ask, "Is this reasonable? Is this at least approximately correct? Does this make sense?"

Check answers to computation, particularly division and subtraction. When you have completed a division or subtraction example, do a quick, approximate check. Your check should confirm your answer. If not, your answer is probably not reasonable.

Circle Important Information and Key Words
Eliminate Extra Information

This approach will draw your attention to the information needed to answer the question. A common mistake is to use facts from the question that have nothing to do with the solution.

In the morning, a train travels at a constant speed over an 800 kilometer distance. In the afternoon the train travels back over this same route. There is less traffic and the train travels four times as fast as it did that morning. However, there are more people on the train during the afternoon. Which of the following do you know about the train's afternoon trip?

Ⓐ The time is divided by four
Ⓑ The time is multiplied by four
Ⓒ The rate and time are divided by four
Ⓓ The rate is divided by four
Ⓔ The distance is the same, so the rate is the same

To solve the problem you just need to know that the speed is constant, four times as fast, and the same route was covered. Circle this information you need to solve the problem.

The distance traveled or that there were more people in the afternoon is extra information. Cross off this extra information, which may interfere with your ability to solve the problem.

In the morning, a train travels at a ⸤constant speed⸥ over an 800 kilometer distance. In the afternoon the train travels back over this ⸤same route.⸥ There is less traffic and the train travels ⸤four times as fast as⸥ it did that morning. However, there are more people on the train during the afternoon. Which of the following do you know about the train's afternoon trip?

The correct answer is (A), the time is divided by four. The route is the same, but the train travels four times as fast. Therefore, the time to make the trip is divided by four. Rate means the same thing as speed, and we know that the speed has been multiplied by four.

Words to Symbols Problems

Before you solve a problem, you may have to decide which operation to use. You can use key words to help you decide which operation to use.

Key Words

Addition	sum, and, more, increased by
Subtraction	less, difference, decreased by
Multiplication	of, product, times
Division	per, quotient, shared, ratio
Equals	is, equals

You cannot just use these key words without thinking. You must be sure that the operation makes sense when it replaces the key word. For example,

19 and 23 is 42	16 is 4 more than 12	30% of 19 is 5.7?
$19 + 23 = 42$	$16 = 4 + 12$	$0.3 \times 19 = 5.7$

three more than y	$y + 3$	The product of 3 and y	$3y$
y increased by 3	$y + 3$	3 times y	$3y$
y more than 3	$3 + y$	3% of y	$0.03y$

3 less than y	$y-3$	3 divided by y	$\dfrac{3}{y}$
y decreased by 3	$y-3$	y divided by 3	$\dfrac{y}{3}$
3 decreased y	$3-y$	ratio of 3 to y	$\dfrac{3}{y}$
The opposite of y	$-y$	The reciprocal of y	$\dfrac{1}{y}$

EXAMPLES

A. 18 divided by what number is 3?

$18 \div y = 3$ $\qquad$ $18 = 3y$ $\qquad$ $y = 6$

B. 25 less 6 is what number?

$25 - 6 = y$ $\qquad$ $y = 19$

C. A student correctly answered 80% of 120 mathematics problems. How many mathematics problems did he answer correctly?

$0.8 \times 120 = y$ $\qquad$ $y = 96$

The student correctly answered 96 problems.

D. The product of a number and its opposite is –25. What is the number?

$(y) \times (-y) = -25$ $\qquad$ $y = 5$ or $y = -5$

The number is either 5 or –5.

Practice

Solve the problems.

1. What number decreased by 9 is 25?

2. What is 60% of 90?

3. Bob lives $\dfrac{2}{3}$ mile from Gina and $\dfrac{1}{2}$ mile from Sam. Bob's walk to the school is three times the sum of these distances. How far is Bob's walk to school?

4. The ratio of two gears is 20 to y. If the ratio equals 2.5, what is the value of y?

5. The sum of 5 and the reciprocal of another number is $5\dfrac{1}{8}$. What is the other number?

6. Car A travels at a constant speed of 60 mph for 2.5 hours. Car B travels at a constant speed of 70 mph for 2 hours. What is the total distance traveled by both cars?

(Answers on page 205.)

Finding and Interpreting Patterns

SEQUENCES

Arithmetic Sequence

A sequence of numbers formed by adding the same nonzero number.

3, 11, 19, 27, 35, 43, 51	Add 8 to get each successive term.
52, 48, 44, 40, 36, 32	Add (−4) to get each successive term.

Geometric Sequence

A sequence of numbers formed by multiplying the same nonzero number.

3, 15, 75, 375	Multiply by 5 to get each successive term.
160, 40, 10, $2\frac{1}{2}$	Multiply by $\frac{1}{4}$ to get each successive term.

Harmonic Sequence

A sequence of fractions with a numerator of 1 in which the denominators form an arithmetic sequence.

$$\frac{1}{2} \quad \frac{1}{9} \quad \frac{1}{16} \quad \frac{1}{23} \quad \frac{1}{30}$$

Each numerator is 1. The denominators form an arithmetic sequence.

Relationships

Linear Relationships

Linear relationships are pairs of numbers formed by adding or multiplying the same number to the first term in a pair. Here are some examples.

(3, 12), (5, 14), (11, 20), (15, 24)	Add 9 to the first term to get the second.
(1, 6), (2, 12), (3, 18), (4, 24), (5, 30)	Multiply the first term by 6 to get the second.
(96, 12), (72, 9), (56, 7), (24, 3), (16, 2)	Multiply the first term by $\frac{1}{8}$ to get the second.

EXAMPLES

A. What term is missing in this number pattern?

$$2 \quad 5 \quad 10 \quad 17 \quad \underline{\quad}$$
$$+3 \quad +5 \quad +7 \quad +9$$

26 is the missing term.

B. These points are all on the same line.
Find the missing term.

$$(-7, -15) \left(\frac{2}{3}, \frac{1}{3} \right) (2, 3) \ (4, 7) \ (8, \underline{\quad})$$

Multiply the first term by 2 and subtract 1.
The missing term is (8, 15).

Practice

Find the missing term in each pattern below.

1. 4, 2, 0, −2, −4, ___ −8, −10 ___

2. 4, 6.5, 9, 11.5, ___

3. 120, 60, 30, 15, ___

4. 1, 2, 6, 24, 120, ___

5. 5, 9, 13, 17 ___

The points in each sequence below are on the same line. Find the missing term.

6. (4, 12), (2, 10), (10, 18), (18, 26), (22, ___)

7. (100, 11), (70, 8), (90, 10), (40, 5), (30, ___)

8. (3, 9), (7, 49), (2, 4), (100, 10,000), (5, ___)

9. A meteorologist placed remote thermometers at sea level and up the side of the mountain at 1,000, 2,000, 5,000, and 6,000 feet. Readings were taken simultaneously and entered in the following table. What temperatures would you predict for the missing readings?

Temperature

0	1,000	2,000	3,000	4,000	5,000	6,000	7,000	8,000	9,000	10,000
52°	49°	46°			37°	34°				

10. Consider another example. A space capsule is moving in a straight line and is being tracked on a grid. The first four positions on the grid are recorded in the following table. Where will the capsule be on the grid when the x position is 13?

x-value	1	2	3	4
y-value	1	4	7	10

(Answers on page 206.)

Estimation Problems

Follow these steps.

1. Round the numbers.
2. Use the rounded numbers to estimate the answer.

EXAMPLE

It takes a person about $7\frac{1}{2}$ minutes to run a mile. The person runs 176 miles in a month. What is a reasonable estimate of the time it takes for the person to run that distance?

Round $7\frac{1}{2}$ to 8.

Round 174 to 180.

$180 \times 8 = 1,440$ minutes or 24 hours.

24 hours is a reasonable estimate of the answer.

Practice

1. A class took a spelling quiz and the grades were 93, 97, 87, 88, 98, 91. What is a reasonable estimate of the average of these grades?

2. To build a sandbox, you need lumber in the following lengths: 12 ft, 16 ft, 18 ft, and 23 ft. What is a reasonable estimate of the total length of the lumber?

3. Each batch of cookies yields 11 dozen. You need 165 dozen. What is a reasonable estimate for the number of batches you will need?

4. It takes 48 minutes for a commuter to travel back and forth from work each day. If the commuter drives back and forth 26 days a month, what is a reasonable estimate of the number of hours that are spent driving?

(Answers on page 206.)

Chart Problems

Follow these steps:

1. Identify the data in the chart.
2. Add when necessary to find the total probability.

EXAMPLE

	Air Express	Rail	Truck
5 pounds and over	0.07	0.34	0.18
Under 5 pounds	0.23	0.02	0.16

The table shows the percent of packages shipped by the method used and the weight classes.

What is the probability that a package picked at random was sent Air Express?

Add the two decimals for Air Express.

$$0.07 + 0.23 = 0.30$$

The probability that a randomly picked package was sent Air Express is 0.3.

What is the probability that a package picked at random weighed under five pounds?

Add the three decimals for under five pounds.

$$0.23 + 0.02 + 0.16 = 0.41.$$

The probability that a randomly chosen package weighed under five pounds is 0.42.

What is the probability that a package picked at random weighs under five pounds and was sent by rail?

Look at the cell in the table where *under five pounds* and *rail* intersect.
That decimal is 0.02.

The probability that a randomly chosen package is under five pounds and was sent by rail is 0.02.

Practice

Use the table on page 174.

1. What is the probability that a package was sent by truck?

2. What is the probability of a package five pounds and over being randomly chosen?

3. What is the probability that a package picked at random is five pounds and over and was sent by Air Express?

4. What is the probability of randomly choosing a package that is under five pounds and was sent other than by rail?

(Answers on page 206.)

Frequency Table Problems

PERCENT

Percent tables show the percent or proportion of a particular score or characteristic. You can see from the table below that 13% of the students got a score from 90 through 100.

EXAMPLE

Scores	Percent of Students
0–59	2
60–69	8
70–79	39
80–89	38
90–100	13

Which score interval contains the median?

The cumulative percentage of 0–79 is 49%.

The median is in the interval in which the cumulative percentage of 50% occurs. The score interval 80–89 contains the median.

What percent of the students scored above 79?

Add the percentiles of the intervals above 79.

$$38 + 13 = 51$$

51% of the students scored above 79.

PERCENTILE RANK

The percentile rank shows the percent of scores below a given value. You can see from the table below that 68% of the scores fell below 60.

EXAMPLE

Standardized Score	Percentile Rank
80	99
70	93
60	68
50	39
40	22
30	13
20	2

What percent of the scores are below 50?

The percentile rank next to 50 is 39. That means 39% of the scores are below 50.

What percent of the scores are at least 30 and less than 70?

Subtract the percentile rank for 30 from the percentile rank for 70.

$93\% - 13\% = 80\%$. 80% of the scores are at least 30 and less than 70.

What percent of the scores are at or above 60?

Subtract the percentile rank for 60 from 100%.

$100\% - 68\% = 32\%$. 32% of the scores are at or above 60.

Practice

Use the table on page 175 and the table above.

Table 1 (on page 175)

1. What percent of the scores are below 70?

2. In which score interval is the median?

3. What percent of the scores are from 80 to 100?

Table 2 (on page 176)

4. The lowest passing score is 50. What percent of the scores are passing?

5. What percent of the scores are from 20 to 50?

(Answers on page 207.)

Formula Problems

Concentrate on substituting values for variables. If you see a problem to be solved with a proportion, set up the proportion and solve.

EXAMPLES

A. A mechanic uses this formula to estimate the displacement (P) of an engine. $P = 0.8 (d^2)(s)(n)$ where d is the diameter, s is the stroke length of each cylinder, and n is the number of cylinders. Estimate the displacement of a 6-cylinder car whose cylinders have a diameter of 2 inches and a stroke length of 4 inches.

1. Write the formula.	$P = 0.8(d^2)(s)(n)$
2. Write the values of the variables.	$d = 2, s = 4, n = 6$
3. Substitute the values for the variables.	$P = 0.8(2^2)(4)(6)$
4. Solve.	$P = 0.8(4)(24) = (3.2)(24)$
	$P = 76.8$

The displacement of the engine is about 76.8 cubic inches.

B. The accountant calculates that it takes $3 in sales to generate $0.42 in profit. How much cost does it take to generate a profit of $5.46?

1. Write a proportion
   Use s for sales. $\qquad\qquad \dfrac{3}{0.42} = \dfrac{s}{5.46}$

2. Cross multiply. $\qquad\qquad 0.42s = 16.38$

3. Solve. $\qquad\qquad\qquad s = \dfrac{16.38}{0.42}$

   $\qquad\qquad\qquad\qquad s = 39$

It will take $39 in sales to generate $5.46 in profits.

Practice

1. A retail store makes a profit of $3.75 for each $10 of goods sold. How much profit would the store make on a $45 purchase?

2. The formula for calculating average speed is $d/(T_2 - T_1)$. If T_1 (start time) is 5:00 P.M. and T_2 (end time) is midnight the same day, and 287 miles were traveled, what was the average speed?

3. A car purchased for $12,000 ($O$) depreciates 10% ($P$) a year ($Y$). If the car is sold in 3 years, what is its depreciated value if $V = O - POY$?

4. There is a square grid of dots. A figure is made of line segments that connect the dots. The formula for the area of a figure on the grid is $\dfrac{T-2}{2} + I$. T is the number of dots touching the figure, and I is the number of dots inside. What is the area of a figure with 14 dots touching and 5 dots inside?

(Answers on page 207.)

Pythagorean Theorem Problems

Follow these steps to solve this type of problem.

1. Sketch and label the right triangle.
2. Use the Pythagorean formula.
3. Solve the problem.

EXAMPLE

A radio tower sticks 40 feet straight up into the air. Engineers attached a wire with no slack from the top of the tower to the ground 30 feet away from the tower. If it costs $95 a foot to attach the wire, how much did the wire cost?

1. Sketch and label the right triangle.

2. Use the Pythagorean formula.

    $a^2 + b^2 = c^2$
    $(40)^2 + (30)^2 = c^2$
    $1,600 + 900 = c^2$
    $2,500 = c^2$
    $50 = c$
    The wire is 50 feet long.

3. Solve the problem.

    50 feet at $95 a foot.
    $50 \times 95 = 4,750$. The wire costs $4,750 to install.

Practice

1. A 20-foot ladder is leaning against the side of a tall apartment building. The bottom of the ladder is 15 feet from the wall. At what height on the wall does the top of the ladder touch the building?

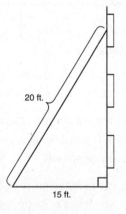

20 ft.

15 ft.

2. A truck ramp is shaped like a right triangle. The base of the ramp is 300 feet long. The ramp itself is 340 feet long. How high is the third side of the ramp?

3. A 25-meter telephone pole casts a shadow. The shadow ends 17 meters from the base of the pole. How long is it straight from the top of the pole to the end of the shadow?

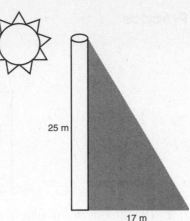

25 m

17 m

4. You are building a staircase. The wall is 14 feet wide and the stairs are 40 feet long. How high is the wall where it touches the top of the stairs?

40

14

(Answers on page 207.)

Geometric Figure Problems

Follow these steps to solve this type of problem.

1. Identify the figure or figures involved.
2. Use the formulas for these figures.
3. Use the results of the formulas to solve the problem.

EXAMPLE

A circular pool with a radius of 10 feet is inscribed inside a square wall. What is the area of the region outside the pool but inside the fence?

10

1. There is a square with $s = 20$ and a circle with $r = 10$. The side of the square is twice the radius of the circle.

2. Find the areas.
   Square: $(A = s^2)$ (20) × (20) = 400
   Circle: $(A = \pi r^2)$ 3.14 × 10^2 = 3.14 × 100 = 314

3. Subtract to find the area inside the square but outside the circle.
   400 − 314 = 86

Practice

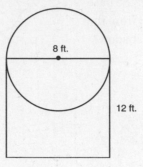

1. The dimensions of part of a basketball court are shown in the diagram above. One pint of paint covers 35 square feet. How much paint would it take to paint the inside region of this part of the court?

2. A roofer uses one bushel of shingles to cover 1,200 square feet. How many bushels of shingles are needed to cover these three rectangular roofs?

   Roof 1: 115 ft by 65 ft
   Roof 2: 112 ft by 65 ft
   Roof 3: 72 ft by 52 ft

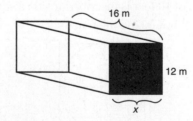

3. The bricks in the wall pictured here measure 2 inches by 4 inches by 8 inches. What is the volume of the bricks in this section of the wall?

4. A circular cone has a radius of 4 cm. If the volume is 134 cm³, what is the height?

5. The official basketball has a radius of 6.5 inches. What is the volume?

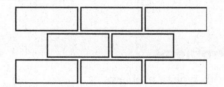

6. The rectangular solid shown here has a volume of 1,920 m³. What is the area of the shaded side?

(Answers on page 208.)

Interpreting Remainder Problems

When you divide to solve a problem there may be both a quotient and a remainder. You may need to (1) use only the quotient, (2) round the quotient to the next greater whole number, or (3) use only the remainder.

EXAMPLE

Stereo speakers are packed 4 to a box. There are 315 stereo speakers to be packed.

Questions:

1. How many boxes can be filled?
2. How many boxes would be needed to hold all the stereo speakers?
3. How many stereo speakers will be in the box that is not completely full?

Divide 315 by 4.

$$
\begin{array}{r}
78 \text{ R}3 \\
4\overline{)315} \\
-28\downarrow \\
\hline
35 \\
-32 \\
\hline
3
\end{array}
$$

Answers:

1. Use only the quotient—78 of the boxes can be filled.
2. Round the quotient to the next higher number. It would take 79 boxes to hold all the stereo speakers.
3. Use only the remainder. Three stereo speakers would be in the partially filled box.

Practice

At the quarry, workers are putting 830 pounds of sand into bags that hold 25 pounds.

1. How much sand is left over after the bags are filled?

2. How many bags are needed to hold all the sand?

3. How many bags can be completely filled with sand?

(Answers on page 208.)

STRATEGIES FOR PASSING THE MATHEMATICS TEST

The mathematics tested is the kind you probably had in high school and in college. It is the kind of mathematics you will use as you teach and go about your everyday life. Computational ability alone is expected but is held to a minimum. Remember to use the general test strategies discussed in the Introduction.

Write on the Scrap Paper Provided

It is particularly important to use the provided scrap paper while taking the mathematics portion of the test.

Draw Diagrams and Figures on the Scrap Paper

When you come across a geometry problem or related problem, draw a diagram on the scrap paper to help.

All sides of a rectangle are shrunk in half. What happens to the area?

Ⓐ Divided by 2
Ⓑ Divided by 4
Ⓒ Multiplied by 2
Ⓓ Multiplied by 6
Ⓔ Multiplied by 16

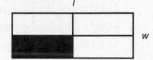

Answer (B), divided by 4, is the correct answer. The original area is evenly divided into four parts.

Work from the Answers

If you do not know how to solve a formula or relation try out each answer choice until you get the correct answer. Look at this example.

What percent times $\frac{1}{4}$ is $\frac{1}{5}$?

Ⓐ 25%
Ⓑ 40%
Ⓒ 80%
Ⓓ 120%
Ⓔ 160%

Just take each answer in turn and try it out.

$$0.25 \times \frac{1}{4} = \frac{1}{4} \times \frac{1}{4} = \frac{1}{16} \quad \text{That is not it.}$$

$$0.40 \times \frac{1}{4} = \frac{4}{10} \times \frac{1}{4} = \frac{4}{40} = \frac{1}{10} \quad \text{That is not it either.}$$

$$0.8 \times \frac{1}{4} = \frac{4}{5} \times \frac{1}{4} = \frac{4}{20} = \frac{1}{5}$$

You know that 0.8 is the correct answer, so choice (C) is correct.

Try Out Numbers

Look at the preceding question.

Work with fractions at first. Ask: What number times $\frac{1}{4}$ equals $\frac{1}{5}$?

Through trial and error you find out that $\frac{4}{5} \times \frac{1}{4} = \frac{1}{5}$. The answer in fractions is $\frac{4}{5}$.

$$\frac{4}{5} = 0.8 = 80\%$$

The correct choice is (C).

In this example, you can find the answer without ever solving an equation by trying out numbers until you find the one that works.

Eliminate and Guess

Use this approach when all else has failed. Begin by eliminating the answers you know are wrong. Sometimes you know with certainty that an answer is incorrect. Other times, an answer looks so unreasonable that you can be fairly sure that it is not correct.

Once you have eliminated incorrect answers, a few will probably be left. Just guess among these choices. There is no method that will increase your chances of guessing correctly.

There is nothing better than mathematics practice. This targeted test is designed to help you practice the problem-solving and test-taking strategies presented in this chapter. For that reason, questions may have a different emphasis than the actual test, and the actual test will certainly be more complete. Answers are on pages 209–213.

> **Directions:** Mark your choice, then check your answers. You may use a calculator, like the one used on the test.

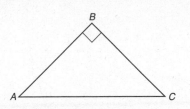

1. This is an isosceles triangle. What is the measure of angle *A*?

   Ⓐ 10°

   Ⓑ 40°

   Ⓒ 90°

   Ⓓ 45°

   Ⓔ 180°

2. After a discount of 25 percent, the savings on a pair of roller blades was $12.00. What was the sale price?

   Ⓐ $48.00

   Ⓑ $36.00

   Ⓒ $24.00

   Ⓓ $25.00

   Ⓔ $60.00

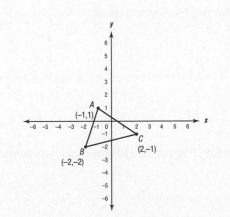

3. In the graph above, the triangle is shifted up 3 units and to the right 6 units. What would be the coordinates of point *B* after that shift?

   Ⓐ (1, –6)

   Ⓑ (1, 3)

   Ⓒ (3, 2)

   Ⓓ (4, 1)

   Ⓔ (1, 4)

4. Chad rolls a fair die. The sides of the die are numbered from 1 to 6. Ten times in a row he rolls a 5. What is the probability that he will roll a 5 on his next roll?

  Ⓐ $\frac{1}{5}$

  Ⓑ $\frac{1}{6}$

  Ⓒ $\frac{1}{50}$

  Ⓓ $\frac{1}{11}$

  Ⓔ $\frac{1}{10}$

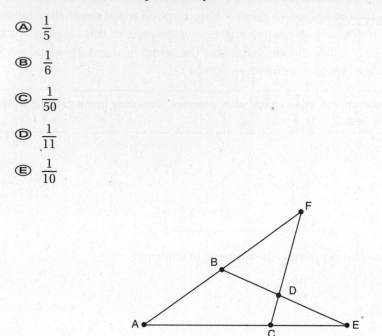

5. Which of the following set of points do not form an angle in the diagram?

  Ⓐ ABF
  Ⓑ ABE
  Ⓒ AFC
  Ⓓ ABC
  Ⓔ CDE

6. An apple costs (C). You have (D) dollars. What equation would represent the amount of apples you could buy for the money you have?

  Ⓐ *C/D*
  Ⓑ *CD*
  Ⓒ *C + D*
  Ⓓ *D/C*
  Ⓔ *C + 2D*

7. If a worker gets $144.00 for 18 hours' work, how much would that worker get for 32 hours' work?

  Ⓐ $200.00
  Ⓑ $288.00
  Ⓒ $400.00
  Ⓓ $432.00
  Ⓔ $256.00

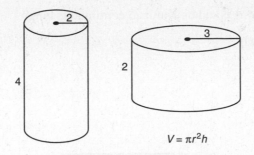

$$V = \pi r^2 h$$

8. Find the difference between the volumes of these two cylinders.

    (A) 2π
    (B) 4π
    (C) 9π
    (D) 16π
    (E) 18π

9. r = regular price
   d = discount
   s = sale price

   What equation would represent the calculations for finding the discount?

    (A) $d = r - s$
    (B) $d = s - r$
    (C) $d = sr$
    (D) $d = s + r$
    (E) $d = \frac{1}{2}r$

10. A printing company makes pamphlets that cost $.75 per copy plus $5.00 as a setter's fee. If $80 were spent printing a pamphlet, how many pamphlets were ordered?

    (A) 50
    (B) 75
    (C) 100
    (D) 150
    (E) 225

11. Which is farthest from $\frac{1}{2}$ on a number line?

    (A) $\frac{1}{12}$

    (B) $\frac{7}{8}$

    (C) $\frac{3}{4}$

    (D) $\frac{2}{3}$

    (E) $\frac{5}{6}$

12. Which of the following could be about 25 centimeters long?

    Ⓐ a human thumb
    Ⓑ a doorway
    Ⓒ a car
    Ⓓ a house
    Ⓔ a notebook

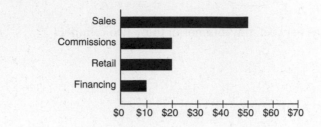

13. The sales department staff draws its salary from four areas of the company's income. Using the above graph, determine what percentage is drawn from the retail fund.

    Ⓐ 10%
    Ⓑ 20%
    Ⓒ 25%
    Ⓓ 30%
    Ⓔ 15%

14. If 250 is lowered by 40%, what percent of the new number is 30?

    Ⓐ 5%
    Ⓑ 10%
    Ⓒ 20%
    Ⓓ 25%
    Ⓔ 50%

15. For a fund-raiser the Science and Technology Club is selling raffles at the cost of six raffles for $5.00. It cost the club $250.00 for the prizes and tickets that will be given away. How many raffles will the club have to sell in order to make $1,000.00?

    Ⓐ 300
    Ⓑ 600
    Ⓒ 750
    Ⓓ 1,200
    Ⓔ 1,500

16. What value for n makes the number sentence true?

$$5.3 \times 10^4 = 0.0053 \times 10^n$$

    Ⓐ 4
    Ⓑ 5
    Ⓒ 6
    Ⓓ 7
    Ⓔ 8

17. Which of the following represents complementary angles?

Ⓐ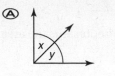

Ⓑ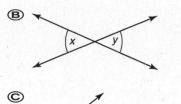

Ⓒ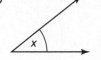

Ⓓ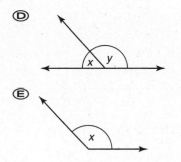

Ⓔ

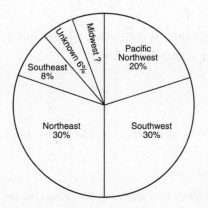

18. The above graph shows the percentage of students who attend college by the location of their home towns. How many more college students come from the Northeast than come from the Midwest?

   Ⓐ twice as many
   Ⓑ three times as many
   Ⓒ half as many
   Ⓓ five times as many
   Ⓔ ten times as many

19. Each rectangle has a total area of 1 square unit. What number represents the area of the shaded regions?

(A) $\frac{5}{6}$ square units

(B) $\frac{7}{8}$ square units

(C) $1\frac{3}{4}$ square units

(D) $1\frac{1}{3}$ square units

(E) $1\frac{5}{24}$ square units

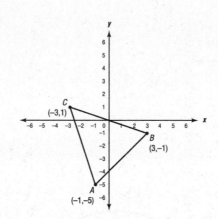

20. In the graph above, the triangle is shifted left 2 units and down 4 units. What would be the coordinates of point *A* after that shift?

(A) (1, 1)
(B) (2, 4)
(C) (−2, −4)
(D) (−8, −3)
(E) (−3, −9)

21. The sum of the measures of two angles is 90°. What do we know about these two angles?

(A) They are right angles.
(B) They are supplementary angles.
(C) They are acute angles.
(D) They are obtuse angles.
(E) They are straight angles.

22. Three very bright light beams go out into space from the same spot on Earth. None of the beams are parallel and none point in the same direction. What conclusion can we reach?

Ⓐ All three beams will cross at the same point.

Ⓑ Exactly two of the beams will cross.

Ⓒ At least two of the beams will cross.

Ⓓ Two of the beams are perpendicular.

Ⓔ At least two of the beams may be skewed.

23. Bob walked about 2,750 meters to school every day. About how many kilometers is that?

Ⓐ 2.750

Ⓑ 27.50

Ⓒ 275

Ⓓ 275,000

Ⓔ $27.5 \times 1,000$

24. You buy 20 shares of stock on March 10 for $17\frac{7}{8}$ a share. You sell the 20 shares of the same stock on May 5 for $19\frac{5}{8}$ a share. How much in dollars and cents did you make on the stock sale?

Ⓐ $75.00

Ⓑ $4.50

Ⓒ $37.50

Ⓓ $35.00

Ⓔ $3.50

25. Alpha Centauri is about 4 light years from Earth. Light travels about 186,000 miles in a second. About how far is it from Alpha Centauri to Earth?

Ⓐ 23 quintillion miles

Ⓑ 23 quadrillion miles

Ⓒ 23 trillion miles

Ⓓ 23 billion miles

Ⓔ 28 million miles

26. An unusual plant is 10 feet tall when planted and then, starting the next day, grows 20 percent of each of the previous day's final height. About how tall is the tree at the end of the fourth day after planting?

Ⓐ 8 feet

Ⓑ 19.4 feet

Ⓒ 18 feet

Ⓓ 16 feet

Ⓔ 20.7 feet

27. A block of stone is 9 feet wide by 12 feet long by 8 feet high. A stone mason cuts the stone to form the biggest cube possible. What is the volume of the cube?

   Ⓐ 864 cubic feet
   Ⓑ 144 cubic feet
   Ⓒ 81 cubic feet
   Ⓓ 526 cubic feet
   Ⓔ 512 cubic feet

USE THE INFORMATION BELOW FOR QUESTIONS 28 AND 29.

An archaeologist was investigating the books of an old civilization. She found the following table, which showed the number of hunters on top and the number of people they could feed on the bottom. For example, 3 hunters could feed 12 people. The archaeologist found a pattern in the table.

Hunters	1	2	3	4	5	6	7
Eaters	2	6	12	20	30		

28. Look for the pattern. How many eaters can 6 hunters feed?

   Ⓐ 42
   Ⓑ 40
   Ⓒ 30
   Ⓓ 36
   Ⓔ 34

29. What is the formula for the pattern:

H stands for hunters and
E stands for eaters?

   Ⓐ $E = 3 \times H$
   Ⓑ $E = 4 \times H$
   Ⓒ $E = H^2 + H$
   Ⓓ $E = 3 \times (H + 1)$
   Ⓔ $E = (H + 1)(H + 1)$

---

30. The school is planning a class trip. They will go by bus. There will be 328 people going on the trip, and each bus holds 31 people. How many buses will be needed for the trip?

   Ⓐ 7
   Ⓑ 8
   Ⓒ 9
   Ⓓ 10
   Ⓔ 11

1	2	3	4	5	6	7	8	9	10
11	12	13	14	15	16	17	18	19	20
21	22	23	24	25	26	27	28	29	30
31	32	33	34	35	36	37	38	39	40
41	42	43	44	45	46	47	48	49	50
51	52	53	54	55	56	57	58	59	60
61	62	63	64	65	66	67	68	69	70
71	72	73	74	75	76	77	78	79	80
81	82	83	84	85	86	87	88	89	90
91	92	93	94	95	96	97	98	99	100

31. Cross off the multiples of 2, 3, 4, 5, 6, 7, and 8 in the above hundreds square. Which numbers in the 80s are not crossed off?

Ⓐ 83, 87

Ⓑ 81, 89

Ⓒ 83, 89

Ⓓ 81, 83, 89

Ⓔ 82, 85, 88

USE THE GRAPH BELOW TO ANSWER QUESTIONS 32 AND 33.

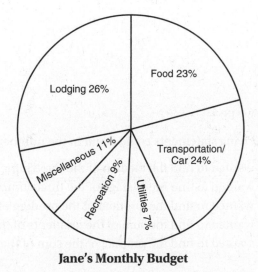

Jane's Monthly Budget

32. Jane spends $2,600 in the month of March. How much did she spend on food?

Ⓐ $624

Ⓑ $598

Ⓒ $312

Ⓓ $400

Ⓔ $600

33. Jane spends $2,600 in May. She needs $858 that month for transportation/car expenses, which is more than the budget allows. Any needed money will come from miscellaneous. When she recalculates her budget chart, what percent is left for miscellaneous?

    Ⓐ   13 percent
    Ⓑ   11 percent
    Ⓒ   9 percent
    Ⓓ   6 percent
    Ⓔ   2 percent

---

34. The bakers make brownies and cookies in a ratio of 2 : 9. Today the bakers made 1,350 cookies. How many brownies did the bakers make?

    Ⓐ   150
    Ⓑ   300
    Ⓒ   675
    Ⓓ   2,750
    Ⓔ   3,000

35. A tent standing on level ground is 40 feet high. A taut rope extends from the top of the tent to the ground 30 feet from the bottom of the tent. About how long is the rope?

    Ⓐ   26.455 feet
    Ⓑ   50 feet
    Ⓒ   63.255 feet
    Ⓓ   70 feet
    Ⓔ   2,500 feet

36. $(123 + 186 + 177) \div (3) =$

Which of the following statements could result in the number sentence given above?

    Ⓐ   The athlete wanted to find the median of the three jumps.
    Ⓑ   The athlete wanted to find the average of the three jumps.
    Ⓒ   The athlete wanted to find the quotient of the product of three jumps.
    Ⓓ   The athlete wanted to find the sum of the quotients of the three jumps.
    Ⓔ   The athlete wanted to find the product of the sum of the quotients.

37. Renee, Lisa, and Jan are all on the basketball team. Renee is the tallest player on the team. Lisa is not the shortest player on the team. Jan is not shorter than Lisa.

Which of the following conclusions can be drawn from this statement?

    Ⓐ   Jan is taller than Lisa.
    Ⓑ   Jan is the second-tallest player on the team.
    Ⓒ   Jan is not the shortest player on the team.
    Ⓓ   Either Jan or Lisa is the second tallest player on the team.
    Ⓔ   Lisa is the tallest player.

38. If $x = \frac{5}{6}$, which of the following inequalities is correct?

    Ⓐ $\frac{5}{9} < x < \frac{7}{9}$

    Ⓑ $\frac{5}{8} < x < \frac{3}{4}$

    Ⓒ $\frac{3}{4} < x < \frac{7}{8}$

    Ⓓ $\frac{7}{8} < x < \frac{15}{16}$

    Ⓔ $\frac{5}{6} < x < \frac{9}{10}$

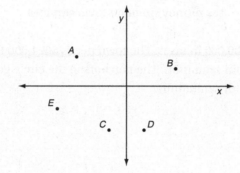

39. Which letter on the coordinate grid above could represent the point (–2, –5)?

    Ⓐ   *A*

    Ⓑ   *B*

    Ⓒ   *C*

    Ⓓ   *D*

    Ⓔ   *E*

40. The disaster relief specialist found that 289, or 85%, of the houses on the beach had been damaged by the storm. How many houses were on the beach?

    Ⓐ   294

    Ⓑ   332

    Ⓒ   340

    Ⓓ   400

    Ⓔ   420

41. Light travels about 186,000 miles in a second. How would you find out how far light travels in an hour?

    Ⓐ   Multiply 186,000 by 24.

    Ⓑ   Multiply 186,000 by 60.

    Ⓒ   Multiply 186,000 by 360.

    Ⓓ   Multiply 186,000 by 3,600.

    Ⓔ   Multiply 186,000 by 2,400.

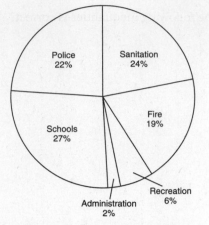

Tax money spent on town services

42. A town collects $2,600,000 in taxes. The town needs $624,000 for police. Any needed money will come from sanitation. The percents in the circle graph are recalculated. What percent is left for sanitation?

    (A) 22%

    (B) 20%

    (C) 19%

    (D) 18%

    (E) 16%

43. A person flips a fair penny twice and it lands heads up each time. What is the probability that the penny will land heads up on the next flip?

    (A) 1

    (B) $\frac{1}{2}$

    (C) $\frac{1}{4}$

    (D) $\frac{1}{8}$

    (E) $\frac{1}{16}$

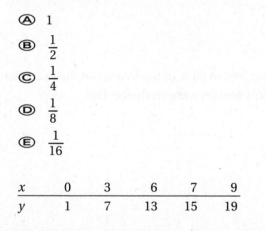

x	0	3	6	7	9
y	1	7	13	15	19

44. Which of the following expressions shows the relationship between x and y in the table above?

    (A) $y = 3x - 2$

    (B) $y = 2x + 1$

    (C) $y = x + 3$

    (D) $y = 2x - 2$

    (E) $y = 4x + 1$

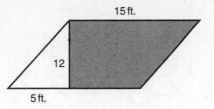

45. What is the area of the shaded portion in the figure above?

    (A) 45 square feet

    (B) 270 square feet

    (C) 170 square feet

    (D) 180 square feet

    (E) 150 square feet

46. $2n + 3n^2 - 5n \times 3 - 6n^2 =$

    (A) $-12n$

    (B) $-13n - 3n^2$

    (C) $13n + 3n^2$

    (D) $-6n^2$

    (E) $-15n - n^2$

47. The formula for converting a kilogram weight (K) to a pound weight (P) is
$P = 2.2$ K. If a dog weighs 15.6 pounds, how many kilograms does the dog weigh?

    (A) 3.43 kg

    (B) 34.32 kg

    (C) 7.09 kg

    (D) 70.9 kg

    (E) .709 kg

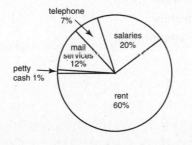

48. The pie chart preceding this question represents the monthly expenses of a small
business for August. In what area is the most money spent?

    (A) mail services, telephone, and salaries

    (B) salaries, telephone, and petty cash

    (C) petty cash and salaries

    (D) rent

    (E) petty cash, salaries, and mail services

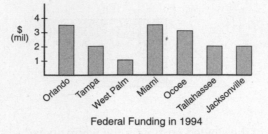

Federal Funding in 1994

49. In the bar graph that precedes this question, which city or cities likely represent the mode?

Ⓐ Orlando
Ⓑ Ocoee
Ⓒ West Palm
Ⓓ Tallahassee
Ⓔ Miami

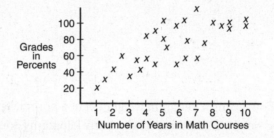

50. The graph shows the grade distribution on a standardized mathematics test. Which of the following best describes the relationships between test score and number of years in mathematics courses?

Ⓐ People who took fewer years of math scored highest.
Ⓑ People who took more math courses scored lower.
Ⓒ There is a negative relationship.
Ⓓ There is no relationship.
Ⓔ There is a positive relationship.

51.   Which of the following expressions represents the area of the figure below?

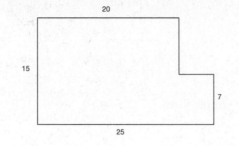

Choose all that apply.

A $(15 \times 20) + (7 \times 5)$
B $(20 \times 15) + (7 \times 25)$
C $(25 \times 15) - (8 \times 5)$
D $(20 \times 15) - (25 \times 7)$
E $(25 \times 15) + (7 \times 5)$

52.   A rectangle is 48 inches wide with an area greater than 57 square feet. Which of the lengths listed below could be the length of the rectangle.

Choose all that apply.

A   12 feet
B   14 feet, 9 inches
C   14 feet, 3 inches
D   60 inches
E   175 inches

Final Exam Grades

Percent Correct	Class A	Class B	Class C	Class D	Class E
90–100	9	4	1	2	4
80–89	2	8	4	5	3
70–79	8	2	5	4	4
60–69	2	3	8	0	5
Below 60	5	11	2	6	7

53.   The passing grade for a college course requires a score of at least 70% on the final exam. Which of the following classes has more than 60% of the students passing the course?

Choose all that apply.

A   Class A
B   Class B
C   Class C
D   Class D
E   Class E

54. If $a > 0$ and $b > 0$, evaluate the expression below when $a = 2$ and $b = 3$.

$$\frac{(b^2 - a^2)^3 + 3}{(a + 2b)^2}$$

55. Write the fraction in simple form.

$$\frac{\frac{1}{4}}{\frac{2}{3} - \frac{1}{2}}$$

56. Write the expression below as a fraction in lowest terms.

$$\left(\frac{2}{3}\right)^3 \cdot \left(\frac{3}{5}\right)^2$$

ANSWERS FOR MATHEMATICS PRACTICE

Understanding and Ordering Whole Numbers, page 122

1. $2 < 3$
2. $4 > 1$
3. $8 < 9$
4. $1 = 1$
5. $7 > 6$
6. 9,037
7. 2,851
8. The hundreds place and the ones place each contain a 7.
9. 1, 2, 3, 4, 5, 6, 7, 8, 9, 10, 11, 12, 13, 14 The problem asks for the numbers between 0 and 15, so 0 and 15 are not included.
10. There are 49. (1, 2, 3, . . . , 47, 48, 49)

Positive Exponents, page 123

1. 241
2. 729
3. 8
4. 900
5. 35
6. 51
7. $4^6 = 4{,}096$
8. $2^5 = 32$
9. 44
10. 1,000
11. $4^4 = 256$
12. 72

Scientific Notation, page 123

1. $0.0564 = 5.64 \times 10^{-2}$
2. $0.00897 = 8.97 \times 10^{-3}$
3. $0.06501 = 6.501 \times 10^{-2}$
4. $0.000354 = 3.54 \times 10^{-4}$
5. $545 = 5.45 \times 10^{2}$
6. $7{,}790 = 7.79 \times 10^{3}$
7. $289{,}705 = 2.89705 \times 10^{5}$
8. $1{,}801{,}319 = 1.801319 \times 10^{6}$

Comparing Whole Numbers and Decimals, page 124

1. $0.02 > 0.003$
2. $4.6 > 1.98$
3. $0.0008 > 0.00009$
4. $1.0 = 1$
5. $7.6274 > 7.6269$
6. 2.586

7. 90310.0704
8. The hundredths place and the hundred thousandths place each contain a 3.
9. 0.0, 0.1, 0.2, 0.3, 0.4, 0.5, 0.6, 0.7, 0.8, 0.9, 1.0
10. There are 99—0.01, 0.02, 0.03, . . . , 0.50, 0.51, 0.52, . . . , 0.97, 0.98, 0.99

Rounding Whole Numbers and Decimals, page 125

1. 23,500
2. 74.151
3. 980,000
4. 302.8
5. 495,240
6. 1,500
7. 13.10
8. 200,000
9. 52
10. 23,500

Rational and Irrational Numbers and Fractions, page 127

1. $\dfrac{2}{3} = 0.666\ldots$
2. $\dfrac{9}{12} = \dfrac{3}{4} = .75$
3. $\dfrac{5}{9} = 0.555\ldots$
4. $\dfrac{7}{12} = 0.58333\ldots$
5. 7π is close to $7 \times \dfrac{22}{7}$, which is approximately equal to 22.
6. $105\sqrt{2}$ is close to $105 \times \dfrac{99}{70}$, or approximately 1.5×99, and approximately 148.5.

Understanding and Ordering Fractions, page 129

1. $1\dfrac{2}{3}$
2. $2\dfrac{1}{7}$
3. $2\dfrac{2}{3}$
4. $\dfrac{41}{5}$
5. $\dfrac{55}{8}$
6. $\dfrac{68}{7}$
7. $\dfrac{3}{7} < \dfrac{4}{9}$
8. $\dfrac{5}{6} = \dfrac{25}{30}$
9. $\dfrac{4}{5} < \dfrac{7}{8}$

Order of Operations, page 130

1. $4 \times 5 + 4 \div 2 = 20 + 2 = 22$
2. $(5 + 7 - 9) \times 8^2 + 2 = 3 \times 8^2 + 2 = 194$
3. $((7 + 4) - (1 + 4)) \times 6 = (11 - 5) \times 6 = 36$
4. $6^2 + 3(9 - 5 + 7)^2 = 36 + 3 \times 11^2 = 399$
5. $51 - 36 = 15$
6. $40 + 4 - 4 = 40$
7. $-50 + 7 = -43$
8. $(49 + 16) \times 8 = 520$

Common Factors and Multiples, page 132

1. 13: 1 and 13
2. 26: 1, 2, 13, and 26
3. 40: 1, 2, 4, 5, 8, 10, 20, 40
4. 23: 1 and 23
5. 12
6. 60
7. 35
8. 28
9. 6
10. 5
11. 32
12. 28

Whole Number Computation, page 134

1. 98,405
2. 27,079
3. 95,809
4. 66,184
5. 16,013
6. 34,099
7. 34,688
8. 42,209
9. 13,680
10. 27,482
11. 29,725
12. 5,256
13. 8
14. 4 R4
15. 29
16. 32 R2

Properties of Operations, page 135

1. Commutative property
   $$\frac{6}{8} \times \frac{7}{9} = \frac{7}{9} \times \frac{6}{8}$$
2. Associative property
   $(2 + 3) + 4 = 2 + (3 + 4)$
3. This equation represents the distributive property.
4. The distributive property creates the expression $a(6 + 3)$.

5. The commutative property creates this expression.
6. (A) is not true for all real numbers. In fact, the answer to $A \times (1/A)$ is always 1.

Add, Subtract, Multiply, and Divide Decimals, page 136

1. 26.09
2. 72.617
3. 988.39
4. 5473.2
5. 8.2
6. 71.0096
7. 453.97
8. 1767.87
9. .6225
10. 163.45
11. 3680.538
12. 3761.514
13. 4.8
14. 9.6
15. 33.6
16. 125.63

Multiply, Divide, Add, and Subtract Fractions and Mixed Numbers, page 138

1. $\frac{5}{27}$
2. $\frac{1}{6}$
3. $13\frac{59}{64}$
4. $8\frac{8}{35}$
5. $\frac{6}{7}$
6. $\frac{18}{35}$
7. $2\frac{22}{91}$
8. $\frac{7}{19}$
9. $1\frac{2}{9}$
10. $1\frac{1}{5}$
11. $4\frac{1}{14}$
12. $12\frac{1}{2}$
13. $\frac{1}{21}$
14. $\frac{1}{40}$
15. $\frac{2}{3}$
16. $3\frac{58}{63}$

Square Roots, page 138

1. $\sqrt{256} = 16$
2. $\sqrt{400} = 20$
3. $\sqrt{576} = 24$
4. $\sqrt{900} = 30$
5. $\sqrt{1225} = 35$
6. $\sqrt{48} = \sqrt{16 \times 3} = 4\sqrt{3}$
7. $\sqrt{245} = \sqrt{49 \times 5} = 7\sqrt{5}$
8. $\sqrt{396} = \sqrt{36 \times 11} = 6\sqrt{11}$
9. $\sqrt{567} = \sqrt{81 \times 7} = 9\sqrt{7}$
10. $\sqrt{832} = \sqrt{64 \times 13} = 8\sqrt{13}$

Ratio and Proportion, page 140

1. 14 vacuum cleaners for 280 buyers
2. 4 teachers for 32 children
3. 21 rest stops for 140 miles
4. Yes. $\frac{7}{9} = \frac{28}{36}$ because $7 \times 36 = 252 = 9 \times 28$

Percent, page 141

1. 35.9%
2. 78%
3. 21.5%
4. 4.1%
5. $11\frac{1}{9}\%$
6. 62.5%
7. 30%
8. $44\frac{4}{9}\%$
9. $\frac{29}{50}$
10. $\frac{79}{100}$
11. $\frac{213}{250}$
12. $\frac{487}{500}$

Three Types of Percent Problems, page 142

1. $\square \times 240 = 120$

   $\square = \frac{120}{240}$

   $\square = .5 = 50\%$

2. $.15 \times 70 = \square$

   $.15 \times 70 = 10.5$

   $\square = 10.5$

3. $.6 \times 300 = \square$

   $.6 \times 300 = 180$

   $\square = 180$

4. $\square \times 60 = 42$

   $\square = \frac{42}{60}$

   $\square = 70\%$

5. $\square\% \times 25 = 2.5$

   $\square\% = \frac{25}{25}$

   $\square = 10\%$

6. $40\% \times \square = 22$

   $\square = \frac{22}{.4}$

   $\square = 55$

7. $.7 \times \square = 85$

   $\square = \frac{85}{.7}$

   $\square = 121\frac{3}{7}$

8. $25\% \times 38 = \square$

   $.25 \times 38 = 9.5$

   $\square = 9.5$

9. $.35 \times \square = 24$

   $\square = \frac{24}{.35}$

   $\square = 68\frac{4}{7}$

10. $24 = \square \times 80$

    $\frac{24}{80} = \square$

    $\square = 30\%$

Percent of Increase and Decrease, page 143

1. Amount of increase $\$35 - \$25 = \$10$

   $\frac{10}{25} = 0.4 = 40\%$

   Percent of increase = 40%

2. Discount: $\$100 \times .25 = \$25$

   $\$100 - \$25 = \$75$

   Sale price = \$75

3. Discount $\$80 \times 15\% = \$12$

   $\$80 - \$12 = \$68$

   New price = \$68

4. Amount of increase $\$150 - \$120 = \$30$

   $\frac{30}{120} = \frac{1}{4} = 25\%$

   Percent of increase = 25%

5. Discount $\$75 \times 10\% = \$7.50$

   $\$75 - \$7.50 = \$67.50$

   Sale price = \$67.50

6. Amount of decrease $18 − $6 = $12

$$\frac{12}{18} = \frac{2}{3} = 66\frac{2}{3}\%$$

Percent of decrease $= 66\frac{2}{3}\%$

7. Amount of decrease $225 − $180 = $45

$$\frac{45}{225} = 0.2 = 20\%$$

Percent of decrease $= 20\%$

8. Discount $150 = x − 0.25x$
   $150 = 0.75x$
   $x = \$200$
   Original price: $200

Probability, page 145

1. There are 10 socks in the drawer. 7 of the 10 are not black.

   $P\,(\text{not black}) = \dfrac{7}{10}$

2. There are 6 goldfish; 2 of the 6 are male.

   $P\,(\text{male}) = \dfrac{2}{6} = \dfrac{1}{3}$

3. There are 52 cards in a deck. There are 4 kings and 4 queens.
   $P\,(\text{king or queen}) =$
   $P\,(\text{king}) + P\,(\text{queen})$

   $= \dfrac{4}{52} + \dfrac{4}{52} = \dfrac{8}{52} = \dfrac{2}{13}$

4. There are 6 different names.
   $P\,(\text{Carl and Phyllis}) =$
   $P\,(\text{Carl}) \times P\,(\text{Phyllis}) =$

   $\dfrac{1}{6} \times \dfrac{1}{6} = \dfrac{1}{36}$

5. $\dfrac{1}{2}$ The prime numbers are 2, 3, and 5.

6. This is an "and" problem. Multiply the probability.

   $\left(\dfrac{1}{2}\right)\left(\dfrac{1}{2}\right)\left(\dfrac{1}{2}\right)\left(\dfrac{1}{2}\right)\left(\dfrac{1}{2}\right) = \dfrac{1}{32}$

Permutations and Combinations, page 146

1. There are 6 combinations of 2 people to sit in the chairs.

2. There are 5,040 possible arrangements of the 7 books on the shelf.

3. 67,600 license plates
   $(26 \times 26 \times 10 \times 10)$

4. The positions on the bus are not specified. Order does not matter. This is a combination problem.

   Four students   A   B   C   D
   ABC   ABD   ACD   BCD

   There are four ways for three of four students to board the bus.

Statistics, page 147

1. mode 80

2. mean (average) 35.5

3. median 9 (Remember to arrange the numbers in order.)

4. 16 is the median, the mode, and very close to the mean.

5. mean 89

6. mode 30

Scatter Plots, page 148

1.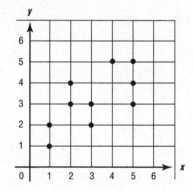

2. The scatter plot shows a trend from lower left to upper right, and it is generally a positive correlation.

3. The correlation will always be positive although the plot might look a little different.

Selecting Unbiased Samples, page 150

1. Good Sampling Techniques

   Randomly ask people at work about their child care needs.

   Randomly sample parents who have their children in day care.

   Poor Sampling Techniques

   Randomly sample women with children.

   Randomly sample people who have no children.

2. Good Sampling Technique

   Randomly sample residents identified as senior citizens.

   Poor Sampling Technique

   Randomly sample residents of senior housing.

Add, Subtract, Multiply, and Divide Integers, page 151

1. 15
2. 1
3. −69
4. −9
5. 1
6. 54
7. 22
8. −80
9. 99
10. −650
11. 1829
12. −1470
13. 15
14. −17
15. 44
16. −22

Polynomials, page 153

1. $3x^2 + 3x^2y + 10y$

2. $3x^2y + 24x + 3yx^2 + 7x^2y^2 = 7x^2y^2 + 6x^2y + 24x$

3. $(3x^5 + 3x^2 - 5x^2y + 6xy^2) + (3x^5 - 2x^2 + 4x^3y - x^2y + 3xy^3 - y^2) = \underline{3x^5 + 3x^5} + \underline{3x^2 - 2x^2} \; \underline{- 5x^2y - x^2y} + 6xy^2 + 4x^3y + 3xy^3 - y^2 = 6x^5 + x^2 - 6x^2y + 6xy^2 + 4x^3y + 3xy^3 - y^2$

4. $(x^4 - 4x^3 + 2x^2y^2 - 4xy^2) + (3x^5 - 7x^4 + 3x^3 - 2x^2y^3 + 7xy^2) = x^4 \underline{- 4x^3 + 3x^3} + 2x^2y^2 \; \underline{- 4xy^2 + 7xy^2} + 3x^5 - 7x^4 - 2x^2y^3 = 3x^5 - 6x^4 - x^3 + 2x^2y^2 + 3xy^2 - 2x^2y^3$

5. $(6x^7 + 9x^4 - 3x^2y + 5xy^3) - (6x^8 - 15x^4 - 3x^3y + x^2y) = (6x^7 + 9x^4 - 3x^2y + 5xy^3) + (-6x^8 + 15x^4 + 3x^3y - x^2y) = 6x^7 + 9x^4 + 15x^4 \underline{- 3x^2y - x^2y} + 5xy^3 - 6x^8 + 3x^3y = -6x^8 + 6x^7 + 24x^4 + 3x^3y - 4x^2y + 5xy^3$

6. $(7x^2 - 9x + 3xy^2 + 3y^3 - 12) - (x^3 - 9x^2 + 2xy^2 - 3y^5 - 18) = (7x^2 - 9x + 3xy^2 + 3y^3 - 12) + (-x^3 + 9x^2 - 2xy^2 + 3y^5 + 18) = 7x^2 + 9x^2 - 9x + 3xy^2 - 2xy^2 + 3y^3 - 12 + 18 - x^3 + 3y^5 = 16x^2 - 9x + xy^2 + 3y^3 + 6 - x^3 + 3y^5 = -x^3 + 16x^2 - 9x + xy^2 + 3y^3 + 3y^5 + 6$

Formulas, page 156

1. πr^2

   $3.14 \times (9)^2 =$

   $\quad 3.14 \times 81 = 254.34 \text{ m}^2$

2. $b = 3, h = 2.6$

   $\left(\dfrac{1}{2}\right)(3)(2.6) = 3.9$

   $4 \times 3.9 = 15.6 \text{ in}^2$

3. Hexagon is 6-sided

   $6 \times 5 \text{ ft} = 30 \text{ ft perimeter}$

4.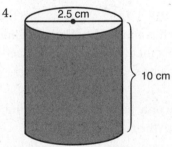

   $\begin{array}{cccc} 2 & \pi & r & h \end{array}$

   $2\,(3.14)(1.25)(10)$

   $= 78.5 \text{ cm}^2$

5. $(x + 5) + (x + 5) + x + x = 90$

   $4x + 10 = 90$

   $4x = 80 \quad x = 20$

   length $= x + 5$

   length $= 25 \text{ ft}$

6. Area of each side $= 25 \text{ cm}^2$

   Cube is 6-sided

   $6 \times 25 = 150 \text{ cm}^2$

7. $x = 12$

8. $A = 32.5$ in.^{2}

9. $V = 4186.\overline{6}$ $\left(4186\frac{2}{3}\right)$ cm^3

10. $V = 3375$ in.^{3}

Solving Linear Equations and Inequalities, page 157

1. $x = 16\frac{3}{5}$

2. $y > -5\frac{1}{3}$

3. $x > \frac{15}{4}$

4. $y = -11$

Symmetry, page 159

1. The numerals 8 and 0 have line and rotational symmetry.
   The numeral 3 has only line symmetry. The other numerals have neither type of symmetry.

2. The most obvious pattern is shown below.
   2   3   4   2   3   4

Circles, page 161

1. A circle has an infinite number of line segments that form a diameter. Each of these line segments is the same length.

2. Yes. The only parts of a chord on the circle are the two endpoints.

3. No. Two radii must form a single line segment across the circle to form a diameter. However, the sum of lengths of two radii are always equal to the length of a diameter.

4. No. A diameter consists of a single chord.

Polygons, page 162

1. trapezoid

2. $m\angle 2 = 135°$

3. $m\angle ABC = 50° = m\angle ACB$

4.

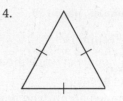

5. An octagon (8 sides) has two more sides than a hexagon (6 sides).

6. A right angle, which has a measure of 90°.

7. (Picture may vary)

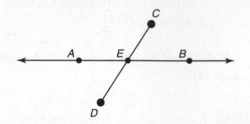

The new figure is $\angle BAC$.

8. (Picture may vary)

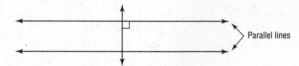

9. (Picture may vary)

Parallel lines

10. The sum of the measures is 180° ($m\angle A + m\angle B + m\angle C = 180°$).

Similar Triangles, page 164

1. Yes, the ratios of the lengths of corresponding sides are equal.

   $\frac{PR}{ST} = \frac{2}{4}$; $\frac{PQ}{SV} = \frac{5}{10}$; $\frac{2}{4} = \frac{5}{10}$

   (Also, $\frac{RQ}{TV} = \frac{3.5}{7}$; $\frac{3.5}{7} = \frac{5}{10}$)

2. The measures of corresponding angles are equal.
   Find the measure of the angle in K.
   Angle b in triangle J is the same size.
   $180 - (50 + 55) = 75$.
   The measure of angle b is 75°.

3. A. Both are right angles because the triangles are right triangles. Choices (B), (C), and (D) are false because the triangles are not similar.

Coordinate Grid, page 165

1. A (3, −2)
   B (−2, −4)
   C (−5, 5)
   D (3, 3)
   E (0, 2)
   F (−5, 0)

2.

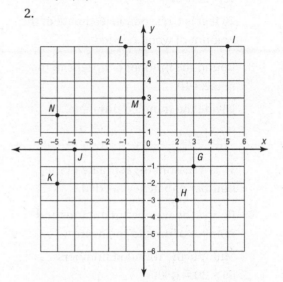

3.

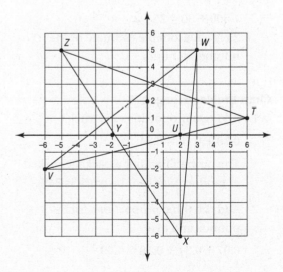

Translations on a Coordinate Grid, page 167

1. (−4, −4)
2. (2, 1)
3. (−4, −2)
4. You know that at least one of the vertices will have the same x value as point B and that at least one will have the same y value as point B. You cannot be sure about anything else.

Deductive Reasoning, page 168

1. False—Some sports, such as hockey, do not use a ball.
2. True—For example, 35 is divisible by both 5 and 7.
3. False—For example, 12 is divisible by 3.
4. True—For example, 2 is both prime and divisible by 2.

Words to Symbols Problems, page 171

1. 34; 34 − 9 = 25
2. 0.6 × 90 = 54
3. Add: $\frac{2}{3} + \frac{1}{2} = \frac{7}{6}$

   Multiply: $\frac{7}{6} \times 3 = \frac{21}{6}$

   Divide: $21 \div 6 = 3\frac{3}{6} = 3\frac{1}{2}$.

   Bob's walk to school is $3\frac{1}{2}$ miles.

4. $\frac{20}{y} = 2.5$ $20 = 2.5y$ $y = 8$

5. $5\frac{1}{x} = 5\frac{1}{8}$ $x = 8$

   The number is 8.

6. Multiply: 60 × 2.5 = 150
   70 × 2 = 140
   Add: 150 + 140 = 290
   The cars traveled a total distance of 290 miles.

Finding and Interpreting Patterns, page 173

1. **−6** is the missing term. Subtract 2 from each term.

2. **14** is the missing term. Add 2.5 to each term.

3. **7.5** is the missing term. Divide each term by 2 to get the next term.

4. **720** is the missing term. The sequence follows the pattern
$(1 \times 1)(1 \times 2)(1 \times 2 \times 3)(1 \times 2 \times 3 \times 4)...$

5. **21** is the missing term. Add 4 to find the next term.

6. **(22, 30)** is the missing term. Add 8 to the first term to find the second term.

7. **(30, 4)** is the missing term. Divide the first term by 10 and add 1 to find the second term.

8. **(5, 25)** is the missing term. Square the first term to get the second term.

9. The temperatures drops 3° from 52° to 49° and from 49° to 46°. If it drops at the same rate, the temperature drop at 3,000 feet would be 43° and at 4,000 feet would be 40° (followed by 37° and 34°). Continue to fill in the table accordingly, as follows.

Temperature

0	1,000	2,000	3,000	4,000	5,000
52°	49°	46°	43°	40°	37°

6,000	7,000	8,000	9,000	10,000
34°	31°	28°	25°	22°

10. Multiply three times the x value, subtract 2, and that gives the y value. The rule is y equals three times x −2, so that the equation is $y = 3x − 2$. Substitute 13 for x:

$$y = 3(13) − 2 = 39 − 2 = 37$$

The capsule will be at position (13, 37).

Estimation Problems, page 174

1. Round all the scores and add the rounded scores.

$90 + 100 + 90 + 90 + 100 + 90 = 560$

Divide by the number of scores.

$560 \div 6 = 93.3$

93 is a reasonable estimate of the average.

2. Round the lengths and add the rounded lengths.

$10 + 20 + 20 + 20 = 70$

70 feet is a reasonable estimate of the amount of wood needed.

3. Round the number of dozens to the nearest 10.

Divide the rounded numbers.

$$\frac{170}{10} = 17$$

17 is a reasonable estimate of the number of batches needed.

4. Round the number of minutes and number of days to the nearest 10.

Multiply the rounded numbers.

$50 \times 30 = 1,500$

Divide to find hours.

$1,500 \div 60 = 25$

25 is a reasonable estimate of the number of hours.

Chart Problems, page 175

1. Add two proportions for truck.

$0.18 + 0.16 = 0.34$

The probability that a package picked at random was sent by truck is 34%.

2. Add the three proportions for 5 pounds and over.

$0.07 + 0.34 + 0.18 = 0.59$

3. The proportion for Air Express over 5 pounds is 0.07.

4. Add proportions for under 5 pounds by Air Express and under 5 pounds by truck.

$$0.23 + 0.16 = 0.39$$

Frequency Table Problems, page 176

1. Add the percentiles of the intervals below 70.

   $$2 + 8 = 10$$

   10% of the students scored below 70.

2. The median score is in the interval 80–89.

3. The percent of scores from 80 to 100 is

   $$38 + 13 = 51$$

   51% of the students scored from 80 to 100.

4. The question is asking for the number of scores that are above 50. The percentile rank next to 50 is 39. So 39% of the scores are below 50; 39% failed. $100 - 39 = 61$. 61% passed.

5. The percent of the scores from 20 to 50 is the percentile rank for 50, less the percentile rank for 20.

   $$39 - 2 = 37$$

   37% of the scores are from 20 to 50.

Formula Problems, page 177

1. $P =$ about $16.88
2. $s = 41$ mph
3. $V = $0,400$
4. $A = 11$

Pythagorean Theorem Problems, page 178

1.

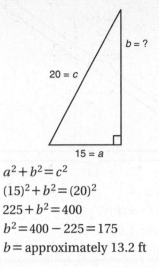

$$a^2 + b^2 = c^2$$
$$(15)^2 + b^2 = (20)^2$$
$$225 + b^2 = 400$$
$$b^2 = 400 - 225 = 175$$
$$b = \text{approximately } 13.2 \text{ ft}$$

2.

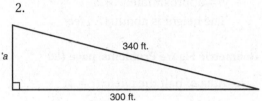

$$a^2 + b^2 = c^2$$
$$a^2 + (300)^2 = (340)^2$$
$$a^2 = 115,600 - 90,000 = 25,600$$
$$a = 160 \text{ ft}$$

The ramp is 160 feet high.

3.

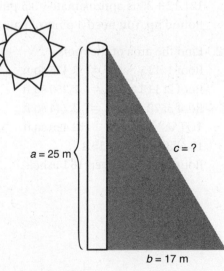

$$a^2 + b^2 = c^2$$
$$(25)^2 + (17)^2 = c^2$$
$$625 + 289 = c^2$$
$$c^2 = 914, c = \text{approximately } 30.2 \text{ m}$$

4.

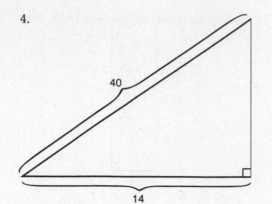

$a^2 + b^2 = c^2$

$(14)^2 + b^2 = (40)^2$

$196 + b^2 = 1{,}600$

$b^2 = 1{,}404$

b = approximately 37.5

The height is about 37.5 feet.

Geometric Figure Problems, page 180

1. Area of half the circle ($r = 4$)

   $\frac{1}{2}(3.14)(16) = (3.14)(8)$ is

   approximately 25.12 sq ft

   Area of the rectangle

   $12 \times 8 = 96$ sq ft

   Area of the entire figure

   $25.12 + 96 = 121.12$ sq ft

   $121.12 \div 35$ is approximately 3.5 pints

   Round up. You need 4 pints of paint.

2. Find the area of the roofs.

   Roof 1: $115 \times 65 \ = \ \ 7{,}475$ sq ft

   Roof 2: $112 \times 65 \ = \ \ 7{,}280$ sq ft

   Roof 3: $72 \times 52 \ \ = \ \ \underline{3{,}744}$ sq ft

   TOTAL $\qquad\qquad 18{,}499$ sq ft

   $18{,}499 \div 1{,}200 = 15.4$

   Round up. You need 16 bushels.

3. Volume of a brick $= lwh$

   $V = 2 \times 4 \times 8 = 64$ in.^{3}

   8×64 in.$^3 = 512$ in.^{3}

4. Volume of a cone $= \frac{1}{3}\pi r^2 h$

   $134 \approx \frac{1}{3}(3.14)(4)^2\,h$

   $134 \approx 16.7\,h$

   $h \approx 8$ cm

5. Volume of a sphere $= \frac{4}{3}\pi r^3$

   $V = \frac{4}{3}(3.14)(274.6)$

   $V = 1149.76$ in.^{3}

6. Volume of a rectangular solid $= lwh$

   $1920 = (16)(12)\,w$

   $1920 = 192\,w$

   $w = 10$

   Shaded area $= 12 \times 10 = 120$ m^2

Interpreting Remainder Problems, page 181

1. 5 pounds
2. 34 bags
3. 33 bags

TARGETED MATHEMATICS TEST ANSWERS EXPLAINED

1. **(D)** $(180 - 90) \div 2 = 45°$. There is a total of 180° in a triangle. If it is an isosceles right triangle, that means one angle is 90° and the other two angles are equivalent.

2. **(B)** 25% of $48 = $12
   $48 − $12 = $36

3. **(D)** Focus on point B. Recall that a shift up moves the y-coordinate and a shift right moves the x-coordinate. Shifting up 3 units from $y = -2$ takes you to $y = 1$. Shifting right 3 units from $x = -2$ takes you to $x = 4$. Write the result as an (x, y) ordered pair (4, 1).

4. **(B)** The probability of rolling a "5" is $\frac{1}{6}$, regardless of what happened on previous rolls.

5. **(D)** An angle is not formed because point B and point C are not connected in this diagram.

6. **(D)** Divide the money by the cost of an item to find the number of items you can afford.

7. **(E)** Estimate. 32 hours is not twice 18 hours, so eliminate (B), (C), and (D). 32 hours is about 75% more than 18 hours. 75% more than $144 is about $250. Choice (E) must be correct.

8. **(A)** $\pi(3^2 \times 2) - \pi(2^2 \times 4) = (9 \times 2 - 4 \times 4)\pi = 2\pi$

9. **(A)** The discount is the regular price minus the sale price.

10. **(C)** $80 − $5 = $75
    $75 ÷ $0.75 = 100

11. **(A)** The fraction farthest from $\frac{1}{2}$ will be closest to 0 or closest to 1. The answer is $\frac{1}{12}$ because it is closest to 0 compared to the other choices, which are greater than $\frac{1}{2}$ but closer to $\frac{1}{2}$ than 1.

12. **(E)** 25 centimeters is about 10 inches, a reasonable length for a notebook.

13. **(B)** The total spent was $100. Retail was $20. $20 \div 100 = .2 = 20\%$.

14. **(C)** $250 − .4 \times 250 = 150$. 30 out of $150 = 30 \div 150 = .2 = 20\%$.

15. **(E)** $1,000 + $250 = $1,250, needed to make $1,000.
    $1,250 ÷ $5 = 250
    $250 \times 6 = 1,500$ tickets

16. **(D)** $5.3 \times 10^4 = 53,000$. 0.0053 needs to have the decimal moved right 7 places.

17. **(A)** Complementary angles total 90°, the number of degrees in this right angle.

18. **(D)** $100\% − 94\% = 6\%$ (Midwest). Northeast $= 30\%$. $6\% \times 5 = 30\%$.

19. **(E)** $\frac{1}{2} + \frac{1}{3} + \frac{3}{8} = \frac{12}{24} + \frac{8}{24} + \frac{9}{24} = \frac{29}{24} = 1\frac{5}{24}$.

20. **(E)** Focus on point A. Recall that a shift left moves the x-coordinate and a shift down moves the y-coordinate. Shifting left 2 units from $x = -1$ takes you to $x = -3$. Shifting down 4 units from $y = -5$ takes you to $y = -9$. Write the result as an (x, y) ordered pair (−3, −9).

21. **(C)** Each angle must measure less than 90° to total 90°. Acute angles have measures less than 90°.

22. **(E)** We just know that since the beams are not parallel and do not point in the same direction, at least two of them may be skewed (not touch).

23. **(A)** There are 1,000 meters in a kilometer. So, divide 2,750 by 1,000 to find the answer.

24. **(D)** The difference in the two stock prices $(19\frac{5}{8} - 17\frac{7}{8})$ is $1\frac{3}{4}$ dollars or \$1.75. Multiply \$1.75 by 20 to find the answer.

25. **(C)** There are about $(60) \times (60) \times (24)$ or 86,400 seconds in a day. There are about $(365) \times (86,400)$ or 31,536,000 seconds in a year. There are about $(4) \times (31,536,000)$ or 126,144,000 seconds in 4 years. Light travels about $(186,000) \times (126,144,000)$ or about 23,000,000,000,000 (23 trillion) miles in 4 years.

26. **(E)** 10 feet + 20% = 12 feet + 20% = 14.4 feet +

           first   second

    20% = 17.28 feet + 20% = 20.736 or

          third   fourth

    about 20.7 feet.

27. **(E)** The maximum length of the side of the cube is the shortest of the three dimensions. The volume of the cube is 8^3 or 512.

28. **(A)** The correct answer is 42. The pattern increases by 4, 6, 8, 10, and then 12.

29. **(C)** This formula gives the correct answer. The formula $H \times (H+1)$ is equivalent to this formula.

30. **(E)** Round the quotient (10) to 11 to have room for all the people to go on the class trip.

31. **(C)** This process crosses off all numbers but the prime numbers. The numbers in choice (C) are all the prime numbers in the 80s.

32. **(B)** Multiply 0.23 and \$2,600 to find \$598.

33. **(E)** Divide \$858 by \$2,600 to find the percent (33 percent) needed for transportation. Subtract the current transportation percentage from 33 percent to find the percent to be taken from miscellaneous (33% − 24% = 9%). Subtract 11% − 9% = 2% to find the percent left for miscellaneous.

34. **(B)** Solve a proportion. $\frac{2}{9} = \frac{x}{1,350}$

    $9x = 2,700 \ x = 300$

35. **(B)** This question asks you to apply the Pythagorean theorem $a^2 + b^2 = c^2$.
    $$30^2 + 40^2 = 50^2$$
    The rope is 50 feet long.

36. **(B)** The number sentence corresponds to finding an average. To find an average, you add the terms and divide by the number of terms.

37. **(C)** Jan is either the same height as Lisa or she is taller than Lisa. Because Lisa is not the shortest player, Jan cannot be the shortest player.

38. **(C)** You can cross multiply to find that $\frac{5}{6} > \frac{3}{4}$, but that $\frac{5}{6} < \frac{7}{8}$. You can also use a calculator to find that $\frac{5}{6} = 0.833$, and see that this decimal comes between $\frac{3}{4} = 0.75$ and $\frac{7}{8} = 0.875$.

39. **(C)** Only points in this quadrant of the coordinate grid have a negative x-value and a negative y-value. Point C is closer to $(-2, -5)$ than point E, which might be closer to $(-5, -2)$.

40. **(C)** This is another calculator problem.
    Think of the percent equation.
    $85\% \times \square = 289$
    So, $\square = 289 \div 0.85$
    Divide 289 by 0.85 to find how many houses there were altogether.
    $289 \div 0.85 = 340$

41. **(D)** There are 60 seconds in a minute and 60 minutes in an hour. So there are $60 \times 60 = 3600$ seconds in an hour. $186{,}000 \times 3600$ is about how far light travels in an hour.

42. **(A)** Use your calculator to find this answer. Divide to find what percent \$624,000 is of \$2,600,000. $624{,}000 \div 2{,}600{,}000 = 0.24 = 24\%$. The town needs 24% for police, 2% more than in the pie chart. Take the 2% from sanitation, leaving 22% for sanitation.

43. **(B)** The probability that a "fair" penny will land heads up is always $\frac{1}{2}$ regardless of what has occurred on previous flips.

44. **(B)** Multiply x by 2 and then add 1. Some of the other choices work for individual values of x, but only this choice works for all the values of x.

45. **(E)** To find the area of a triangle, use the formula $A = \frac{1}{2} bh = 30$.

    To find the area of a parallelogram, use the formula $A = (bh) = 180$.
    Subtract: Area (parallelogram) $-$ Area (triangle) $=$ Area (shaded portion)
    $$180 - 30 = 150$$

46. **(B)** Use the order of operations to combine to simplest terms.
    $$2n + 3n^2 - 5n \times 3 - 6n^2 = 2n + 3n^2 - 15n - 6n^2 = -13n - 3n^2$$

47. **(C)** Use formula $P = 2.2K$
    $$K = P \div 2.2$$
    $$K = 15.6/2.2$$
    $$K = 7.09$$

48. **(D)** Rent represents 60% of the monthly expenses, greater than all the other expenses combined.

49. **(D)** The mode is the amount that occurs most often. Tampa, Tallahassee, and Jacksonville have graphs of almost identical heights and most likely represent the mode. None of the other answer choices lists cities with nearly matching graphs.

50. **(E)** There is a positive relationship between the test score and the number of years in math courses.

51. **(A, C)** Choice (A): Complete the missing measurements on the figure as shown below. Then use the area formula $A = l \times w$ to find the larger area (15×20) and the smaller area (7×5). Add the two areas as shown in the answer.

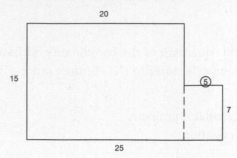

Choice (C): Find that the area of the larger rectangle shown below is (25×15) and find the area of the "missing piece" is (5×8). Then subtract the area of the missing piece from the area of the larger rectangle as shown in the answer.

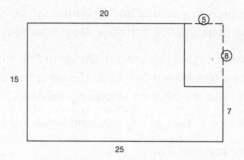

52. **(B, E)** Notice that 48 inches is 4 feet. Divide the area (57 square feet) by the width (4 feet). The result is 14.25 feet (14 feet, 3 inches). That means the length must be more than 14 feet, 3 inches (171 inches). Choice (B) is correct because 14 feet, 9 inches is greater than 14 feet, 3 inches. Choice (E) is correct because 175 inches is greater than 171 inches. Choice (A) is incorrect because 12 feet is less than 14 feet, 3 inches. Choice (C) is incorrect because 14 feet, 3 inches is not greater than 14 feet, 3 inches. Choice (D) is incorrect because 60 inches is less than 171 inches.

53. **(A, D)** Find the total number of students in each class. (A = 26, B = 28, C = 20, D = 17, E = 23). Calculate 60% of each class: A = 15.6, B = 16.8, C = 12, D = 10.2, E = 13.8. Next, find the sum of students from each class that scored 70% or higher. Compare this number to the 60% number for each class. If it is greater, it is the correct solution. Choice (A) is correct because 19 > 15.6. Choice (B) is incorrect because 14 < 16.8. Choice (C) is incorrect because 10 < 12. Choice (D) is correct because 11 > 10.2. Choice (E) is incorrect because 11 < 13.8.

54. **(2)** Follow these steps:

Substitute the given values for a and b.
$$\frac{\left(3^2 - 2^2\right)^3 + 3}{\left(2 + 2 \cdot 3\right)^2}$$

Compute inside the ( ).
$$\frac{(9-4)^3 + 3}{8^2} = \frac{5^3 + 3}{64}$$

Raise to the given powers and simplify.
$$\frac{125 + 3}{64} = \frac{128}{64} = 2$$

55. $\left(\dfrac{3}{2}\right)$ Do the computation in the denominator first.

$$\frac{\dfrac{1}{4}}{\dfrac{2}{3}-\dfrac{1}{2}}=\frac{\dfrac{1}{4}}{\dfrac{4}{6}-\dfrac{3}{6}}=\frac{\dfrac{1}{4}}{\dfrac{1}{6}}$$

Do the indicated division.

$$\frac{1}{4}\div\frac{1}{6}=\frac{1}{4}\times\frac{6}{1}$$

Simplify and multiply as indicated.

$$\frac{1}{\underset{2}{4}}\times\frac{\overset{3}{\cancel{6}}}{1}=\frac{3}{2}$$

56. $\left(\dfrac{8}{75}\right)$ Remove the ( ) applying the exponent to both the numerators and denominators of each factor.

$$\frac{8}{27}\cdot\frac{9}{25}$$

Simplify the fractions and multiply.

$$\frac{8}{\underset{3}{\cancel{27}}}\cdot\frac{\overset{1}{\cancel{9}}}{25}=\frac{8}{75}$$

PART III
Practice Core Tests
with Answers Explained

Practice Core 1

6

TEST INFO BOX

Reading	56 items	85 minutes
Writing Multiple-Choice	40 items	40 minutes
Writing Essays	2 responses	30 minutes each
Mathematics	56 items	85 minutes

Take this test in a realistic, timed setting. You should not take this practice test until you have completed your review.

The setting will be most realistic if another person times the test and ensures that the test rules are followed exactly. If another person is acting as test supervisor, he or she should review these instructions with you and say "Start" when you should begin a section and "Stop" when time has expired.

Mark your answers on the test. Use a computer without the spell or grammar check function to type your essays.

Once the test is complete, review the answers and explanations for each item.

READING TEST (5712)

56 ITEMS   85 MINUTES

> **Directions:** You will read selections followed by one or more questions. Most items have five answer choices with one correct answer. A few items may have one or more correct answers. The answer choices for these questions will be within boxes. Select the best answer choices based on what the selection states or implies and mark that letter on the test.

1. The computers in the college dormitories are actually more sophisticated than the computers in the college computer labs, and they cost less. It seems that the person who bought the dormitory computers looked around until she found powerful computers at a low price. The person who runs the labs just got the computers offered by the regular supplier.

   The best statement of the main idea of this paragraph is

   Ⓐ it is better to use the computers in the dorms.
   Ⓑ it is better to avoid the computers in the labs.
   Ⓒ the computers in the dorms are always in use so, for most purposes, it is better to use the computers in the labs.
   Ⓓ it is better to shop around before you buy.
   Ⓔ wholesale prices are usually better than retail prices.

QUESTIONS 2–4 ARE BASED ON THIS PASSAGE.

Researchers were not sure at first what caused AIDS or how it was transmitted. They did know early on that everyone who developed AIDS died. Then researchers began to understand that the disease is caused by the HIV virus, which could be transmitted through blood and blood products. Even after knowing this, some blood companies resisted testing blood for the HIV virus. Today we know that the HIV virus is transmitted through blood and other bodily fluids. Women may be more susceptible than men, and the prognosis hasn't changed.

2. The main purpose of this passage is to

   Ⓐ show that blood companies can't be trusted.
   Ⓑ detail the history of AIDS research.
   Ⓒ detail the causes and consequences of AIDS.
   Ⓓ warn women that they are susceptible to AIDS.
   Ⓔ raise awareness about AIDS.

3. Which of the following questions could be answered from this passage?

   Ⓐ How do intravenous drug users acquire AIDS?
   Ⓑ How many AIDS diagnoses were recorded last year?
   Ⓒ Through what mediums is AIDS transmitted?
   Ⓓ How do blood companies test for AIDS?
   Ⓔ What does AIDS mean?

4. Which of the following would be the best conclusion for this passage?

   Ⓐ AIDS research continues to be underfunded in the United States.

   Ⓑ Sexual activity and intravenous drug use continue to be the two primary ways that AIDS is transmitted.

   Ⓒ People develop AIDS after being HIV positive.

   Ⓓ Our understanding of AIDS has increased significantly over the past several years, but we are no closer to a cure.

   Ⓔ It is better to be transfused with your own blood, if possible.

---

5. The retired basketball player said that, while modern players were better athletes because there was so much emphasis on youth basketball and increased focus on training, he still believed that the players of his day were better because they were more committed to the game, better understood its nuances, and were more dedicated to team play.

In this passage, the retired basketball player believed that which of the following factors led to today's basketball players being better athletes?

   Ⓐ More dedication

   Ⓑ Increased salaries

   Ⓒ Better nutrition

   Ⓓ Youth basketball

   Ⓔ More commitment

6. The way I look at it, Robert E. Lee was the worst general in the Civil War—he was the South's commanding general, and the South lost the war.

What assumption does the writer of this statement make?

   Ⓐ War is horrible and should not be glorified.

   Ⓑ Pickett's charge at Gettysburg was a terrible mistake.

   Ⓒ A general should be judged by whether he wins or loses.

   Ⓓ The South should have won the Civil War.

   Ⓔ Slavery is wrong.

7. Advances in astronomy and space exploration during the past twenty-five years have been significant, and we now know more answers to questions about the universe than ever before, but we still cannot answer the ultimate question, "How did our universe originate?"

Which of the following best characterizes the author's view of how the advances in astronomy and space exploration affect our eventual ability to answer the ultimate question?

   Ⓐ We now know more answers than ever before.

   Ⓑ All the questions have not been answered.

   Ⓒ Eventually we will probably find out.

   Ⓓ The question can't be answered.

   Ⓔ We will have the answer very soon.

The Board of Adjustment can exempt a person from the requirements of a particular land use ordinance. Several cases have come before the Board concerning three ordinances. One ordinance states that religious and other organizations cannot build places of worship or meeting halls in residential zones. A second ordinance states that any garage must be less than 25 percent of the size of a house on the same lot, while a third ordinance restricts a person's right to convert a one-family house to a two-family house.

It is interesting to note how a person can be in favor of an exemption in one case but opposed to exemption in another. For example, one homeowner applied to build a garage 45 percent of the size of her house but was opposed to a neighbor converting his house from a one-family to a two-family house. This second homeowner was opposed to a church being built in his neighborhood. The woman opposed to his proposal was all for the church construction project.

The pressure on Board of Adjustment members who also live in the community is tremendous. It must sometimes seem to them that any decision is the wrong one. But that is what Boards of Adjustment are for, and we can only hope that this example of America in action will best serve the community and those who live there.

8. Which of the following sentences is the author of the passage most likely to DISAGREE with?

   Ⓐ These Boards serve a useful purpose.
   Ⓑ No exemptions should be granted to any zoning ordinance.
   Ⓒ People can be very fickle when it comes to the exemptions they favor.
   Ⓓ Some people may try to influence Board of Adjustment members.
   Ⓔ The garage the woman wanted to build was about twice the allowable size.

9. The author finds people's reactions to exemption requests interesting because

   Ⓐ so many different types of exemptions are applied for.
   Ⓑ a person's reaction is often based on religious principles and beliefs.
   Ⓒ a person can both support and not support requested exemptions.
   Ⓓ people put so much pressure on Board members.
   Ⓔ men usually oppose exemptions sought by women.

10. In which of the following publications would you expect this passage to appear?

   Ⓐ A government textbook
   Ⓑ A local newspaper
   Ⓒ A national newspaper
   Ⓓ A civics textbook
   Ⓔ A news magazine

11. We can infer from this passage that the actions of a Board of Adjustment

    Ⓐ oppress religious and community groups.
    Ⓑ favor men over women.
    Ⓒ enforce town ordinances.
    Ⓓ are examples of America in action.
    Ⓔ exempt people from property taxes.

12. Which of the following does the passage convey?

    Ⓐ A person should be consistently for or against Board exemptions.
    Ⓑ The Board of Adjustment should act only when all agree.
    Ⓒ People are interested in their own needs when it comes to zoning.
    Ⓓ Board of Adjustment members should not be from town.
    Ⓔ The Board of Adjustment should not approve any of the requests.

   _____

13. The college sororities are "interviewed" by students during rush week. Rush week is a time when students get to know about the different sororities and decide which ones they want to join. Each student can pledge only one sorority. Once students have chosen the three they are most interested in, the intrigue begins. The sororities then choose from among the students who have chosen them.

   Which of the following strategies will help assure a student that she will be chosen for at least one sorority and preferably get into a sorority she likes?

   Select all that apply.

    Ⓐ Choose at least one sorority she is sure will choose her
    Ⓑ Choose one sorority she wants to get into
    Ⓒ Choose her three favorite sororities
    Ⓓ Choose three sororities she knows will choose her

14. During a Stage 4 alert, workers in an energy plant must wear protective pants, a protective shirt, and a helmet, except that protective coveralls can be worn in place of protective pants and shirt. When there is a Stage 5 alert, workers must also wear filter masks in addition to the requirements for the Stage 4 alert.

   During a Stage 5 alert, which of the following could be worn?

   Select all that apply.

    Ⓐ masks, pants, helmet
    Ⓑ coveralls, helmet, mask
    Ⓒ coveralls, mask

Using percentages to report growth patterns can be deceptive. If there are 100 new users for a cereal currently used by 100 other people, the growth rate is 100 percent. However, if there are 50,000 new users for a cereal currently used by 5,000,000 people, the growth rate is 1 percent. It seems obvious that the growth rate of 1 percent is preferable to the growth rate of 100 percent. So while percentages do provide a useful way to report growth patterns, we must know the initial number the growth percentage is based on before we make any conclusions.

15. Which of the following statements about growth rates is the author most likely to agree with?

 Ⓐ Lower growth rates mean higher actual growth.
 Ⓑ Higher growth rates mean higher actual growth.
 Ⓒ The growth rate depends on the starting point.
 Ⓓ The growth rate does not depend on the starting point.
 Ⓔ A lower starting point means a higher growth rate.

16. Which of the following can be inferred from this passage?

 Ⓐ Don't believe any advertisements.
 Ⓑ Question any percentage growth rate.
 Ⓒ Percentages should never be used.
 Ⓓ Any growth rate over 50 percent is invalid.
 Ⓔ Percentages are deceptive advertising.

---

17. (1) The science fiction story started with a description of the characters.
 (2) Some of the descriptions were hard for me to understand.
 (3) The book was about time travel in the 22nd century, an interesting subject.
 (4) The authors believed time travel would be possible by then.

In these four sentences, a person describes a science fiction book. Which of the following choices most accurately characterizes these statements made by the person describing the book?

 Ⓐ (2) alone states an opinion
 Ⓑ (1) and (4) alone state facts
 Ⓒ (3) states both facts and opinion
 Ⓓ (1), (3), and (4) state facts only
 Ⓔ (4) states an opinion

18. The public schools in Hinman have devoted extra resources to mathematics instruction for years. Their programs always reflect the most current thinking about the way mathematics should be taught, and the schools are always equipped with the most recent teaching aids. These extra resources have created a mathematics program that is now copied by other schools throughout America.

The mathematics program at the Hinman schools is copied by other schools because

Ⓐ their programs always reflect the most current thinking about the way mathematics should be taught.

Ⓑ the schools are always equipped with the most recent teaching aids.

Ⓒ the schools use the NCTM standards.

Ⓓ extra resources were devoted to mathematics instruction.

Ⓔ their successful programs were publicized to other schools.

QUESTIONS 19–24 APPLY TO THIS PASSAGE.

Computer graphing programs are capable of graphing almost any equations, including advanced equations from calculus. The student just types in the equation and the graph appears on the computer screen. The graphing program can also show the numerical solution for any entered equation. I like having a computer program that performs the mechanical aspects of these difficult calculations. However, these programs do not teach about graphing or mathematics because the computer does not "explain" what is going on. A person could type in an equation, get an answer, and have not the slightest idea what either meant.

Relying on this mindless kind of graphing and calculation, students will be completely unfamiliar with the meaning of the equations they write or the results they get. They will not be able to understand how to create a graph from an equation or to understand the basis for the more complicated calculations.

It may be true that a strictly mechanical approach is used by some teachers. There certainly is a place for students who already understand equations and graphing to have a computer program that relieves the drudgery. But these computer programs should never and can never replace the teacher. Mathematical competence assumes that understanding precedes rote calculation.

19. What is the main idea of this passage?

Ⓐ Mechanical calculation is one part of learning about mathematics.

Ⓑ Teachers should use graphing programs as one part of instruction.

Ⓒ Graphing programs are not effective for initially teaching mathematics.

Ⓓ Students who use these programs won't learn mathematics.

Ⓔ The programs rely too heavily on a student's typing ability.

20. Which of the following questions could be answered from the information in the passage?

   Ⓐ How does the program do integration and differentiation?
   Ⓑ What type of mathematics learning experiences should students have?
   Ⓒ When is it appropriate to use graphing programs?
   Ⓓ Why do schools buy these graphing programs?
   Ⓔ Which graphing program does the author recommend?

21. If the reasoning about learning to use a graphing calculator was applied to all learning, then all learning should emphasize

   Ⓐ competence.
   Ⓑ thoroughness.
   Ⓒ teaching.
   Ⓓ mathematics.
   Ⓔ understanding.

22. What can we infer about the aspect of graphing programs that the author of the passage likes?

   Ⓐ That you just have to type in the equation
   Ⓑ That the difficult mechanical operations are performed
   Ⓒ That the calculations and graphing are done very quickly
   Ⓓ That you don't have to know math to use them
   Ⓔ That they can't replace teachers

23. Which of the following could be used in place of the first sentence of the last paragraph?

   Ⓐ It may be true that some strict teachers use a mechanical approach.
   Ⓑ It may be true that some teachers use only a mechanical approach.
   Ⓒ It may be true that a stringently mechanical approach is used by some teachers.
   Ⓓ It may be true that inflexible mechanical approaches are used by some teachers.
   Ⓔ It may be true that the mechanical approach used by some teachers is too rigorous.

24. Which of the following conclusions is supported by the passage?

   Ⓐ Programs that display the graph of an equation are useful in the schools.
   Ⓑ Relying on mindless graphing and calculation can still help students learn mathematics.
   Ⓒ Strictly mechanical approaches are used by most teachers.
   Ⓓ Using programs to graph equations can replace understanding.
   Ⓔ Being able to type in equations can help students understand the solution.

25. An analysis of models of potential space vehicles prepared by engineers revealed that the parts of the hull of the vehicles that were strongest were the ones that had the most potential for being weak.

Which of the following statements about hull design is the author most likely to agree with?

(A) The parts of the hull that are potentially strongest should not receive as much attention from engineers as those that are potentially weakest.

(B) The potentially weaker parts of the hull are stronger in models than the potentially stronger parts of the hull.

(C) Being potentially weaker, these parts of the hull appear relatively stronger in a model.

(D) Potentially weaker parts of the hull have the most potential for being stronger.

(E) The parts of the hull that are potentially weakest receive less attention from engineers than those parts that are potentially stronger.

QUESTIONS 26 AND 27 ARE BASED ON THIS PASSAGE.

The growth of the town led to a huge increase in the number of students applying for kindergarten admission. Before this time, students had been admitted to kindergarten even if they were "technically" too young. At first the school administrators considered a testing plan for those applicants too young for regular admission, admitting only those who passed the test. Luckily the administrators submitted a plan that just enforced the official, but previously ignored, birth cut-off date for kindergarten admission. This decision set the stage for fairness throughout the town.

26. What main idea is the author trying to convey?

(A) Testing of young children doesn't work.
(B) All children should be treated equally.
(C) Tests are biased against minority children.
(D) The testing program would be too expensive.
(E) Age predicts a child's performance level.

27. Which of the following is the primary problem with this plan for the schools?

(A) Parents will sue.
(B) Parents will falsify birth certificates to get their children in school.
(C) Next year the schools will have to admit a much larger kindergarten group.
(D) Missing kindergarten because a child is born one day too late doesn't seem fair.
(E) Parents would not be able to dispute the results of an objective testing plan.

28. A person who is not treated with respect cannot be expected to be a good worker.

Which of the following can be concluded from this statement?

Ⓐ A person treated with respect can be expected to be a good worker.
Ⓑ A person who is expected to be a good worker should be treated with respect.
Ⓒ A person who cannot be expected to be a good worker is not treated with respect.
Ⓓ A person not treated with respect can still be expected to be a good worker.
Ⓔ A person who is not a good worker can't expect to be treated with respect.

QUESTIONS 29 AND 30 ARE BASED ON THESE CIRCUMSTANCES.

The state highway department has sets of regulations for the number of lanes a highway can have and how these lanes are to be used. A summary of these regulations follows.

- All highways must be five lanes wide and either three or four of these lanes must be set aside for passenger cars only.
- If four lanes are set aside for passenger cars, then one of these lanes must be set aside for cars with three or more passengers, with a second lane of the four passenger lanes also usable by school vehicles such as buses, vans, and cars.
- If three lanes are set aside for passenger cars, then one of these lanes must be set aside for cars with two or more passengers, except that school buses, vans, and cars may also use this lane.

29. Officials in one county submit a plan for a five-lane highway, with three lanes set aside for passenger cars, and school buses able to use the lane set aside for cars with two or more passengers. Based on their regulations, which of the following is most likely to be the state highway department's response to this plan?

Ⓐ Your plan is approved because you have five lanes with three set aside for passenger cars and one set aside for passenger cars with two or more passengers.
Ⓑ Your plan is approved because you permitted school buses to use the passenger lanes.
Ⓒ Your plan is disapproved because you don't include school vans and school cars among the vehicles that can use the lane for cars with two or more passengers.
Ⓓ Your plan is disapproved because you include school buses in the lane for passenger cars with two or more passengers.
Ⓔ Your plan is disapproved because you set aside only three lanes for passenger cars when it should have been four.

30. County officials send a list of three possible highway plans to the state highway department. Using their regulations, which of the following plans would the state highway department approve?

Select all that apply.

A 4 lanes—3 for passenger cars, 1 passenger lane for cars with 3 or more passengers, school buses and vans can also use the passenger lane for 3 or more people

B 5 lanes—4 for passenger cars, 1 passenger lane for cars with 3 or more passengers, 1 of the 4 passenger lanes can be used by school buses, vans, and cars

C 4 lanes—3 for passenger cars, 1 passenger lane for cars with 2 or more passengers, school vehicles can also use the passenger lane for 2 or more passengers

---

QUESTIONS 31–34 ARE BASED ON THIS PASSAGE.

The choice of educational practices sometimes seems like choosing fashions. Fashion is driven by the whims, tastes, and zeitgeist of the current day. The education system should not be driven by these same forces. But consider, for example, the way mathematics is taught. Three decades ago, teachers were told to use manipulative materials to teach mathematics. In the intervening years, the emphasis was on drill and practice. Now teachers are being told again to use manipulative materials. This cycle is more akin to random acts than to sound professional practice.

31. What does the author most likely mean by the word *zeitgeist* in the second sentence?

Ⓐ Tenor
Ⓑ Emotional feeling
Ⓒ Fabric availability
Ⓓ Teaching methods
Ⓔ Intelligence

32. Which of the following sentences contains an opinion?

Ⓐ "But consider for example . . . ."
Ⓑ "Three decades ago . . . ."
Ⓒ "In the intervening years . . . ."
Ⓓ "Now teachers are being told . . . ."
Ⓔ "This cycle is more akin . . . ."

33. Which of the following best describes how this passage is organized?

Ⓐ The author presents the main idea followed by examples.
Ⓑ A comparison is made between two dissimilar things followed by the author's main idea.
Ⓒ The author describes chronological events followed by an explanation of those events.
Ⓓ The author presents a trend and explains why that trend will not continue.
Ⓔ The author describes effective techniques and then gives examples of those techniques.

34. Which of the following could be substituted for the phrase "random acts" in the last sentence?

   Ⓐ Unsound practice
   Ⓑ A fashion designer's dream
   Ⓒ The movement of hemlines
   Ⓓ A fashion show
   Ⓔ Pressure from mathematics manipulative manufacturers

---

35. Empty halls and silent walls greeted me. A summer day seemed like a good day for me to take a look at the school in which I would student teach. I tiptoed from door to door looking. Suddenly the custodian appeared behind me and said, "Help you?" "No sir," I said. At that moment, he could have been Aristotle or Plato for all I knew. Things worked out.

Which of the following best describes the main character in the passage?

   Ⓐ Timid and afraid
   Ⓑ Confident and optimistic
   Ⓒ Pessimistic and unsure
   Ⓓ Curious and respectful
   Ⓔ Careful and quiet

QUESTIONS 36–38 ARE BASED ON THE FOLLOWING READING.

       I remember my childhood vacations at a bungalow colony near a lake. Always bare-foot, my friend and I spent endless hours playing and enjoying our fantasies. We were pirates, rocket pilots, and detectives. Everyday objects were transformed into swords,
Line ray guns, and two-way wrist radios. With a lake at hand, we swam, floated on our crude
(5)   rafts made of old lumber, fished, and fell in. The adult world seemed so meaningless while our world seemed so full. Returning years later I saw the colony for what it was—tattered and torn. The lake was shallow and muddy. But the tree that had been our lookout was still there. And there was the house where the feared master spy hid from the FBI. There was the site of the launching pad for our imaginary rocket trips. The
(10) posts of the dock we had sailed from many times were still visible. But my fantasy play did not depend on this place. My child-mind would have been a buccaneer wherever it was.

36. Which of the following choices best characterizes this passage?

   Ⓐ An adult describes disappointment at growing up.
   Ⓑ A child describes the adult world through the child's eyes.
   Ⓒ An adult discusses childhood viewed as a child and as an adult.
   Ⓓ An adult discusses the meaning of fantasy play.
   Ⓔ An adult describes a wish to return to childhood.

37. The sentence "The adult world seemed so meaningless while our world seemed so full," (lines 5–6) is used primarily to

Ⓐ emphasize the emptiness of most adult lives.

Ⓑ provide a transition from describing childhood to describing adulthood.

Ⓒ show how narcissistic children are.

Ⓓ describe the difficulty this child had relating to adults.

Ⓔ emphasize the limited world of the child compared to the more comprehensive world of the adult.

38. Which of the following best characterizes the last sentence in the passage?

Ⓐ The child would have been rebellious, no matter what.

Ⓑ Childhood is not a place but a state of mind.

Ⓒ We conform more as we grow older.

Ⓓ The writer will always feel rebellious.

Ⓔ A part of us all stays in childhood.

QUESTIONS 39 AND 40 APPLY TO THIS PASSAGE.

Sometimes parents are more involved in little league games than their children. I remember seeing a game in which a player's parent came on the field to argue with the umpire. The umpire was not that much older than the player.

Before long, the umpire's mother was on the field. There the two parents stood, toe to toe. The players and the other umpires formed a ring around them and looked on in awe.

Of course, I have never gotten too involved in my children's sports. I have never yelled at an umpire at any of my kid's games. I have never even—well, I didn't mean it.

39. What other "sporting" event is the author trying to re-create in the second paragraph?

Ⓐ Bullfight

Ⓑ Wrestling match

Ⓒ Boxing match

Ⓓ Football game

Ⓔ Baseball game

40. The author portrays herself as "innocent" of being too involved in her children's sports. How would you characterize this portrayal?

Ⓐ False

Ⓑ A lie

Ⓒ Tongue in cheek

Ⓓ Noble

Ⓔ Self-effacing

In the 1796 presidential election, John Adams eked out a victory over Thomas Jefferson. In the controversial XYZ affair, France sought bribes from America. Concern about France led to the Alien and Sedition acts. These acts put pressure on noncitizens and forbade writing that criticized the government. Some Western states opposed those acts and wanted to nullify those acts for their state. This Nullification Theory, and the states' rights mentioned in the Tenth Amendment to the Constitution, raised issues still important today.

41. Which of the following best summarizes the Nullification Theory?

Ⓐ Individual states' rights are superior to federal government rights.
Ⓑ Individual states could nullify their statehood and leave the Union.
Ⓒ Individual states' rights did not apply to noncitizens.
Ⓓ Individual states could decide which laws applied in their states.
Ⓔ Individual states could nullify treaties made with foreign governments.

My love falls on silence nigh
I am alone in knowing the goodbye
For while a lost love has its day
A love unknown is a sadder way

42. The word *nigh* in the first line most nearly means

Ⓐ clear
Ⓑ complete
Ⓒ near
Ⓓ not
Ⓔ missing

43. I grew up in Kearny New Jersey, now known as Soccer Town USA. I played football in high school and barely knew that the soccer team existed. However, a look back at my high school yearbook revealed that the soccer team won the state championship, while the football team had a .500 record. So much for awareness.

The author wrote the passage to

Ⓐ describe a situation.
Ⓑ reflect on past events.
Ⓒ present a point of view.
Ⓓ express irony.
Ⓔ narrate a story.

44. Lyndon Johnson was born in a farmhouse in central Texas in 1908. He grew up in poverty and had to work his way through college. He was elected to the U.S. House of Representatives in 1937, and served in the U.S. Navy during World War II. Following twelve years in the House of Representatives, he was elected to the U.S. Senate, where he was the youngest person chosen by any party to be its Senate leader.

According to this passage, Lyndon Johnson

Ⓐ lived in a farmhouse when he went to college.
Ⓑ was the youngest person elected to the U.S. Senate.
Ⓒ joined the Navy while a U.S. Representative.
Ⓓ served in the Senate for twelve years.
Ⓔ was born in the 1930s.

45. Population experts estimate that there may be 300 million inhabitants in South America. About 7 percent of the inhabitants speak native languages, and pockets of native civilization can still be found in the countryside. Most of the inhabitants with European origins trace their roots to Portugal, Spain, and Italy.

When the passage refers to native languages, it most likely means

Ⓐ spoken by those born in South America.
Ⓑ of those residents of South America who are native to Portugal, Spain, and Italy.
Ⓒ of those living in the pockets of civilization in the countryside.
Ⓓ of those born in South America with European origins who are not from Portugal, Spain, or Italy.
Ⓔ of those natives of Europe who came to South America.

46. The space vehicle identification program is designed to show that the vehicle meets all design and performance specifications. The <u>verification</u> program also seeks to ensure that all hazards and sources of failure have been eliminated or reduced to acceptable levels. The specific spaceship verification is based on a series of carefully monitored testing protocols. The verification tests are conducted under the strictest controls, including temperature and stress levels.

Which of the following words could be used in place of the word *verification*, underlined in the second sentence?

Ⓐ Elimination
Ⓑ Corroboration
Ⓒ Allocation
Ⓓ Renovation
Ⓔ Containment

QUESTIONS 47–52 ARE BASED ON THE FOLLOWING PASSAGES.

I.

The United States has the world's largest reserves of coal. Coal is the most common fuel for generating electricity in the United States. Recently, 42 percent of the country's nearly 4 trillion kilowatt hours of electricity used coal as its source of energy. That such *Line* an important resource is abundantly available in this country provides one road to
(5) energy independence, with the promise of economic growth and jobs.

Coal has gotten a bad name. However, coal-fired plants have become more efficient; recent advances have developed coal furnaces that operate at 91 percent efficiency. Coal is primarily carbon, and in particular, older plants have had significant carbon dioxide emissions. But the argument that our abundant supply of coal
(10) should be abandoned is nonsense, just as it would be nonsense to suggest that cars be abandoned because they kill about thirty thousand Americans each year at an estimated cost approaching $300 billion.

II.

Burning coal to produce energy is widespread and dangerous. During combustion, the reaction between coal and air emits CO_2 (a greenhouse gas), oxides of sulfur (mainly
(15) sulfur dioxide; SO_2), and various oxides of nitrogen (NO_x). Hybrids and nitrides of carbon and sulfur are also produced during the combustion of coal in air. These include hydrogen cyanide (HCN), sulfur nitrate (SNO_3), and other toxic substances.

The World Health Organization reports pollution caused by coal likely shortens over twenty thousand lives a year in the United States. Coal mining itself has signifi-
(20) cant adverse environmental health impacts, including underground coal fires, some of which are still burning in Pennsylvania.

The argument that this country should use coal just because it has a lot of it does not hold up.

47. Which of the following best describes the relationship of these passages?

Ⓐ Both passages emphasize that coal is an important source of energy.

Ⓑ The first passage emphasizes more the harmful environmental impact of coal more than the second passage.

Ⓒ The first passage emphasizes the potential uses of coal in transportation while the second passage does not.

Ⓓ The second passage opposes the use of coal to produce energy compared to the first passage.

Ⓔ The passages provide equal evidence about the dangers of coal.

48. The meaning of the word *combustion* in context (line 13) is

Ⓐ mixing.

Ⓑ burning.

Ⓒ crushing.

Ⓓ igniting.

Ⓔ washing.

PRACTICE CORE 1 233

49. Both passages mention carbon dioxide, which is referred to in the second passage as

   (A) NO_x.
   (B) HCN.
   (C) SNO_3.
   (D) CO_2.
   (E) SO_3.

50. Choose the word below that the authors each associate with coal-fired furnaces.

   (A) Dangerous
   (B) Helpful
   (C) Emissions
   (D) Heat
   (E) Light

51. Which of the following sentences, if added to the end of the second passage, would most strengthen the author's position?

   (A) Besides, clean-burning natural gas is replacing coal-fired plants.
   (B) It is true that using coal supports the mining sector of the economy.
   (C) Things get worse when you take the plight of the miners into account.
   (D) There might be some ways to use coal efficiently.
   (E) It is striking that the United States has so much coal.

52. The essence of each passage addresses

   (A) the disadvantages of using coal.
   (B) the advantages of using coal.
   (C) emissions created by coal-burning plants.
   (D) U.S. coal reserves.
   (E) using coal to create energy.

Sun	Mon	Tue	Wed	Thu	Fri	Sat
	1 8:00 A.M. History 10:00 A.M. Algebra 2:00 P.M. Physics	**2** 9:00 A.M. English 1:00 P.M. Theater	**3** 8:00 A.M. History 10:00 A.M. Algebra 3:00 P.M. Physics	**4** 11:00 A.M. English 1:00 P.M. Theater	**5** 11:00 A.M. Physics Lab A	**6**
7	**8** 8:00 A.M. History 10:00 A.M. Algebra 2:00 P.M. Physics	**9** 9:00 A.M. English 1:00 P.M. Theater	**10** 8:00 A.M. History 10:00 A.M. Algebra 3:00 P.M. Physics	**11** 10:00 A.M. English 1:00 P.M. Theater	**12** 11:00 A.M. Physics Lab B	**13** 8:00 P.M. PLAY
14	**15** 8:00 A.M. History 10:00 A.M. Algebra 2:00 P.M. Physics	**16** 9:00 A.M. English 1:00 P.M. Theater	**17** 8:00 A.M. History 10:00 A.M. Algebra 3:00 P.M. Physics	**18** 10:00 A.M. English 1:00 P.M. Theater	**19** 11:00 A.M. Physics Lab A	**20**
21	**22** 8:00 A.M. History 10:00 A.M. Algebra 2:00 P.M. Physics	**23** 9:00 A.M. English 1:00 P.M. Theater	**24** 8:00 A.M. History 10:00 A.M. Algebra 3:00 P.M. Physics	**25** 10:00 A.M. English 1:00 P.M. Theater	**26** 11:00 A.M. Physics Lab B	**27** 8:00 P.M. PLAY

The calendar shows when courses and labs are scheduled during the month. Each class meets twice a week.

53. Quinn has to participate in a play following three theater classes, and he wants to participate in the play on the 13th. Which of the following is the best reason for skipping a class on the fourth day of the month?

    (A) That choice would permit Quinn to participate in the play on the 27th.
    (B) That choice would let Quinn be there for the beginning of class and practice just before the play.
    (C) That choice would let Quinn skip English on the 4th and give him the day off to prepare for the physics lab on the 5th.
    (D) Thursday is the day Quinn plans to take a trip to visit his family.
    (E) Most students will be absent on the first day of class.

54. Quinn has to attend two meetings of lab A OR two meetings of lab B. Which of the following is the best explanation of why Quinn would choose lab A?

    Ⓐ Lab A meets during the first week of class.
    Ⓑ Lab B meets on the next-to-last-day of the term.
    Ⓒ There is a play on the 13th.
    Ⓓ There is no play on the 20th.
    Ⓔ Lab B is more difficult than lab A.

55. Based on the calendar, which of the following activities could Quinn have participated in *just one* single time?

Select all that apply.

    A An English class at 11:00 A.M.
    B Algebra on the 22nd
    C A play on the 27th

Music consists of pitch, the actual frequency or sound of a note, and duration. A tone has a specific pitch and duration. Different tones occurring simultaneously are called chords. A melody is the tones that produce the distinctive "sound" of the music. Harmony is chords with a duration. Pitches separated by specific intervals are called a scale. Most music is based on the diatonic scale found on a piano's white keys (C, D, E, F, G, A, B). The chromatic scale includes the seven notes on the diatonic scale with the five sharps and flats corresponding to the white and black keys on a piano.

56. According to the passage, the chromatic scale

    Ⓐ corresponds to the white keys on a piano.
    Ⓑ consists of the flats and sharps not contained in the diatonic scale.
    Ⓒ is contained in the diatonic scale.
    Ⓓ can be played only on a piano.
    Ⓔ includes notes corresponding to seven letters of the alphabet.

WRITING TEST (5722)

40 ITEMS   **40 MINUTES**
2 CONSTRUCTED RESPONSES   **60 MINUTES**

Usage

> **Directions:** You will read sentences with four parts underlined and lettered. Determine whether one of the underlined parts contains grammatical, word use, or punctuation errors. If so, mark that letter. If there are no errors, mark E.

1. Disgusted by the trash <u>left behind</u> by picnickers, the <u>town</u> council passed a
         Ⓐ   Ⓑ   Ⓒ

   law <u>requiring convicted litterers</u> to spend five hours cleaning up the town
         Ⓓ

   park. <u>No error.</u>
      Ⓔ

2. The teacher <u>was sure</u> that the child's <u>difficult home</u> life <u>effected</u> her <u>school work.</u>
         Ⓐ   Ⓑ   Ⓒ   Ⓓ

   <u>No error.</u>
    Ⓔ

3. It <u>took</u> Ron a long time <u>to realize</u> that the <u>townspeople</u> <u>were completely</u> opposed
      Ⓐ   Ⓑ   Ⓒ   Ⓓ

   to his proposal. <u>No error.</u>
         Ⓔ

4. A newspaper <u>columnist</u> promised to print the <u>people who</u> were <u>involved in</u>
         Ⓐ   Ⓑ   Ⓒ

   the secret negotiations concerning the <u>sports stadium</u> in the next column.
         Ⓓ

   <u>No error.</u>
    Ⓔ

5. The silent <u>halo</u> of a <u>solar eclipse</u> <u>could be seen</u> by astronomers across <u>asia.</u>
       Ⓐ   Ⓑ   Ⓒ   Ⓓ

   <u>No error.</u>
    Ⓔ

6. <u>Also found</u> during the archaeological dig <u>was</u> a <u>series</u> of animal bone fragments,
    Ⓐ   Ⓑ   Ⓒ

   fire signs, and <u>arrow points.</u> <u>No error.</u>
         Ⓓ   Ⓔ

7. The <u>teacher</u> asked all of <u>her</u> students to bring in <u>they're</u> permission slips <u>to go on</u>
      Ⓐ   Ⓑ   Ⓒ   Ⓓ

the Washington trip. <u>No error.</u>
          Ⓔ

8. The <u>plumber</u> <u>did not go</u> to the dripping water <u>than to</u> the place the water
     Ⓐ   Ⓑ   Ⓒ

<u>seemed to be coming from.</u> <u>No error.</u>
   Ⓓ   Ⓔ

9. The driver realized that she <u>would either</u> have to <u>go completely out of</u>
                Ⓐ   Ⓑ

the <u>way</u> or have to wait for the <u>swollen creek</u> to subside. <u>No error.</u>
   Ⓒ   Ⓓ   Ⓔ

10. The <u>tracker</u> was so <u>good</u> that he could tell the <u>difference between</u> a hoofprint
     Ⓐ   Ⓑ   Ⓒ

made by a horse with a saddle <u>or</u> a hoofprint made by a horse without a
                 Ⓓ

saddle. <u>No error.</u>
    Ⓔ

11. The mayor <u>estimated</u> that it <u>would cost</u> $1,200 for each <u>citizen individually</u> to
        Ⓐ   Ⓑ   Ⓒ

repair the storm damage <u>to the town.</u> <u>No error.</u>
            Ⓓ   Ⓔ

12. <u>Sustaining</u> a <u>month-long</u> winning streak in the town baseball A B league, the
   Ⓐ   Ⓑ

young team <u>pressed on</u> with <u>unwavering determination.</u> <u>No error.</u>
       Ⓒ   Ⓓ   Ⓔ

13. A fire chief, <u>like a police chief,</u> <u>has so much</u> responsibility, that <u>they often have</u>
         Ⓐ   Ⓑ   Ⓒ

a personal <u>driver.</u> <u>No error.</u>
     Ⓓ   Ⓔ

14. A talented chef <u>making customers</u> smack their lips at her <u>great gustatorial delights,</u>
         Ⓐ   Ⓑ

the likes of which <u>are not available</u> in any <u>ordinary restaurant.</u> <u>No error.</u>
       Ⓒ   Ⓓ   Ⓔ

15. The fate of small towns in America, which were <u>popularized</u> in movies when it
    Ⓐ

    seemed that everyone came from a small town <u>and now</u> face <u>anonymity</u> as
    Ⓑ   Ⓒ

    cars on highways speed by, <u>is perilous.</u> <u>No error.</u>
    Ⓓ   Ⓔ

16. The coach <u>not only</u> <u>works with</u> each pitcher and each catcher, but he <u>also has to</u>
    Ⓐ   Ⓑ   Ⓒ

    change <u>him.</u> <u>No error.</u>
    Ⓓ   Ⓔ

17. When I <u>was a child,</u> a wet washcloth was the <u>main method</u> of first <u>aid;</u> it reduced
    Ⓐ   Ⓑ   Ⓒ

    swelling, eliminated pain, <u>and inflammation was reduced.</u> <u>No error.</u>
    Ⓓ   Ⓔ

18. I am going to a <u>World Cup game</u> next week, and I <u>would be surprised</u> if <u>there is even</u>
    Ⓐ   Ⓑ   Ⓒ

    one empty seat <u>in the stadium.</u> <u>No error.</u>
    Ⓓ   Ⓔ

Sentence Correction

> **Directions:** You will read sentences with some or all of the sentence underlined, followed by five answer choices. The first answer choice repeats the underlined portion and the other four present possible replacements. Select the answer choice that best represents standard English without altering the meaning of the original sentence. Mark that letter on the test.

19. The quality of the parts received in the most recent shipment <u>was inferior to parts in the previous shipments, but still in accordance with</u> manufacturers' specifications.

    Ⓐ was inferior to parts in the previous shipments, but still in accordance with
    Ⓑ were inferior to the previous shipments' parts but still in accordance with
    Ⓒ was the inferior of the previous shipments' parts but still in accordance with
    Ⓓ was inferior to the previous parts' shipments but still not on par with
    Ⓔ was inferior to the previous parts' shipments and the manufacturers' specifications

20. <u>The painful rabies treatment first developed by Pasteur</u> saved the boy's life.

    Ⓐ The painful rabies treatment first developed by Pasteur
    Ⓑ The painful rabies treatment which was first discovered by Pasteur
    Ⓒ Pasteur developed the painful rabies treatment
    Ⓓ First developed by Pasteur the treatment for painful rabies
    Ⓔ The fact that Pasteur developed a rabies treatment

21. By 10:00 A.M. every morning, <u>the delivery service brought important papers to the house in sealed envelopes.</u>

 Ⓐ the delivery service brought important papers to the house in sealed envelopes

 Ⓑ important papers were brought to the house by the delivery service in sealed envelopes

 Ⓒ sealed envelopes were brought to the house by the delivery service with important papers

 Ⓓ the delivery service brought important papers in sealed envelopes to the house

 Ⓔ the deliver service brought sealed envelopes to the house containing important papers

22. The shadows shortened as the sun <u>begun the</u> ascent into the morning sky.

 Ⓐ begun the

 Ⓑ begin the

 Ⓒ began the

 Ⓓ begun that

 Ⓔ begun an

23. Liz and Ann spent all day climbing the mountain, and <u>she was almost</u> too exhausted for the descent.

 Ⓐ she was almost

 Ⓑ they were almost

 Ⓒ they were

 Ⓓ she almost was

 Ⓔ was

24. The embassy announced that at the present time, they could neither confirm <u>nor deny that the ambassador would return home in the event that</u> hostilities broke out.

 Ⓐ nor deny that the ambassador would return home in the event that

 Ⓑ or deny that the ambassador would return home in the event that

 Ⓒ nor deny that the ambassador would return home if

 Ⓓ nor deny that the ambassador would leave

 Ⓔ nor deny that ambassador will return home in the event that

25. Every person <u>has the ultimate capacity to</u> control his or her own destiny.

 Ⓐ has the ultimate capacity to

 Ⓑ ultimately has the capacity to

 Ⓒ has the capacity ultimately to

 Ⓓ can

 Ⓔ could

26. In all likelihood, her mother's absence would be devastating, <u>were it not</u> for the presence of her sister.

   (A) were it not
   (B) it was not
   (C) it were not
   (D) were they not
   (E) was it not

27. She had listened very carefully to all the candidates, and the Independent candidate was the only <u>one who had not said something that did not make sense.</u>

   (A) one who had not said something that did not make sense
   (B) one who did not make sense when he said something
   (C) one who had only said things that made sense
   (D) one to not say something that made sense
   (E) one who never said anything that made no sense

28. The author knew that the book would be finished <u>only by working every day and getting</u> lots of sleep at night.

   (A) only by working every day and getting
   (B) only working every day and getting
   (C) only by working every day and by getting
   (D) only through work and sleep
   (E) only by daily work and by sleepless nights

29. The teacher was sure that Tom's difficult home life affected <u>his school work.</u>

   (A) his school work
   (B) his school's work
   (C) him school work
   (D) his school works
   (E) him school works

30. Small town sheriffs in America, <u>whom were popularized in movies when it seemed that everyone came from a small town,</u> now face anonymity.

   (A) whom were popularized in movies when it seemed that everyone came from a small town
   (B) who were popularized in movies when it seemed that everyone came from a small town
   (C) whom were popularized in movies when it seemed that anyone came from a small town
   (D) whom were popularized in movies when they seemed that everyone came from a small town
   (E) whom were popularized in movies when it seemed that everyone comes from a small town

31. The professor asked the class to consider the development of the human race. She pointed out that, throughout the ages, <u>human beings has learned to communicate by nonverbal means.</u>

    Ⓐ human beings has learned to communicate by nonverbal means

    Ⓑ human beings had learned to communicate by nonverbal means

    Ⓒ human beings has learn to communicate by nonverbal means

    Ⓓ human beings have learn to communicate by nonverbal means

    Ⓔ human beings have learned to communicate by nonverbal means

Revision in Context

Select the best answer.

QUESTIONS 32–36 ARE BASED ON THE FOLLOWING PASSAGE.

Constitution

(1) The Federal Convention convened in the State House (Independence Hall) in Philadelphia on May 14, 1787, to revise the Articles of Confederation. (2) Through discussion and debate it became clear by mid-June that, rather than amend the existing articles, the Convention would draft an entirely new frame of government. (3) All through the summer, in closed sessions, the delegates debated and redrafted the articles of the new Constitution. (4) Among the chief points at issue were how much power to allow the central government, how many representatives in Congress to allow each state, and how these representatives should be elected—directly by the people or by the state legislators. (5) The Constitution stands as a model of cooperative statesmanship and the art of compromise.

(6) For the Constitution to be amended, the amendment must be approved by Congress and sent to the various states to be ratified. (7) A proposed amendment becomes part of the Constitution as soon as it is ratified by three-fourths of the states (38 of 50 states at this time). (8) The first ten amendments were adopted and ratified simultaneously and are known collectively as the <u>Bill of Rights</u>.

(9) The ratification is not described in detail. (10) Rather, appropriate officials follow procedures and customs established by the Secretary of State. (11) The Constitution provides that an amendment may be proposed either <u>by the Congress with a two-thirds majority vote in both the House of Representatives and the Senate</u> or by a constitutional convention called for by two-thirds of the state legislatures. (12) None of the twenty-seven amendments to the Constitution have been proposed by constitutional convention. (13) Six amendments adopted by Congress and sent to the states have not been ratified by the required number of states.

32. Which of the following sentences, added just after sentence 13, would provide the best conclusion to this paragraph?

    Ⓐ It makes you wonder whatever happened to those six amendments floating around somewhere, and whether it is just a few states or a lot of states that still have to ratify them.

    Ⓑ Six amendments out of thirty-three is not that bad.

    Ⓒ A constitutional convention might be a good idea if none of the amendments has ever been approved by Constitutional Convention.

    Ⓓ Four of these amendments are still technically open and pending.

    Ⓔ It makes you wonder about how unimportant state legislatures have become that they have never proposed a constitutional amendment on their own.

33. In the context of this passage, what is the best replacement for the underlined portion of the sentence shown below?

by the Congress with a two-thirds majority vote in both the House of Representatives and the Senate

(A) Leave as is

(B) by a two-thirds majority vote in Congress

(C) by two-thirds of the House of Representatives or Congress

(D) with a majority two-thirds vote of the House of Representatives or Congress

(E) by a two-thirds majority vote

34. In the context of this paragraph, which of the following is the best introduction to sentence 5?

(A) It goes without saying,

(B) Because of the secretiveness, the

(C) State's rights were respected, and

(D) Thankfully,

(E) The work of many minds,

35. Among the following choices, which is the best thing to do with sentence 9?

(A) Delete it.

(B) Change "ratification" to "clarification."

(C) Add "Essentially," at the beginning of the passage.

(D) Add the word *process* as the third word in the sentence.

(E) Change "majority" to plurality.

36. In context, what is the most effective way to revise and combine sentences 6 and 7, reproduced below?

(6) For the Constitution to be amended, the amendment must be approved by Congress and sent to the various states to be ratified. (7) A proposed amendment becomes part of the Constitution as soon as it is ratified by three-fourths of the states (38 of 50 states at this time).

(A) Constitutional amendments require approval by Congress and the states.

(B) Delete sentence (7).

(C) The Constitution can be amended when the proposed amendment is approved by Congress and ratified by three-fourths of the states.

(D) Congress approves proposed amendments and states ratify them.

(E) Constitutional amendments must be ratified by three-fourths of the states. We have 50 so 38 states must ratify, which is really 76 percent of the states.

Research Skills

Select the best answer.

37. Woodman, Bryna L., and Rae Craven, *Growing Up Nashville, 1953–1963* (Nashville, TN: Forest Street Publishing, 2003), p. 52.

    The citation above is from which of the following types of sources?

    Ⓐ An online article
    Ⓑ A newspaper article
    Ⓒ A blog
    Ⓓ A book
    Ⓔ An interview

38. Which of the following would be correctly cited as a secondary source about dinosaurs?

    Ⓐ Dinosaur bones in a museum
    Ⓑ Field notes from a scientist written as dinosaur bones were unearthed
    Ⓒ A book about reptiles by a scientist who is an expert on dinosaurs
    Ⓓ Dinosaur skeletal remains embedded in a rock outcropping
    Ⓔ An ancient drawing on a cave wall depicting dinosaurs

39. You are writing a paper about Benedict Arnold. Which of the following pieces of information is NOT directly relevant to the paper?

    Ⓐ Benedict Arnold was the commander of the American fortifications at West Point.
    Ⓑ Benedict Arnold secretly planned to surrender West Point to British forces.
    Ⓒ A British major was hanged in connection with the proposed West Point plan.
    Ⓓ The British army paid Arnold to desert the American army and join the British army.
    Ⓔ British raids against American forces in Virginia were led by Arnold.

40. A friend is writing a paper about beekeeping. Which of the following could NOT be a primary source for this paper?

    Ⓐ A book about beekeeping from an experienced beekeeper
    Ⓑ A recorded interview with a beekeeper
    Ⓒ A summary of a report about beekeeping
    Ⓓ Images of steps to follow when extracting honey from a bee hive
    Ⓔ A video showing the steps to control bee stings

ARGUMENTATIVE CONSTRUCTED RESPONSE

30 MINUTES

Directions: You have 30 minutes to complete this essay question. Use a computer, but not the spell or grammar check, to type a brief essay based on this topic.

> **To encourage talented people to enter teaching, teachers who score higher on standardized tests should make significantly more money than those teachers who receive lower test scores.**

Describe the extent to which you agree or disagree with this statement. Support your response with specific details, examples, and experiences.

Write a brief outline here.

INFORMATIVE/EXPLANATORY (SOURCE-BASED) CONSTRUCTED RESPONSE

30 MINUTES

> **Directions:** You have 30 minutes to read two position papers on a topic and then type an essay based on the topic. Use a computer, but not the spell or grammar check. The essay should discuss the important points in the topic.
>
> Read the topic and sources below. It is good to spend time organizing your thoughts and planning your essay before you start to write. You MUST write on the given topic, and you MUST include references to the sources.
>
> This essay gives you a chance to demonstrate how well you can write and include sources in your writing. That means you should focus on writing well, and using examples and references, all while being sure to cover the topic presented. While how much you write is not a specific scoring criteria, you will certainly want to write several meaningful paragraphs.

Topic

Nuclear power uses nuclear processes to generate heat and electricity. The nuclear fission of elements produces the vast majority of nuclear energy. Nuclear fission power stations produce about 6 percent of the world's energy and 15 percent of the world's electricity. Nuclear fission is efficient, but fission and nuclear waste are radioactive, and there is danger, with short- and long-term health risks. The recent Fukushima nuclear accident at a fifty-year-old reactor has slowed but not stopped the construction of newer and safer reactors worldwide. Attempts, unlikely to yield results before the middle of this century, are ongoing to develop nuclear fusion sources, the type of nuclear energy produced by the sun.

Read the two source passages below. Then type an essay that highlights the most important aspects of each and then explain why they are important. Your essay should refer to EACH of the sources and must CITE the sources as you refer to them or provide direct quotations. You may also use your own experiences and readings.

Nuclear Energy . . . the Best Road to Energy Independence
(Quinson, web access 10/12/2017)

You have heard about problems with nuclear energy from older reactors. What you may not have heard is that it is the most efficient way of using renewable energy to create electricity. It is better than coal, which is still the main way electricity is produced, and it is better than oil or gas or any other non-renewable energy source. You have heard a lot about solar power, but the truth is solar power will not be a commercially viable energy source in this century.

Nuclear power has caused fewer fatalities per unit of energy generated. Nuclear energy produces no greenhouse gases and does not pollute the environment. The new reactors put into service are much safer than the reactors built 50 years ago, and many of those older reactors have already been retired. I am very comfortable living just miles from a reactor that has been safely providing energy to this community for decades with no problems. There are no smokestacks, no trains hauling in coal, and no huge pipeline delivering gas or oil. In truth, the air here is cleaner than in most other parts of the United States because coal used to create electricity in most places is simply not used. Beyond that there are over 150 naval vessels propelled by nuclear power, vessels which never have to be refueled at sea and never have to come into port for fuel. That is the benefit of an energy source that does not have to constantly be renewed.

I want to close this brief paper by mentioning the Fukushima Daiichi nuclear reactor accident in 2011. The universal assessment of this tragedy is that it was essentially man made. That is, all investigations agree that the reactor should never have been built where it was, and that a reactor like that one over 50 years old should have already been retired. About 20,000 people were killed by the tsunami and its aftermath. There will undoubtedly be some aftereffects, but not at the level of the number of people killed in the tsunami. Using this accident to argue against nuclear power production is a failed argument.

Nuclear Energy—a Ticking Atom Bomb
(Patrick, web access 9/28/2017)

Nuclear energy is not all bad, and I can think of some specific situations when it might be appropriate. A ship at sea might be one of them, or perhaps a tiny reactor at some remote location away from a populated area, and where the earthquake and tornado risks are close to zero. But that is about it.

A large reactor built anywhere else is nothing more than a ticking bomb—a nuclear bomb. There have been three major accidents in the last 25 years, and the number of nuclear reactors is steadily increasing. No one really knows the death toll from these accidents or the long-term impact of radiation exposure, but the toll will be in the many tens of thousands, with many more impairments and diseases. And that is the problem with radiation—you often do not see most of the impact for decades. Just to understand the real safety issue, consider if someone blew up a coal generating power plant or a nuclear generating plant. Neither is good, but the impact of a destroyed nuclear plant would be devastation. Millions might be killed and thousands of square miles of land made barren for a century. And all that danger for a power system that serves a tiny portion of electric users.

We do not even have to look at the serious safety issues to question nuclear power. Recently former members of the agency that regulates the nuclear industry have said that nuclear energy is simply not economically viable. They point out that solar energy could fill the void that would be left by the absence of nuclear power. It is just a fact that solar energy could never fill a void left if coal and gas were not available to produce energy. So I guess there is a choice, but I will take the choice that will not lead to the death of millions.

Write a brief outline here.

MATHEMATICS TEST (5732)

56 ITEMS   85 MINUTES

Directions: Choose the correct answer(s) or write the answer in the box(es).

---

1. A fair two-sided coin has a heads side and a tails side. The odds that either side will face up when flipped is exactly $\frac{1}{2}$. Jeanette flips the coin three times and gets three heads. What is the probability that the coin will land heads up on the next flip?

   Ⓐ $\frac{1}{16}$

   Ⓑ $\frac{1}{8}$

   Ⓒ $\frac{1}{4}$

   Ⓓ $\frac{1}{2}$

   Ⓔ 1

2. Which of the expressions below is equivalent to $51 - 3y$ for every value of y?

   Ⓐ $(6 - 2)(y - 17)$
   Ⓑ $(10 + 7)(y - 1)$
   Ⓒ $(-12 - 5)(-3 + \frac{3y}{17})$
   Ⓓ $(51 - 14)(y - 13)$
   Ⓔ $(14 - 51)(3y - 38)$

3. If $3x(5 + 2) = 4(2x + 3)$, what is the value of x? Write your answer below as a fraction.

4. The triangle *ABC* below is shifted 7 units down and 3 units right. What are the coordinates of point *A* after the shifts?

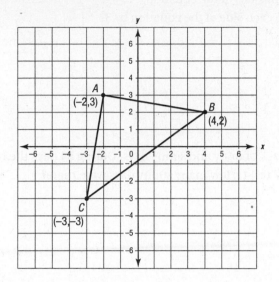

Ⓐ (−7, 0)
Ⓑ (5, −1)
Ⓒ (−6, 1)
Ⓓ (1, −4)
Ⓔ (−1, 6)

5. If $\frac{3}{4}x - 7 = 12$, then $x =$

Ⓐ $6\frac{2}{3}$

Ⓑ $19\frac{2}{3}$

Ⓒ $25\frac{1}{3}$

Ⓓ $36\frac{1}{3}$

Ⓔ $76\frac{1}{3}$

6. The numbers below are listed in order from least to greatest. Choose ALL the following numbers that could be the value of *x*.

$$0.5 \qquad \sqrt{2} \qquad x \qquad \frac{5}{2} \qquad \frac{8}{2}$$

Ⓐ 1.26
Ⓑ 2.333 . . .
Ⓒ $2\frac{3}{8}$
Ⓓ $2\frac{1}{2}$
Ⓔ 4

7. Which of the following equations can be solved using this set of steps?

   1. Add 8 to both sides of the equation.
   2. Then divide each side of the equation by 3.

   Ⓐ $8 - 3x = 3$
   Ⓑ $-8 + 3x = -4$
   Ⓒ $8x - 3 = 3$
   Ⓓ $3x + 8 = 4$
   Ⓔ $-3x - 8 = 3$

8. The class kept track of rainy and sunny days. During 54 days the ratio of rainy days to sunny days was 7 to 14. How many sunny days were there?

   Ⓐ 4
   Ⓑ 8
   Ⓒ 18
   Ⓓ 24
   Ⓔ 36

9. A car traveled along an interstate highway at a constant rate from 11:00 A.M. to 4:00 P.M. During that time the car traveled from mile marker 78 to mile marker 393. How many miles had the car traveled by 2:00 P.M.?

   Ⓐ 126
   Ⓑ 127
   Ⓒ 128
   Ⓓ 189
   Ⓔ 282

10. The expression below represents the total number of two- and three-point baskets a basketball player scored in a season. The team scored a total of 233 points. What fraction of the total number of the team's points were from that player's three-point baskets?

    $$3(\text{two}) + 12(\text{three})$$

    Ⓐ $\dfrac{12(\text{three})}{233}$

    Ⓑ $\dfrac{(\text{three})}{233}$

    Ⓒ $\dfrac{12(\text{three}) - 3(\text{two})}{233}$

    Ⓓ $\dfrac{12(\text{three})}{233 - 3(\text{two})}$

    Ⓔ $\dfrac{233}{3(\text{two}) + 12(\text{three})}$

11. All the letters of the alphabet were written on plastic discs and placed in a bag. The vowels in the bag were A, E, I, O, U. Two letters are randomly chosen and not replaced. Both letters are consonants. What is the probability that the next letter chosen will be a vowel?

Ⓐ $\frac{1}{5}$

Ⓑ $\frac{1}{3}$

Ⓒ $\frac{5}{26}$

Ⓓ $\frac{5}{24}$

Ⓔ $\frac{24}{26}$

12. Accurate readings are taken of the amount of precipitation each day for 10 days. On 2 of the days there was no rainfall. The rainfall amounts in inches on the remaining 8 days are listed below.

0.132, 0.622, 0.093, 0.089, 0.0342, 0.601, 0.009, 0.499

What is the range of the rainfall on these days?

Ⓐ 0.368
Ⓑ 0.499
Ⓒ 0.613
Ⓓ 0.622
Ⓔ 0.754

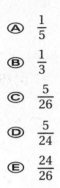

13. The coordinate plane below shows a graph of a linear equation. Which of the tables of values below could create this graph?

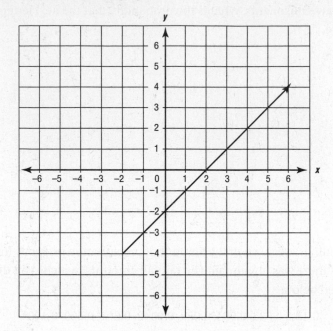

Ⓐ

x	y
2	4
4	6
−2	0
−4	−2

Ⓑ

x	y
0	−2
2	0
1	−1
−3	1

Ⓒ

x	y
1	−1
−1	−3
3	1
6	4

Ⓓ

x	y
4	6
6	4
3	1
1	3

Ⓔ

x	y
3	5
6	4
3	1
0	−3

14. There are four cylinders at the oil tank farm. You can see the first cylinder above. It has a height of 10 feet and a radius of 2 feet. The other three cylinders are hidden behind it. The second cylinder is half the height of this cylinder. The third is $\frac{1}{4}$ the height of this one, and the fourth cylinder is $\frac{1}{8}$ the height of this one. What is the combined volume of all four cylinders?

Use the formula for the volume of a cylinder: volume $= \pi \cdot r^2 \cdot$ height. Use 3.14 for π.

Ⓐ 235.5 cubic feet
Ⓑ 235.555 . . . cubic feet
Ⓒ 284.6 cubic feet
Ⓓ 286.7 cubic feet
Ⓔ 302.4 cubic feet

15. Serena is an account executive. She receives a base pay of $18 an hour plus a 15% bonus for all the sales she generates. Last week she generated $1,200 worth of business. What is the minimum number of hours she could have worked to make $500?

Ⓐ 17
Ⓑ 18
Ⓒ 25
Ⓓ 26
Ⓔ 35

16. If $5a + 3b = 19$ and $4c + 2d = 14$ where a, b, c, and d are whole numbers greater than 0, and where $a < b$ and $c < d$, then what is the value of the expression $(5a + 3c)(4b + 2d)$? The variables a, b, c, and d each has a different value.

Write your answer in the box below.

17. Which of the following scatter plots best represents a positive correlation?

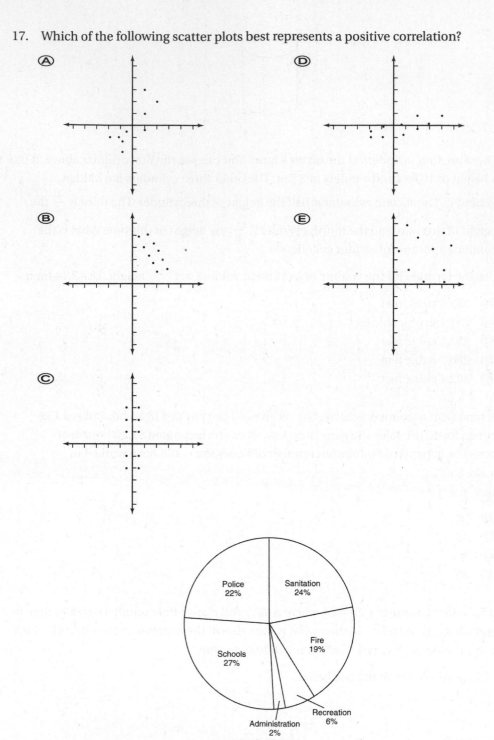

18. A town collects $2,600,000 in taxes. The town needs $624,000 for police. Any needed money will come from sanitation. The percents in the circle graph are recalculated. What percent is left for sanitation?

Ⓐ 22%

Ⓑ 20%

Ⓒ 19%

Ⓓ 18%

Ⓔ 16%

19. Steve pays $520 a month for rent, and his monthly paycheck after taxes is $1,300. Which computation shows the percent of Steve's paycheck that is used to pay rent?

    Ⓐ $(1300 \div 520) \cdot 100$
    Ⓑ $(520 \div 1300) \cdot 100$
    Ⓒ $(5.2 \cdot 1300) \cdot 100$
    Ⓓ $(13 \cdot 520) \cdot 100$
    Ⓔ $(5.2 \cdot 13) \cdot 100$

20. All of the windows in the house are rectangles. None of the windows in the house are squares.

Based on this statement, which of the following conclusions are true?

    Ⓐ Some of the windows have four sides of equal length.
    Ⓑ None of the windows contain right angles.
    Ⓒ None of the windows are parallelograms.
    Ⓓ None of the windows have four sides of equal length.
    Ⓔ All of the windows contain an acute angle.

21. The area of a square is 4 in.^{2}. There is a larger square made up of 49 of these squares. What is the length of one side of the larger square?

    Ⓐ 7 in.
    Ⓑ 14 in.
    Ⓒ 28 in.
    Ⓓ 56 in.
    Ⓔ 112 in.

22. What is the value of the number in the table below that is expressed in scientific notation?

	A	B	C
1.	53794×10^1	537.94×10^4	5.3794×10^1
2.	5379.4×10^1	53.794×10^2	53794×10^2

    Ⓐ 5.37940
    Ⓑ 53794
    Ⓒ 5379.4
    Ⓓ 537.94
    Ⓔ 53.794

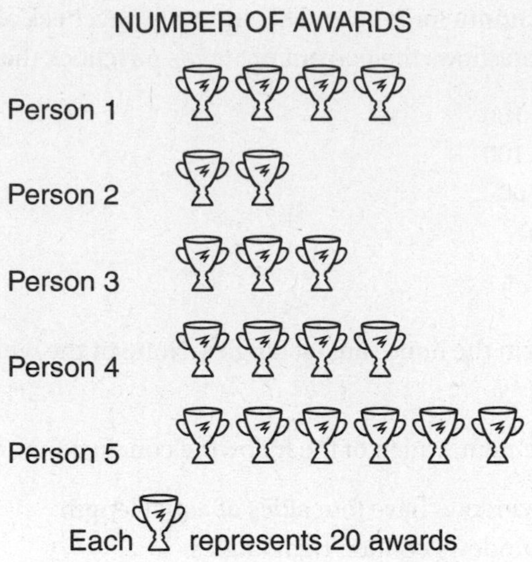
NUMBER OF AWARDS
Person 1
Person 2
Person 3
Person 4
Person 5
Each
represents 20 awards

23. How many more awards did person 5 have than person 3?

Ⓐ 20
Ⓑ 40
Ⓒ 60
Ⓓ 80
Ⓔ 100

24. If the function $B \overset{A}{\triangle} C = A \cdot B + C$, then $2 \overset{-4}{\triangle} 11$

Ⓐ –88
Ⓑ –19
Ⓒ –3
Ⓓ 3
Ⓔ 19

25. The following is a list of the ages of ten different people: 53, 27, 65, 21, 7, 16, 70, 41, 57, and 37.

What is the difference between the mean age and the median age of the group?

Ⓐ 0.4
Ⓑ 4
Ⓒ 39
Ⓓ 39.4
Ⓔ 13

26. A pizza has crust all around the edge. Which of the following figures shows a way to cut the pizza into four pieces where only two have crust?

Ⓐ

Ⓓ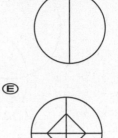

Ⓑ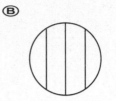

Ⓔ

Ⓒ

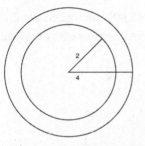

27. What is the difference between the area of the inner circle and the area of the outer circle?

Ⓐ 2π
Ⓑ 4π
Ⓒ 6π
Ⓓ 12π
Ⓔ 14π

28. Frank has 2 dogs, some cats, and 1 bunny. If 62.5 percent of these animals are cats, how many cats are there?

Ⓐ 2
Ⓑ 3
Ⓒ 5
Ⓓ 7
Ⓔ 10

Number of Students on Sports Teams

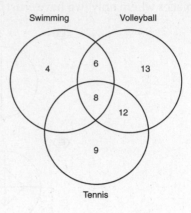

29. How many students participate in all of the sports except swimming?

Ⓐ 4
Ⓑ 8
Ⓒ 14
Ⓓ 30
Ⓔ 34

30. An old laser regenerates in 45,000 microseconds. By which factor does a new laser regenerate if the new laser regenerates every 0.45 microseconds?

Ⓐ 0.1
Ⓑ 0.01
Ⓒ 0.001
Ⓓ 0.0001
Ⓔ 0.00001

31. All of the following numbers are equal except for:

Ⓐ 4/9
Ⓑ 44/90
Ⓒ 404/909
Ⓓ 444/999
Ⓔ 4044/9099

32. Alice arrived at work at 7:45 A.M. and left work at 7 P.M. If she receives $20 an hour salary and no salary for her 1-hour lunch, how much did Alice earn as salary for the day?

Ⓐ $175
Ⓑ $195
Ⓒ $205
Ⓓ $215
Ⓔ $225

33. Which of the following shows a line with x- and y-intercepts equal to 1?

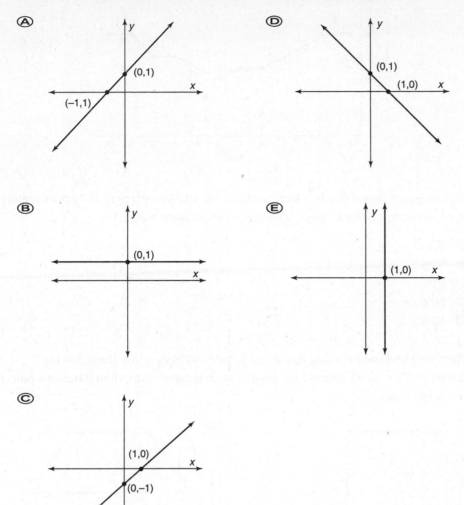

34.

If the lengths of the bases in the trapezoid ($A = \frac{h}{2}(b_1 + b_2)$) above are doubled, the area of the new trapezoid is given by the formula:

Ⓐ $A = \frac{h}{2}(b_1 + b_2)$

Ⓑ $A = 2h(b_1 + b_2)$

Ⓒ $A = \frac{h}{4}(b_1 + b_2)$

Ⓓ $A = h(b_1 + b_2)$

Ⓔ $A = 4h(b_1 + b_2)$

where b_1 and b_2 are the lengths of the original bases.

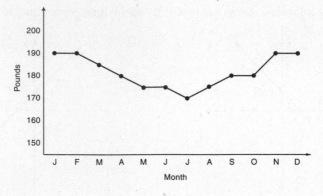

35. The line graph above displays Jack's weight over a 12-month period. Approximately what percentage of Jack's highest weight is Jack's lowest weight?

Ⓐ 97%
Ⓑ 94%
Ⓒ 91%
Ⓓ 89%
Ⓔ 85%

36. Select which of the following figures could be used to disprove the following statement: "If a quadrilateral has one pair of congruent sides, then it has two pairs of congruent sides."

Ⓐ
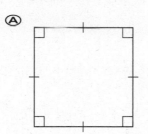

Ⓓ
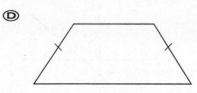

Ⓑ
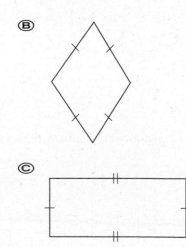

Ⓔ
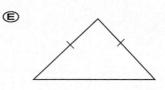

Ⓒ

37. The five shapes seen below are made up of identical semi-circles and identical quarter-circles. Which of the five shapes has the greatest perimeter?

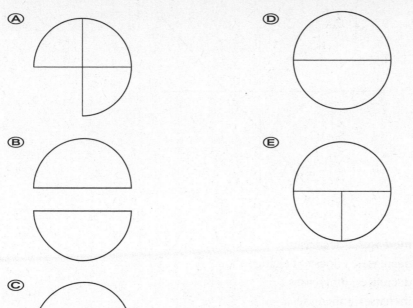

Ⓐ

Ⓑ

Ⓒ

Ⓓ

Ⓔ

38. Which of the following choices is not equivalent to the others?

   Ⓐ $3^4 \times 9 \times 12$
   Ⓑ $3^3 \times 27 \times 12$
   Ⓒ $3^5 \times 36$
   Ⓓ $3^3 \times 9^3 \times 4$
   Ⓔ $3^5 \times 4 \times 9$

39. Company employees just received their earning report. The earnings of 4 individuals in a company are:

     Person 1: $45,250
     Person 2: $78,375
     Person 3: $52,540
     Person 4: $62,325

The total earnings of these individuals, in thousands of dollars, is closest to:

   Ⓐ $237 thousand
   Ⓑ $238 thousand
   Ⓒ $239 thousand
   Ⓓ $240 thousand
   Ⓔ $241 thousand

40. Which of the following is true about the graph seen below?

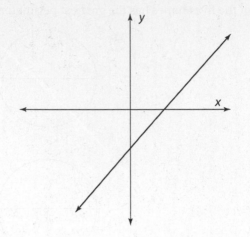

(A) As x increases, y decreases
(B) As x decreases, y does not change
(C) As x decreases, y increases
(D) As x increases, y increases
(E) As x increases, y does not change

41. A computer costs 65 percent of its retail price of $400. What does the computer cost?

(A) $660
(B) $540
(C) $260
(D) $200
(E) $140

42. What is the average of $\frac{1}{2}$, $\frac{2}{3}$, and $\frac{5}{12}$?

(A) $\frac{19}{12}$

(B) $\frac{19}{24}$

(C) $\frac{19}{36}$

(D) $\frac{19}{44}$

(E) $\frac{19}{52}$

43. In a standard deck of 52 cards, what is the probability of being dealt a king, a queen, or a jack?

Ⓐ $\frac{1}{3}$

Ⓑ $\frac{2}{13}$

Ⓒ $\frac{3}{13}$

Ⓓ $\frac{4}{13}$

Ⓔ $\frac{5}{13}$

44. To estimate 2.3×10^5 you could multiply 20 by

Ⓐ 10
Ⓑ 100
Ⓒ 1,000
Ⓓ 10,000
Ⓔ 100,000

45. A circle can be a part of any of the following except a

Ⓐ circle.
Ⓑ sphere.
Ⓒ cylinder.
Ⓓ cone.
Ⓔ cube.

46. The 2:00 P.M. temperature is shown on the thermometer. At 10:00 A.M. the temperature was 8° warmer. If the temperature changed at a constant rate, what was the temperature at noon?

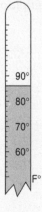

Ⓐ 82°F
Ⓑ 86°F
Ⓒ 90°F
Ⓓ 94°F
Ⓔ 96°F

47. If $6x + 2y = 10$, which of the following choices are possible values for x and y?

    Ⓐ $x = 2, y = -1$
    Ⓑ $x = 2, y = 11$
    Ⓒ $x = 3, y = 4$
    Ⓓ $x = 3, y = 14$
    Ⓔ $x = 4, y = -8$

48. Tickets for a baseball game are \$8 each, or 4 tickets for \$30. What is the lowest cost for 18 tickets?

    Ⓐ \$144
    Ⓑ \$136
    Ⓒ \$132
    Ⓓ \$130
    Ⓔ \$126

49. If $4A + 6 = 2(B - 1)$, then $B = ?$

    Ⓐ $2A + 4$
    Ⓑ $8A + 13$
    Ⓒ $2A + 2$
    Ⓓ $4A + 7$
    Ⓔ $4A + 5$

50. Which of the following measurements is not equal to the others?

    Ⓐ 230,000 millimeters
    Ⓑ 0.23 kilometers
    Ⓒ 23 meters
    Ⓓ 23,000 centimeters
    Ⓔ 2.3 hectometers

51. Which of the following choices is a multiple of 7 when 4 is added to it?

    Ⓐ 58
    Ⓑ 114
    Ⓒ 168
    Ⓓ 78
    Ⓔ 101

52. Ryan has gone $3\frac{1}{5}$ miles of his 5-mile run. How many more miles has he left to run?

    Ⓐ   A little less than 2 miles

    Ⓑ   A little more than 2 miles

    Ⓒ   A little less than 3 miles

    Ⓓ   A little more than 3 miles

    Ⓔ   A little less than 4 miles

53. For every 2 hours that Barbara works she earns $17. How much money will she earn if she works 45 hours?

    Ⓐ $391

    Ⓑ $382.50

    Ⓒ $374

    Ⓓ $365.50

    Ⓔ $357

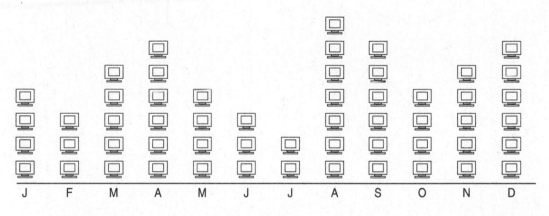

54. The pictograph shows TV sales for each month for all the stores in a chain. About how many times greater is the number of televisions sold in December than the number of televisions sold in January?

    Ⓐ   1.5

    Ⓑ   2

    Ⓒ   2.5

    Ⓓ   3

    Ⓔ   3.5

55. Which of the circles below include measurements that would be possible? (Point *B* is the center of each circle.) Choose all that apply.

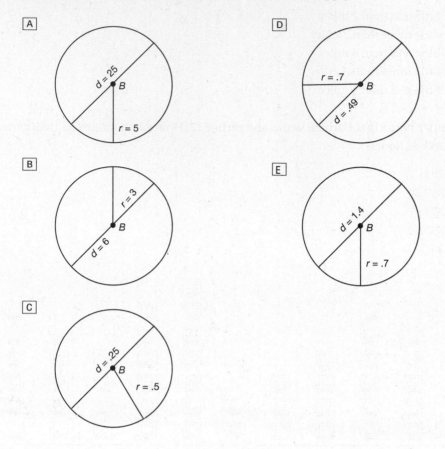

Ice Cream Cone Sales	
Single Scoop	$2.50
Double Scoop	$4.00

56. The sign shows the cost of ice cream cones. A total of 100 cones were sold over a weekend. What additional information would be needed to determine how many double-scoop cones were sold?

Ⓐ The total number of the single-scoop cones sold.
Ⓑ The number of patrons who bought both single- and double-scoop cones.
Ⓒ The total dollar value of the first fifty cones sold.
Ⓓ The total number of cones sold each day.
Ⓔ Amount of ice cream in each scoop.

ANSWER KEY
Practice Core 1

READING TEST

1. **D**	11. **D**	21. **E**	31. **A**	41. **D**	51. **A**
2. **E**	12. **C**	22. **B**	32. **E**	42. **C**	52. **E**
3. **C**	13. **A, B**	23. **B**	33. **B**	43. **D**	53. **B**
4. **D**	14. **B**	24. **A**	34. **C**	44. **C**	54. **B**
5. **D**	15. **C**	25. **B**	35. **D**	45. **C**	55. **A, B, C**
6. **C**	16. **B**	26. **B**	36. **C**	46. **B**	56. **E**
7. **C**	17. **C**	27. **C**	37. **B**	47. **D**	
8. **B**	18. **D**	28. **B**	38. **B**	48. **B**	
9. **C**	19. **C**	29. **C**	39. **C**	49. **D**	
10. **B**	20. **C**	30. **B**	40. **C**	50. **C**	

WRITING TEST
Usage

1. **E**	4. **B**	7. **C**	10. **D**	13. **C**	16. **E**
2. **C**	5. **D**	8. **C**	11. **C**	14. **A**	17. **D**
3. **E**	6. **B**	9. **E**	12. **E**	15. **B**	18. **B**

Sentence Correction

19. **A**	22. **C**	25. **D**	28. **C**	31. **E**
20. **A**	23. **B**	26. **A**	29. **A**	
21. **D**	24. **C**	27. **C**	30. **B**	

Revision in Context

32. **D**	33. **A**	34. **E**	35. **D**	36. **C**

Research Skills

37. **D**	38. **B**	39. **C**	40. **C**

See pages 272–275 for sample responses for the Argumentative and Informative/Explanatory (Source-Based) essays.

MATHEMATICS TEST

1. **D**	10. **A**	20. **D**	30. **E**	40. **D**	50. **C**
2. **C**	11. **D**	21. **B**	31. **B**	41. **C**	51. **E**
3. $\frac{12}{13}$	12. **D**	22. **E**	32. **C**	42. **C**	52. **A**
4. **D**	13. **C**	23. **C**	33. **D**	43. **C**	53. **B**
5. **C**	14. **A**	24. **D**	34. **D**	44. **D**	54. **A**
6. **B, C**	15. **B**	25. **A**	35. **D**	45. **E**	55. **B, E**
7. **B**	16. **286**	26. **C**	36. **D**	46. **C**	56. **A**
8. **E**	17. **A**	27. **D**	37. **B**	47. **A**	
9. **D**	18. **A**	28. **C**	38. **D**	48. **B**	
	19. **B**	29. **E**	39. **B**	49. **A**	

ANSWERS EXPLAINED

Reading Test

1. **(D)** The paragraph describes how careful shopping can result in lower prices.

2. **(E)** The author is trying to raise AIDS awareness and not to present any particular fact.

3. **(C)** The passage explains that AIDS is transmitted through blood and other bodily fluids.

4. **(D)** The sentence for this choice is the best conclusion for this passage.

5. **(D)** The retired basketball player mentions youth basketball as one of the reasons why today's players were better athletes. The passage also mentions an increased focus on training. However, the question does not ask for all the factors the retired player mentioned.

6. **(C)** This writer believes that generals should be judged by results. Even if you do not agree, that is the view of this writer.

7. **(C)** The author writes that the question still cannot be answered. The author does not say that the question can never be answered.

8. **(B)** The author never discusses exemptions but indicates that Boards of Adjustment should do away with exemptions.

9. **(C)** The passage gives an example of a person who both supported and did not support requested exemptions.

10. **(B)** The author is writing about a local issue.

11. **(D)** In the last paragraph the author uses these words to describe Boards of Adjustment.

12. **(C)** The author gives several examples in which people support or don't support exemptions based on their own needs.

13. **(A, B)** Choices (A) and (B), together, assure the student that she will be chosen and give her a chance to get into a sorority she wants.

14. **(B)** Choice (B) is the only list that meets all the requirements.

15. **(C)** The rate, alone, does not provide enough information. You must also know the starting point.

16. **(B)** You should question any growth rate when only the percentage is given.

17. **(C)** Choice (C) is correct. A sentence can state both a fact and an opinion. "(2) alone states an opinion" means that it is the only sentence that states an opinion.

18. **(D)** This choice gives the fundamental reason why the schools' programs are copied. The other reasons grow out of the decision to provide extra resources.

19. **(C)** The author objects to using these programs with students who don't know mathematics.

20. **(C)** This is the only question that can be answered from information in the passage. The answer is that it can be used when students already understand equations and graphing.

21. **(E)** The author emphasizes understanding in the second paragraph with a discussion of the "mindless kind of graphing . . ." that can occur with graphing calculators.

22. **(B)** The author mentions liking this aspect in the middle of the first paragraph.

23. **(B)** Choice (B) replicates the intent of the original sentence.

24. **(A)** The author provides support for this conclusion in the fourth sentence. The conclusions in the other choices are refuted in the passage.

25. **(B)** This is the only choice that reflects the author's observation that potentially weaker spots were actually stronger.

26. **(B)** The author's view is that all children should be treated the same.

27. **(C)** Choice (C) describes the problem. All the students who might have been admitted early this year will be admitted next year along with the other kindergarten students.

28. **(B)** Only this choice is a logical conclusion.

29. **(C)** When there are three lanes for passenger cars, school buses, school vans, and school cars can all use the lane for cars with two or more passengers.

30. **(B)** Only this choice meets all the rules.

31. **(A)** The context tells us that tenor is the best choice to replace "zeitgeist."

32. **(E)** Of the listed sentences, only "This cycle is more akin . . ." contains an opinion.

33. **(B)** The author compares fashion to education, and then finally gets to the main point of the passage. That is, education practices seem random, like fashion, rather than based on sound educational practices.

34. **(C)** Hemlines move without apparent reason, which is this author's point about educational practices.

35. **(D)** The character visited the school and is certainly curious. The character's reaction to the custodian shows respectfulness.

36. **(C)** The author discusses childhood from each of the perspectives described in choice (C). Choice (D) is incorrect because the meaning of fantasy play is never discussed.

37. **(B)** This sentence juxtaposes adulthood and childhood and provides a transition to discussing adulthood.

38. **(B)** The author says that these childhood experiences would have occurred regardless of the location.

39. **(C)** The description of going toe to toe inside a ring reminds us of a boxing match.

40. **(C)** The author is not lying, but the story is obviously not meant to be taken seriously.

41. **(D)** You will find the answer in the third sentence. Some states wanted to nullify acts (laws) so these laws would not apply to their states. Choices (A) and (B) are incorrect because the Nullification Theory applied to laws on a case-by-case basis and were not as sweeping as the answers given in these choices.

42. **(C)** The word *nigh* most nearly means *near*, in time, place, or relationship. The writer's love has fallen on the deaf ears of someone near to the writer.

43. **(D)** Irony means an incongruity between the actual result and the expected result. It is ironic that the writer did not even know about the soccer team in Soccer Town USA.

44. **(C)** The third sentence indicates that he entered the Navy while he was in the House of Representatives.

45. **(C)** The passage indicates that the pockets of native civilizations, where native language would most likely be spoken, are in the countryside. Note that choice (A) is incorrect because births in South America can occur among nonnatives.

46. **(B)** *Corroboration* means "evidence of support for a finding," which has the same meaning as *verification*.

47. **(D)** The second passage clearly states opposition to the use of coal, which is supported in the first paragraph.

48. **(B)** *Combustion* means *burning*, which is what happens to coal as it is converted into energy.

49. **(D)** The main clues are the "di" in carbon dioxide, which means 2, the subscript in this answer choice, and that C is the most likely abbreviation for carbon. You may know from your own experience that CO_2 is the abbreviation for carbon dioxide.

50. **(C)** The first passage includes the word *emit*, while the second passage includes the word *emissions*. Each word means the same thing, discharge(s), when applied to coal furnaces.

51. **(A)** The author's main point is that coal is a bad choice to create energy. Adding information about clean-burning natural gas supports that point of view. The other choices tend to weaken the author's anti-coal point of view.

52. **(E)** The common thread that runs through both passages is using coal to create energy.

53. **(B)** This choice is best because it gives Quinn two successive theater classes before the play, and allows him to be there for the first class when he is most likely to choose a part he wants. Choice (D) is incorrect because you do not know to which Thursday this choice refers.

54. **(B)** Quinn chooses lab A to avoid lab B, which comes at the end of the term. Lab A gives him more time off. The plays are not a factor, and you do not know anything about the difficulty of the labs.

55. **(A, B, C)** Quinn could only participate in each of these activities just once. None of the activities conflicts with the other. The other Algebra classes, plays on other days, and the English classes at other times are separate activities.

56. **(E)** The chromatic scale includes the diatonic scale, which includes the notes corresponding to the first seven letters of the alphabet. Remember, the black keys add sharps and flats but not more letters.

Writing Test

USAGE

1. **(E)** This sentence does not contain an error.

2. **(C)** The word *effected* is incorrect. It should be replaced by the word *affected*.

3. **(E)** This sentence also contains no errors. *Townspeople* is an appropriate word.

4. **(B)** You can't print people. The underlined section should be *names of the people*.

5. **(D)** The word *Asia* should be capitalized.

6. **(B)** The correct verb is *were*.

7. **(C)** The contraction *they're* (they are) is used incorrectly. *Their* is the correct word.

8. **(C)** The phrase *than to* is incorrectly used here. *But to* is the correct phrase.

9. **(E)** There are no errors in this sentence.

10. **(D)** The conjunction *or* is incorrectly used here. The correct conjunction is *and*.

11. **(C)** There is no reason to use the word *individually*. Each citizen is an individual. The word *individually* should be removed.

12. **(E)** This sentence does not contain an error.

13. **(C)** The word *they* creates confusion because it could mean that there is one driver for both of them. A better usage is *each often has*.

14. **(A)** *Making* is the wrong verb. *Made* is the correct choice.

15. **(B)** The words *and now* should read *and which now*, in order to clarify just what faces anonymity.

16. **(E)** This sentence contains no errors.

17. **(D)** This part of the sentence does not follow a parallel development. The correct usage is *reduced inflammation*.

18. **(B)** The correct replacement for *would be surprised* is *will be surprised*.

SENTENCE CORRECTION

19. **(A)** The underlined portion is appropriate.

20. **(A)** The underlined portion is appropriate.

21. **(D)** The rewording in Choice (D) clarifies that the papers are in sealed envelopes—not in the house.

22. **(C)** This choice is the best wording from among the five choices available.

23. **(B)** This choice creates an agreement in number between nouns and pronoun.

24. **(C)** This choice replaces the wordy *in the event that* with *if*.

25. **(D)** This wordy expression is replaced by *can*.

26. **(A)** The underlined portion is appropriately worded.

27. **(C)** This choice appropriately replaces the double negative underlined in the original sentence.

28. **(C)** Adding the word *by* creates the desired parallel development in the sentence.

29. **(A)** The sentence is correct. The pronoun *his* agrees with the antecedent *Tom*.

30. **(B)** *Who* correctly shows the subjective case.

31. **(E)** *Have learned* indicates this has occurred and may continue.

REVISION IN CONTEXT

32. **(D)** This sentence clarifies the status of the six unratified amendments and brings this paragraph to a conclusion.

33. **(A)** The existing sentence part is a better choice than any of the suggested replacements. These replacements are all incomplete in some way and do not accurately describe the amendment process.

34. **(E)** This choice captures the cooperation and compromise that led to the Constitution, which was not the work of a single person.

35. **(D)** The word *ratification* refers to the outcome. Adding the word *process* clarifies the sentence and indicates that the sentence describes the steps to ratification.

36. **(C)** The best answer is choice (C). This sentence eliminates some of the wordiness of sentence 6 and sentence 7 and still conveys the essential meaning of these sentences.

RESEARCH SKILLS

37. **(D)** There is only one title and a publisher, indicating that this citation is for a book.

38. **(B)** The field notes are a secondary source. The scientist was not around when the dinosaurs were alive. Choices (A) and (D) are primary sources. Choice (C) is a general reference and not directly a source about dinosaurs. As for choice (E), there were no drawings of any type made showing living dinosaurs.

39. **(C)** This statement about Major Andre is true, but it is not <u>directly</u> related to the topic of Benedict Arnold.

40. **(C)** In general, a summary cannot be a primary source. It is likely that the original report would have been a primary source.

Argumentative Essay

Compare your essay to the sample essay that follows. You may want to show your essay to an English expert for further evaluation.

This essay would likely receive a rating of 5 or 6 out of 6.

Paying Teachers Because They Score High Is a Bad Idea

A higher standardized test score does not tell anything about what a person will be like as a teacher. How many of us have known someone who could do very well on tests, but could not interact effectively with others? The same thing is true of people who do well on tests and can't explain what they know to another person. This does not mean that doing well on tests is a bad thing. It does seem to me that doing well on tests does not by itself mean that someone will be a good teacher. Besides that it is very hard to pay teachers on an incentive basis because there are so many differences among the pupils that teachers work with that you could never tell whether students did well because of a teacher or because of some other reason.

I don't agree that teacher's should be paid more to do something that lasts for a year because they scored higher on a test that lasts for hours, and I don't think it is possible to pay teachers by merit in most situations. I am going to write some things about each of these.

Just try to imagine this situation. There are two first grade teachers. One teacher scored much higher on a standardized test. Both teachers have to help their students learn about reading. But the teacher with the higher score for some reason or another can't deal with these young children. They do not have the patience to work with them all day long. It could be that the teacher with the higher score does not know how to teach reading. The teacher with the lower score is just the opposite. That other teacher works well with the children they have the patience to deal with them and they know how to teach reading. I do not think we could find a person anywhere who would not think that this low scoring teacher is the one we would want in the classroom.

The idea of paying teachers by merit is a part of this question. I think paying teachers in that way would be great if there was any way to tell that a teacher was the reason students were doing better or poorer as they learned. But I do not think there is. I can think of classes I was in where we did better because of the students who were in my class. To be honest the teacher did not help that much. But if you pay by merit then the teacher would have been paid more, not because of the teacher, but because of the students. That is not right.

In conclusion, I disagree with the statement because there is not evidence that indicates that teachers with higher standardized scores are better teachers. If some teachers have higher standardized scores, it is probably something about them and not the scores they received. This idea of paying teachers this way is an idea that should not be used in schools.

Informative/Explanatory (Source-Based) Essay

Compare your essay to the sample essay that follows. You may want to show your essay to an English expert for further evaluation.

Here is an essay that would receive a rating of 5 or 6.

The issues raised in these essays have mainly to do with safety, but also with the continued use of nuclear reactors for power generation. Both authors agree that a strength of nuclear energy is that it is a renewable energy source with low greenhouse emissions.

Each author agrees there can be health risks associated with nuclear power generation. However, the Quinson seeks to minimize the risks, noting that, "Nuclear power has caused fewer fatalities per unit of energy generated." Personally, I don't find that particularly reassuring because the introduction notes that nuclear energy generates just 5% of the world's energy. Patrick takes a more ominous tone pointing out the three major nuclear accidents that occurred in the last 25 years writing ". . . nuclear reactor . . . is a ticking time bomb—a nuclear bomb." (Patrick)

The authors quite unusually each downplay the role of nuclear power in energy production. Quinson points out that coal is far and away the fuel used most often to produce power. Patrick seconds this idea, noting that solar power could fill the void left by the absence of nuclear energy but never the void left by the absence of coal.

Quinson brings in an additional point that there are "over 150 naval vessels powered by nuclear energy." (Quinson) Quite unusually, it seems to me, Patrick also believes a "ship at sea" (Patrick) might be an appropriate use of nuclear power.

Frankly, a somewhat confusing picture appears from these position papers. Quinson indicates that nuclear power is generally good, with some reservations. On the other hand

Patrick says nuclear reactors are like nuclear bombs, most of the time. Each author likes nuclear power's reliability and absence of greenhouse emissions. I am drawn to Patrick's point that if some cataclysmic event occurs the results could be catastrophic. It's this final point that convinces me that Patrick's position is most appropriate.

Discussion

This essay identifies the main issues and notes that the issue of nuclear safety is the most prominent issue. The essay uses information from the two position papers, both by paraphrasing and by quoting, and in each case cites the appropriate position paper. This paper helps the reader see where the authors of the position papers actually agree and brings the essay writer's own perspectives to the issue. The essay is long enough for a rater to place it in the upper third, uses language well, and is free of any meaningful English errors.

This essay would receive a rating of 3 or 4.

The best way to look at and see the main points about nuclear energy is to take each author's position one at a time..It seems that you either think it's good or you think it is bad. We can see that Quinson supports nuclear energy, while it looks like Patrick mainly opposes it.

As I see it Quinson mainly shows his support for nuclear energy by going to great lengths to explain off the nuclear accident with that tusomi in Japan. In this position paper. "Universal assessment of this tragedy is that it was essentially man made." I mean that may be true but it does not seem that should make much difference. The problem would not have happened if the reactor was not there. So what difference does it make. But this position paper sticks to its guns and add to "all investigations agree that the reactor should never have been built where it was." Quinson also brings all the ships that use reactors to make them work, but even Patrick seems to think that is OK too.

Patrick uses a title that shows opposition right away with the words "Nuclear Energy—A Ticking Atom Bomb." But when you start to read the paper it is hard to tell for sure that Patrick really is opposed. That's because of the fact that the first paragraph lists some ways that nuclear energy could be useful.

That all changes in the second paragraph. That is when we read that there "been three major accidents in the last 25 years." (Patrick) I remember reading about the one in Japan and it seemed pretty bad to me. Then Patrick goes further, "No one really knows the death toll from these accidents, and the long term impact of radiation exposure." I agree with that. I think that people were effected by the radiation from first atom bomb for decades and decades after the bomb was dropped. That would have to be true for other nuclear accidents.

Quinson is really on the defensive from the very beginning, and Patrick starts out too with a few positive things to say about nuclear power. But when you read on it seems that Quinson's paper is based on what Quinson believes, and that Patrick's paper provides more factual information.

Discussion

This essay lays out each position paper's point of view and frequently brings in the writer's own experiences. The essay mentions information from both sources and usually cites the source of the information. The essay summarizes the writer's opinion of the strength of the argument in each position paper. The essay does not fully integrate a discussion of the issues. While grammar and usage are generally fine, there are errors including sentence fragments, wordiness, and grammar. The appropriate references, completeness of the essay, and usage earn this essay a rating of 4.

This essay would earn a rating of 2.

The way I read these essays, the authors of the paper each agree that nuclear energy is a problem. One says nuclear energy is a ticking time bomb. The other says that nuclear energy is not all bad but doesn't that mean that it's at least somewhat bad. They writing about different stuff.

It's pretty hard to argue that radiation from a generator is not like radiation from a bomb. Once you see that the rest of it is just talk. These authors know how to make their own points, but is that the reason for writing a paper to show that you know how to make a point.

They each agree that nuclear energy is dangerous, it's just that one tries to convince you that it is not as dangerous as you might think it is. OK, I get it nuclear energy is dangerous.

Discussion

Even a well-written essay that cited sources, but was this short, could never earn a rating above 3. The absence of any citations and the poor development mean that the highest rating possible is a 2. The rating could not be higher unless both the development and the citations were significantly improved.

Mathematics Test

1. **(D)** The coin is a fair coin so no matter how many times you flip it the probability that the coin will land heads up is always $\frac{1}{2}$.

2. **(C)** Here is the best way to solve this problem. Find a product that equals 51.

   To see this only occurs in choice (C), multiply $(-12 - 5) \times -3$ (the first term in the second expression). $(-12 - 5) \times -3 = -17 \times -3 = 51$

   To find out if (C) is correct, work out the entire problem. Remember to do the work in parentheses first.

   $$(-12 - 5)\,(-3 + \frac{3y}{17}) =$$

   $$-17\,(-3 + \frac{3y}{17}) =$$

   $$(-17)\,(-3) + (-17)\,(\frac{3y}{17}) = \text{(That is the distributive property.)}$$

   $$= 51 - \frac{(17)(3y)}{17} = 51 - 3y$$

3. $\left(\dfrac{12}{13}\right)$ Solve the equation.

   $$3x(5 + 2) = 4(2x + 3) = 15x + 6x = 8x + 12 \quad 21x = 8x + 12$$

   Subtract $8x$ from each side of the equation.

   $$
   \begin{array}{rl}
   21x = & 8x + 12 \\
   -8x & -8x \\
   \hline
   13x = & 12 \\
   \end{array}
   $$

   $$x = \frac{12}{13}$$

4. **(D)** Remember that "up" (add) and "down" (subtract) describe the movement of the y-coordinate, while "left" (subtract) and "right" (add) describe the movement of the x-coordinate.

The original coordinates of point A are $(-2, 3)$

Add 3 to find the x-coordinate $-2 + 3 = 1$. Subtract 7 to find the y-coordinate: $3 - 7 = -4$

The coordinates of point A after the translation are $(1, -4)$.

You can trace the movement on the graph to confirm your answer.

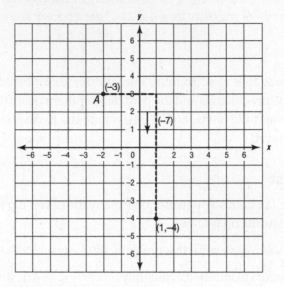

5. **(C)** Solve the equation.

$$\frac{3}{4}x - 7 = 12$$

(First add 7 to each side.) $\quad \frac{3}{4}x - 7 \,(+7) = 12 \,(+7)$

$$\frac{3}{4}x = 19$$

(Next multiply both sides by $\frac{4}{3}$.) $\quad \left(\frac{4}{3}\right)\left(\frac{3}{4}x\right) = 19 \times \frac{4}{3}$

$$x = 19 \times \frac{4}{3}$$

$$x = \frac{76}{3}$$

$$x = 25\frac{1}{3}$$

6. **(B, C)** $\sqrt{2}$ is just to the left of x.

First use the calculator square root key to estimate that $\sqrt{2}$ is about 1.41.
x will be greater than 1.41.

$\frac{5}{2}$ is just to the right of x. x will be less than $2\frac{1}{2}$.

Look at each number in turn.

(A) 1.26; No, 1.26 is less than 1.41

(B) 2.333 . . . (= $2\frac{1}{3}$); Yes, $2\frac{1}{3}$ is more than 1.42 and less than $2\frac{1}{2}$.

(C) $2\frac{3}{8}$; Yes, $2\frac{3}{8}$ is more than 1.41 and less than $2\frac{1}{2}$ $(2\frac{4}{8})$.

(D) $2\frac{1}{2}$; No, $2\frac{1}{2} = \frac{5}{2}$.

(E) 4; No, 4 is greater than $\frac{5}{2}$.

7. **(B)** These steps solve this equation.

Here are the steps for the other equations.

(A) Subtract 8 from each side and then divide each side by –3.
(C) Add 3 to each side and divide each side by 8.
(D) Subtract 8 from each side and then divide each side by 3.
(E) Add 8 to each side and then divide each side by –3.

8. **(E)** The ratio 7 to 14 (7 : 14) can be expressed as 1 : 2. Use the equation $x + 2x = 54$, where x represents the number of rainy days and $2x$ the number of sunny days. The total number of days equals 54, so $x + 2x = 54$ and $3x = 54$, $x = 18$.

$x = 18$, the number of rainy days

$2x = 36$, the number of sunny days

$18 + 36 = 54$. That checks.

9. **(D)** The car traveled for a total of 5 hours. Subtract to find how far the car traveled: $393 - 78 = 315$ miles. Divide by 5 to find the rate per hour: $315 \div 5 = 63$. The rate is 63 miles an hour. At 2:00 P.M. the car traveled for 3 hours. Multiply $63 \times 3 = 189$ to find how many miles the car had traveled at 2:00 P.M.

10. **(A)** The answer is a fraction with the total number of the team's points in the denominator and the total number of the player's three-point baskets in the numerator. There is no equation to solve.

11. **(D)** There are 26 letters in the alphabet. When 2 consonants were removed that left 24 letters, 5 of which were vowels. The probability of randomly picking a vowel is $\frac{5}{24}$.

12. **(D)** First find the lowest and highest rainfall amounts. The lowest amount is 0; there were two days with no rainfall.

To find the highest amount look first in the tenths place. The largest digit in the tenths place is 6. There are two rainfall amounts with 6 in the tenths place: 0.622 and 0.601.

0.622 is the largest of these two numbers.

Subtract the smallest amount of rainfall from the largest amount to find the range.

$$0.622 - 0 = 0.622$$

13. **(C)** First look at the graph to find two points where the graph crosses the intersection of two coordinate lines. The most obvious ones in this graph are (3, 1) and (–1, –3). Find a table with these two sets of values. There is just one table with these two points, choice (C). Check out the other two points to be sure they fit the pattern. They do. This is the correct choice.

14. **(A)** First find the volume of the main tank shown in the diagram.

Use the calculator. Remember the answer is in cubic feet.

$$V = \pi \cdot r^2 \cdot h$$

$$V = 3.14 \times 2^2 \times 10 = 3.14 \times 40 = 125.6 \text{ cubic feet}$$

Now add to find the total size of all four cylinders.

$$1 + \frac{1}{2} + \frac{1}{4} + \frac{1}{8} = 1 + \frac{4}{8} + \frac{2}{8} + \frac{1}{8} = 1\frac{7}{8}$$

It turns out $\frac{7}{8}$ has a decimal representation of 0.875. You would get the same answer if you used the fraction $\frac{7}{8}$.

The total size of all four tanks is 1.875.

Multiply $1.875 \times 125.6 = 235.5$. (Remember you have a calculator.)

The total volume of all four tanks is 235.5 cubic feet.

15. **(B)** Multiply to find her bonus: $\$1{,}200 \times 15\% = \$180$

She needs to work enough hours to make $\$500 - \$180 = \$320$.

Divide to find the number of hours: $\dfrac{\$320}{18} = 17 \text{ R}14$

17 hours would be too few so she would have to work a minimum of 18 hours.

Notice that choices (C), (D), and (E) are incorrect because they are *more* than the minimum number of hours she needed to work.

16. **(286)** You could probably see that you cannot find the values of a, b, c, and d directly. You need to use trial and error. We know that the numbers will be from the set 1, 2, 3, 4, 5, 6, 7, 8, 9, 10, 11, 12, 13, 14, 15 . . . That's going to make it a lot easier.

$5a + 3b = 19$. Just a few guesses will show us that $a = 2$ and $b = 3$.

$4c + 2d = 14$ Just a few more guesses shows us that $c = 1$ and $d = 5$.

Substitute these values in the expression.

$$(5a + 3c)\,(4b + 2d) =$$
$$(5 \cdot 2 + 3 \cdot 1)\,(4 \cdot 3 + 2 \cdot 5) =$$
$$(10 + 3)\,(12 + 10) = \text{(Use the order of operations.)}$$
$$= 13 \cdot 22 = 286$$

17. **(A)** The "tight" diagonal pattern from lower left to upper right best shows a positive correlation. Choice (B) shows a negative correlation. Choices (C) and (E) show no correlation. Choice (D) suggests a slight positive correlation but not the strong positive correlation found in choice (A).

18. **(A)** Divide to find what percent $\$624{,}000$ is of $\$2{,}600{,}000$. $624{,}000 \div 2{,}600{,}000 = 0.24 = 24$ percent. The town needs 24 percent for police, 2 percent more than in the pie chart. Take 2 percent from sanitation, leaving 22 percent for sanitation.

19. **(B)** To find what percent 520 is of 1300, divide 520 by 1300 to get the decimal representation of percent. Then multiply by 100 to get the answer into percent form.

20. **(D)** Choice (A) is not true because none of the windows are squares. All of the windows are rectangles, so choices (B), (C), and (E) are not true. Choice (D) alone meets both of the requirements.

21. **(B)** The larger square has seven of the smaller squares along each side. The area of the smaller square is 4 in.^{2}, so each side of the smaller square is 2 in. The length of one side of the larger square is 2 in. $\times$ 7 $=$ 14 in.

22. **(E)** The only number in the table written in scientific notation is (1C) 5.3794 $\times$ 10^1. Scientific notation is written as a number between 1 and 10 times a power of 10. Choice (E) is the value of 5.3794 $\times$ 10^1.

23. **(C)** Person 5 had 3 more awards than person 3. Therefore person 5 had 3 $\times$ 20 $=$ 60 more awards than person 3.

24. **(D)** $A \cdot B + C = -4 \cdot 2 + 11 = -8 + 11 = 3$

25. **(A)** The mean is 39.4 while the median is 39. The difference is 0.4 of a year.

26. **(C)** Only choice (C) has four pieces where two have crusts.

27. **(D)** The formula for the area of a circle is πr^2.

$$\text{Area of the inner circle} = \pi(2)^2 = 4\pi$$
$$\text{Area of the outer circle} = \pi(4)^2 = 16\pi$$
$$16\pi - 4\pi = 12\pi$$

That is the area for the portion of the outer circle outside the inner circle. Choices (A), (B), and (C) are all incorrect because these choices do not show the correct area.

28. **(C)** If 62.5 percent are cats, then 37.5 percent are not cats. Divide 37.5 by 3 to find that each animal is 12.5 percent of the total. Then divide 62.5 percent by 12.5 percent (62.5 ÷ 12.5 = 5) to find there are 5 cats.

29. **(E)** Add the numbers that are outside the "swimming circle." 13 + 12 + 9 = 34, the number of students who participate in sports except swimming.

30. **(E)** You are looking for the number multiplied by 45,000 that equals 0.45. Divide: 0.45 ÷ 45,000 = 0.00001.

31. **(B)** The decimal equivalents of each answer choice are:

(A) $0.\overline{4}$

(B) $0.4\overline{8}$

(C) $0.\overline{4}$

(D) $0.\overline{4}$

(E) $0.\overline{4}$

Choices (A), (C), (D), and (E) are equal.

32. **(C)** It is $11\frac{1}{4}$ hours from 7:45 A.M. to 7:00 P.M. Subtract 1 hour for lunch. That leaves $10\frac{1}{4}$ work hours.

$$10\frac{1}{4} \times \$20 = \$205$$

33. **(D)** $(0, 1)$ shows a *y*-intercept of 1. $(1, 0)$ shows an *x*-intercept of 1.

34. **(D)** The formula for the area of a trapezoid is $A = \dfrac{h}{2}(b_1 + b_2)$.

    However, in the new trapezoid the length of each base is doubled; therefore, the formula is

$$A = \frac{h}{2}(2b_1 + 2b_2) = \frac{h}{2} \cdot 2(b_1 + b_2) = h(b_1 + b_2)$$

35. **(D)** Jack's lowest weight is 170 pounds and Jack's highest weight is 190 pounds.

$$170 \div 190 \approx 0.89 \approx 89\%$$

36. **(D)** The trapezoid, choice (D), has only one pair of congruent sides.

37. **(B)** Each diameter in choice (B) is part of the perimeter. When answering this question, consider only the perimeter and not any segments within a figure.

38. **(D)**

    (A) $3^4 \times 9 \times 12 = 3^4 \times 9 \times 4 \times 3 = 3^5 \times 4 \times 9$

    (B) $3^3 \times 27 \times 12 = 3^3 \times 9 \times 3 \times 4 \times 3 = 3^5 \times 4 \times 9$
    This is also choice (A).

    (C) $3^5 \times 36 = 3^5 \times 4 \times 9$
    This is also choice (A).

    (D) $3^3 \times 9^3 \times 4 = 3^3 \times 3^2 \times 9^2 \times 4 = 3^5 \times 4 \times 9^2 \neq 3^5 \times 4 \times 9$
    This is **not** choice (A).

    (E) $3^5 \times 4 \times 9$
    This is also choice (A). We do not need to calculate.

    Choice (D) is the only choice not equivalent to the others.

39. **(B)** $45{,}250 + 78{,}375 + 52{,}540 + 62{,}325 = 238{,}490 \approx 238{,}000$

40. **(D)** The *y*-value (vertical axis) moves up as the *x*-value (horizontal axis) moves right.

41. **(C)** $65\% = 0.65 \qquad (0.65) \cdot \$400 = \$260$

42. **(C)** $\dfrac{1}{2} = \dfrac{6}{12}, \ \dfrac{2}{3} = \dfrac{8}{12}, \ \dfrac{5}{12}$

$$\left(\frac{6}{12} + \frac{8}{12} + \frac{5}{12} \right) \div 3 = \frac{19}{12} \div 3 = \frac{19}{12} \cdot \frac{1}{3} = \frac{19}{36}$$

43. **(C)** In a standard deck of cards there are 12 "face cards"—4 kings, 4 queens, and 4 jacks out of 52 possible cards.

$$P(\text{face card}) = \frac{12}{52} = \frac{3}{13}$$

44. **(D)** Change 2.3 to 23 and then round to 20. (This involves multiplying by 10.) 10^5 means multiply by 100,000. So you need to move the decimal four more places to the right.

45. **(E)** Figures A, B, C, and D show a circle within a circle, a sphere, a cylinder, and a cone. A cube, represented in Figure E, does not contain a circle.

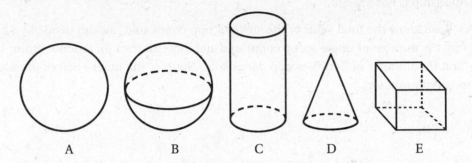

A   B   C   D   E

46. **(C)** The temperature on the thermometer is 86°F. It moved down 8° from 10:00 A.M. when it was 94°F. The temperature moved at a constant rate of 2° an hour, which means it moved down 4° from 10:00 A.M. to a noon temperature of 90°F. Be careful. The problem says the temperature is getting lower as the day goes on.

47. **(A)** $6(2) + 2(-1) = 12 - 2 = 10$

48. **(B)** There are 18 tickets and you can buy 16 of the tickets for $120 (4 · $30) and the remaining two tickets at $16.

$$\$120 + \$16 = \$136$$

49. **(A)** $4A + 6 = 2(B - 1)$

Divide by 2 on both sides: $2A + 3 = B - 1$
Add 1 to both sides: $2A + 4 = B$

$$B = 2A + 4$$

50. **(C)** Use this chart

Kilo	Hecto	Deka	Unit	Deci	Centi	Milli
1,000	100	10	1	0.1	0.01	0.001

Given below is each answer choice in meters.

(A) 230 meters
(B) 230 meters
(C) 23 meters
(D) 230 meters
(E) 230 meters

Choice (C) is not equal to the others.

51. **(E)** $101 + 4 = 105 = 7 \cdot 15$

52. **(A)** $5 - 3\frac{1}{5} = 1\frac{4}{5}$, which is a little less than 2 miles.

53. **(B)** If Barbara earns $17 every 2 hours, she earns $\frac{\$17}{2} = \$8.50$ per hour. In 45 hours she earns $\$8.50 \cdot 45 = \$382.50$.

54. **(A)** There are 4 pictures of televisions in January and 6 pictures of televisions in December; $\frac{6}{4} = 1.5$. It does not matter how many televisions each picture represents, the answer will still be the same.

55. **(B, E)** The diameter of a circle is twice the radius. This relationship is correctly shown in both choice (B) and choice (E). Choices (A), (C), and (D) are incorrect because this relationship is not present.

56. **(A)** If we know the total value of the single-scoop cones sold, we can divide by $2.50 to find the number of single-scoop cones sold and then subtract that number from 100 to find the number of double-scoop cones sold. None of the other choices produces enough information.

Practice Core 2

7

Directions: You will read selections followed by one or more questions. Most items have five answer choices with one correct answer. A few items may have one or more correct answers. The answer choices for these questions will be within boxes. Select the best answer choices based on what the selection states or implies and mark that letter on the test.

---

1. Cellular phones, once used by the very rich, are now available to almost everyone. With one of these phones, you can call just about anywhere from just about anywhere. Since the use of these phones will increase, we need to find legal and effective ways for law enforcement agencies to monitor calls.

   Which of the following choices is the best summary of this passage?

   Ⓐ Criminals are taking advantage of cellular phones to avoid legal wiretaps.
   Ⓑ The ability to use a cellular phone to call from just about anywhere makes it harder to find people who are using the phones.
   Ⓒ The increase in cellular phone use means that we will have to find legal ways to monitor cellular calls.
   Ⓓ Cellular phones are like regular phones with a very long extension cord.
   Ⓔ Since cellular phones are more available to everyone, they are certainly more available to criminals.

2. The moon takes about 28 days to complete a cycle around Earth. Months, 28 days long, grew out of this cycle. Twelve of these months made up a year. But ancient astronomers realized that it took Earth about 365 days to make one revolution of the sun. Extra days were added to some months and the current calendar was born.

   What details does the author use to support the main purpose of the passage?

   Ⓐ Describes the moon's movement around Earth
   Ⓑ Is based on the sun's position
   Ⓒ Is based on Earth's rotation and position of the moon
   Ⓓ Combines features of the moon's cycle and Earth's revolution
   Ⓔ Was based on the number 12

3. Occasionally, college students will confuse correlation with cause and effect. Correlation just describes the degree of relationship between two factors. For example, there is a positive correlation between poor handwriting and intelligence. However, writing more poorly will not make you more intelligent.

   The author's main reason for writing this passage is to

   Ⓐ explain the difference between correlation and cause and effect.
   Ⓑ encourage improved penmanship.
   Ⓒ explain how college students can improve their intelligence.
   Ⓓ make those with poor penmanship feel more comfortable.
   Ⓔ describe a cause-and-effect relationship.

It is striking how uninformed today's youth are about Acquired Immune Deficiency Syndrome. Because of their youth and ignorance, many young adults engage in high-risk behavior. Many of these young people do not realize that the disease can be contracted through almost any contact with an infected person's blood and bodily fluids. Some do not realize that symptoms of the disease may not appear for ten years or more. Others do not realize that the danger in sharing needles to inject intravenous drugs comes from the small amounts of another's blood injected during this process. A massive education campaign is needed to fully inform today's youth about AIDS.

4. The main idea of this passage is

Ⓐ previous education campaigns have failed.

Ⓑ AIDS develops from the HIV virus.

Ⓒ the general public is not fully informed about AIDS.

Ⓓ people should not share intravenous needles.

Ⓔ young people are not adequately informed about AIDS.

5. Which of the following is the best summary of the statement about what young people don't realize about how AIDS can be contracted?

Ⓐ The symptoms may not appear for ten years or more.

Ⓑ AIDS is contracted because of ignorance.

Ⓒ AIDS is contracted from intravenous needles.

Ⓓ AIDS is contracted through contact with infected blood or bodily fluids.

Ⓔ You will not contract AIDS if you know what to avoid.

6. Which of the following words best describes how the author views young people and their knowledge of AIDS?

Ⓐ Stupid

Ⓑ Unaware

Ⓒ Dumb

Ⓓ Unintelligible

Ⓔ Reluctant

---

7. When Lyndon Johnson succeeded John F. Kennedy, he was able to gain congressional approval for programs suggested by Kennedy but never implemented. These programs, called Great Society programs, included low-income housing and project Head Start. To some, this made Johnson a better president.

Based on this statement, we can conclude that Johnson

Ⓐ was a better president than Kennedy.

Ⓑ gained approval for programs proposed by Kennedy.

Ⓒ was a member of a Great Society.

Ⓓ was president before Kennedy.

Ⓔ originally lived in low-income housing.

QUESTIONS 8 AND 9 ARE BASED ON THIS PASSAGE.

I think women are discriminated against; however, I think men are discriminated against just as much as women. It's just a different type of discrimination. Consider these two facts: Men die about 6 years earlier than women, and men are the only people who can be drafted into the armed forces. That's discrimination!

8. What is the author's main point in writing this passage?

Ⓐ Men are discriminated against more than women are.
Ⓑ Both sexes are discriminated against.
Ⓒ Women are not discriminated against.
Ⓓ On average, men die earlier than women.
Ⓔ Men are not discriminated against.

9. Which of the following could be substituted for the word *drafted* in the next to last sentence?

Ⓐ Inducted against their will
Ⓑ Signed up
Ⓒ Pushed in by society
Ⓓ Drawn in by peer pressure
Ⓔ Serve in a foreign country

_____

QUESTIONS 10 AND 11 ARE BASED ON THIS PASSAGE.

Alice in Wonderland, written by Charles Dodgson under the pen name Lewis Carroll, is full of symbolism, so much so that a book titled *Understanding Alice* was written containing the original text with marginal notes explaining the symbolic meanings.

10. By symbolism, the author of the passage above meant that much of *Alice in Wonderland*

Ⓐ was written in a foreign language.
Ⓑ contained many mathematical symbols.
Ⓒ contained no pictures.
Ⓓ had a figurative meaning.
Ⓔ was set in a special type.

11. Which of the following details does the author use to support the description of *Understanding Alice*?

Ⓐ Explanations of the musical meaning of the text
Ⓑ Notes that may not have been completely correct
Ⓒ Notes written next to the main text
Ⓓ Marginal notes written by Carroll but not included in the original book
Ⓔ An explanation of the text by Alice Liddell, the real Alice

12. Following a concert, a fan asked a popular singer why the songs sounded so different in person than on the recording. The singer responded, "I didn't record my emotions!"

Which of the following conclusions is suggested by this passage?

Ⓐ The singer was probably not in a good mood during that performance.
Ⓑ The fan was being intrusive, and the performer was "brushing her off."
Ⓒ The performance was outdoors where sound quality is different.
Ⓓ The fan didn't realize the controls available for studio recordings.
Ⓔ The performance may vary depending on the mood of the performer.

QUESTIONS 13–18 ARE BASED ON THIS PASSAGE.

The War of 1812 is one of the least understood conflicts in American history. However, many events associated with the war are among the best remembered from American History. The war began when the United States invaded British colo-
Line nies in Canada. The invasion failed, and the United States was quickly put on the
(5) defensive. Most Americans are not aware of how the conflict began. During the war, the *USS Constitution* (Old Ironsides) was active against British ships in the Atlantic. Captain William Perry, sailing on Lake Erie, was famous for yelling to his shipmates, "Don't give up the ship." Most Americans remember Perry and his famous plea, but not where or in which war he was engaged.
(10) Most notably, British troops sacked and burned Washington, D.C. during this conflict. Subsequent British attacks on Fort McHenry near Baltimore were repulsed by American forces. It was during one of these battles that Francis Scott Key wrote the "Star Spangled Banner" while a prisoner on a British ship. The "rockets red glare, bombs bursting in air" referred to ordnance used by the British to attack the fort. Many
(15) Americans mistakenly believe that the "Star Spangled Banner" was written during or shortly after the Revolutionary War.

13. All the following statements can be implied from the passage EXCEPT:

Ⓐ The British did not start the war.
Ⓑ Francis Scott Key was not at Fort McHenry when he wrote the "Star Spangled Banner."
Ⓒ The rockets referred to in the "Star Spangled Banner" were part of a celebration.
Ⓓ The British army entered Washington, D.C., during the war.
Ⓔ The nickname for the *USS Constitution* was Old Ironsides.

14. Which of the following words is the most appropriate replacement for *sacked* in line 10?

Ⓐ Entered
Ⓑ Ravished
Ⓒ Invaded
Ⓓ Enclosed
Ⓔ Encapsulated

15. With which of the following statements would the author agree about the difference referred to in the passage between Perry's involvement in the War of 1812 and the way many Americans remember his involvement?

Ⓐ Perry was a drafter of the Constitution and later served on the *Constitution* in the Atlantic, although many Americans don't remember that.
Ⓑ Perry served in the Great Lakes, but many Americans don't remember that.
Ⓒ Perry served in Washington, D.C., although many Americans don't remember that.
Ⓓ Perry served on the *Constitution* at Fort McHenry during the writing of the "Star Spangled Banner," although many Americans do not remember that.
Ⓔ Perry served on the *Constitution* in the Atlantic, but many Americans don't remember that.

16. What can be inferred about Francis Scott Key from lines 12–13 of the passage?

Ⓐ He was killed in the battle.
Ⓑ All his papers were confiscated by the British after the battle.
Ⓒ He was released by or escaped from the British after the battle.
Ⓓ He returned to Britain where he settled down.
Ⓔ He was a British spy.

17. Based on the passage, which of the following words best describes the United States' role in the War of 1812?

Ⓐ Colonizer
Ⓑ Neutral
Ⓒ Winner
Ⓓ Loser
Ⓔ Aggressor

18. Which of the following questions is best answered from this passage?

Ⓐ Why did the Americans fight the British in the War of 1812?
Ⓑ Why did the Revolutionary War continue into the 1800s?
Ⓒ Why did the British renew the Revolutionary War during the 1800s?
Ⓓ Why were many Americans unaware of events associated with the War of 1812?
Ⓔ Why should Americans remember the treachery of the army that invaded Washington during this war?

QUESTIONS 19–24 ARE BASED ON THIS PASSAGE.

Computer-based word processing programs have spelling checkers and even a thesaurus to find synonyms and antonyms for highlighted words. To use the thesaurus, the student just types in the word, and a series of synonyms and antonyms appears on the computer screen. The program can also show recommended spellings for misspelled words. I like having a computer program that performs these mechanical aspects of writing. However, these programs do not teach about spelling or word meanings. A person could type in a word, get a synonym and have not the slightest idea what either meant.

Relying on this mindless way of checking spelling and finding synonyms, students will be completely unfamiliar with the meanings of the words they use. In fact, one of the most common misuses is to include a word that is spelled correctly but used incorrectly in the sentence.

It may be true that a strictly mechanical approach to spelling is used by some teachers. There certainly is a place for students who already understand word meanings to use a computer program that relieves the drudgery of checking spelling and finding synonyms. But these computer programs should never and can never replace the teacher. Understanding words—their uses and meanings—should precede this more mechanistic approach.

19. What is the main idea of this passage?

   Ⓐ Mechanical spell checking is one part of learning about spelling.
   Ⓑ Programs are not effective for initially teaching about spelling and synonyms.
   Ⓒ Teachers should use word processing programs as one part of instruction.
   Ⓓ Students who use these programs won't learn about spelling.
   Ⓔ The programs rely too heavily on a student's typing ability.

20. Which of the following information is found in the passage?
    Select all that apply.

   Ⓐ The type of computer that runs the word processor
   Ⓑ The two main outputs of spell checking and thesaurus programs
   Ⓒ An explanation of how to use the word-processing program to teach about spelling and synonyms

21. What is the author's attitude toward spell checking and thesaurus programs?

   Ⓐ That you just have to type in the word
   Ⓑ That the synonyms and alternative spellings are done very quickly
   Ⓒ That the difficult mechanical aspects are performed
   Ⓓ That you don't have to know how to spell to use them
   Ⓔ That they can't replace teachers

22. Which of the following questions could be answered from the information in the passage?

   Ⓐ When is it appropriate to use spell checking and thesaurus programs?
   Ⓑ How does the program come up with recommended spellings?
   Ⓒ What type of spelling learning experiences should students have?
   Ⓓ Why do schools buy these word processing programs?
   Ⓔ Which word program does the author recommend?

23. Which of the following statements could be used in place of the first sentence of the last paragraph?

   Ⓐ It may be true that some strict teachers use a mechanical approach.
   Ⓑ It may be true that a stringently mechanical approach is used by some teachers.
   Ⓒ It may be true that inflexible mechanical approaches are used by some teachers.
   Ⓓ It may be true that the mechanical approach used by some teachers is too rigorous.
   Ⓔ It may be true that some teachers use only a mechanical approach.

24. According to this passage, what could be the result of a student's unfamiliarity with the meanings of words or synonyms?

  Ⓐ Using a program to display the alternative spellings
  Ⓑ Relying on mindless ways of checking spelling and finding synonyms
  Ⓒ Strictly mechanical approaches
  Ⓓ Using microcomputers to find synonyms for highlighted words
  Ⓔ Being able to just type in a word

QUESTIONS 25–28 ARE BASED ON THIS PASSAGE.

As a child he read the *Hardy Boys* series of books and was in awe of the author, Franklin Dixon. As an adult, he read a book entitled the *Ghost of the Hardy Boys*, which revealed that there was no Franklin Dixon and that ghost writers had authored the books. The authors were apparently working for a large publishing syndicate.

25. Which of the following is the likely intent of the author of this passage?

  Ⓐ To describe a book-publishing practice
  Ⓑ To contrast fiction and fact
  Ⓒ To contrast childhood and adulthood
  Ⓓ To correct the record
  Ⓔ To dissuade children from reading the *Hardy Boys* books

26. Which of the following best describes the author's attitude as an adult toward Franklin Dixon?

  Ⓐ Awe
  Ⓑ Childlike
  Ⓒ Syndicated
  Ⓓ Disappointment
  Ⓔ Satisfaction

27. What does the word *Ghost* in the title of the second mentioned book refer to?

  Ⓐ A person who has died or was dead at the time the book was published
  Ⓑ A person who writes books without credit
  Ⓒ A person who influences the way a book is written
  Ⓓ The mystical images of the mind that affect the way any author writes
  Ⓔ A person who edits a book after the author has submitted it for publication

28. Which of the following would NOT be an acceptable replacement for the word *awe* in the first sentence?

  Ⓐ Wonder
  Ⓑ Admiration
  Ⓒ Esteem
  Ⓓ Aplomb
  Ⓔ Respect

The Iroquois nation consisted of five main tribes—Cayuga, Mohawk, Oneida, Onondaga, and Seneca. Called the Five Nations or the League of Five Nations, these tribes occupied much of New York State. Since the tribes were arranged from east to west, the region they occupied was called the long house of the Iroquois.

The Iroquois economy was based mainly on agriculture. The main crop was corn, but they also grew pumpkins, beans, and fruit. The Iroquois used wampum (hollow beads) for money, and records were woven into wampum belts.

The Iroquoian Nation had a remarkable democratic structure, spoke a common Algonquin language, and were adept at fighting. These factors had made the Iroquois a dominant power by the early American colonial period. In the period just before the Revolutionary War, Iroquoian conquest had overcome most other Indian tribes in the northeastern United States as far west as the Mississippi River.

During the Revolutionary War, most Iroquoian tribes sided with the British. At the end of the Revolutionary War the tribes scattered, with some migrating to Canada. Only remnants of the Seneca and Onondaga tribes remained on their tribal lands.

29. Which of the following statements drawn from the passage is opinion rather than fact?

    Ⓐ The main crop was corn.
    Ⓑ The Iroquois used wampum (hollow beads) for money.
    Ⓒ These factors made the Iroquois a dominant power.
    Ⓓ Records were woven into wampum belts.
    Ⓔ The Iroquois nation consisted of five main tribes.

30. Which of the following best describes the geographic location of the five Iroquoian tribes?

    Ⓐ The northeastern United States as far west as the Mississippi River
    Ⓑ Southern Canada
    Ⓒ Cayuga
    Ⓓ New York State
    Ⓔ The League of Nations

31. Which of the following best describes why the area occupied by the Iroquois was called the long house of the Iroquois?

    Ⓐ The tribes were arranged as though they occupied different sections of a long house.
    Ⓑ The Iroquois lived in structures called long houses.
    Ⓒ The close political ties among tribes made it seem that they were all living in one house.
    Ⓓ The Iroquois had expanded their original tribal lands through conquest.
    Ⓔ It took weeks to walk the trail connecting all the tribes.

32. According to the passage, which of the following best describes the economic basis for the Iroquoian economy?

    Ⓐ Wampum

    Ⓑ Corn

    Ⓒ Agriculture

    Ⓓ Conquest

    Ⓔ Warfare

QUESTIONS 33–38 ARE BASED ON THIS PASSAGE.

Europeans had started to devote significant resources to medicine when Louis Pasteur was born December 7, 1822. By the time he died in the fall of 1895, he had made enormous contributions to science and founded microbiology. At 32, he was named professor and dean at a French university dedicated to supporting the production of alcoholic beverages. Pasteur immediately began work on yeast and fermentation. He found that he could kill harmful bacteria in the initial brewing process by subjecting the liquid to high temperatures. This finding was extended to milk in the process called pasteurization. This work led him to the conclusion that human disease could be caused by germs. In Pasteur's time, there was a widely held belief that germs were spontaneously generated. Pasteur conducted experiments that proved germs were always introduced and never appeared spontaneously. This result was questioned by other scientists for over a decade. He proved his theory of vaccination and his theory of disease during his work with anthrax, a fatal animal disease. He vaccinated some sheep with weakened anthrax germs and left other sheep unvaccinated. Then he injected all the sheep with a potentially fatal dose of anthrax bacteria. The unvaccinated sheep died while the vaccinated sheep lived. He developed vaccines for many diseases and is best known for his vaccine for rabies. According to some accounts, the rabies vaccine was first tried on a human when a young boy, badly bitten by a rabid dog, arrived at Pasteur's laboratory. The treatment of the boy was successful.

33. What is topic of this passage?

    Ⓐ Microbiology

    Ⓑ Pasteur's scientific discoveries

    Ⓒ Germs and disease

    Ⓓ Science in France

    Ⓔ Louis Pasteur

34. What does the process of pasteurization involve?

    Ⓐ Inoculating

    Ⓑ Experimenting

    Ⓒ Hydrating

    Ⓓ Heating

    Ⓔ Fermenting

35. Which of the following statements could most reasonably be inferred from this passage?

Ⓐ The myth of spontaneous generation was dispelled immediately following Pasteur's experiments on the subject.

Ⓑ The pasteurization of milk can aid in the treatment of anthrax.

Ⓒ Pasteur's discoveries were mainly luck.

Ⓓ Even scientists don't think scientifically all the time.

Ⓔ Injecting sheep with fatal doses of anthrax is one way of vaccinating them.

36. Which of the following statements can be implied from this passage?

Ⓐ That germs do not develop spontaneously was already a widely accepted premise when Pasteur began his scientific work.

Ⓑ Scientists in European countries had made significant progress on the link between germs and disease when Pasteur was born.

Ⓒ Europe was ready for scientific research on germs when Pasteur conducted his experiments.

Ⓓ Most of Pasteur's work was the replication of other work done by French scientists.

Ⓔ The theory that germs could cause human disease was not yet accepted at the time of Pasteur's death.

37. Which of the following choices best characterizes the reason for Pasteur's early work?

Ⓐ To cure humans

Ⓑ To cure animals

Ⓒ To help the French economy

Ⓓ To study germs

Ⓔ To be a professor

38. According to this passage, the rabies vaccine

Ⓐ was developed after Pasteur had watched a young boy bitten by a rabid dog.

Ⓑ was developed from the blood of a rabid dog, which had bitten a young boy.

Ⓒ was developed from the blood of a young boy bitten by a rabid dog.

Ⓓ was developed in addition to the vaccines for other diseases.

Ⓔ was developed in his laboratory where a young boy had died of the disease.

QUESTIONS 39 AND 40 ARE BASED ON THIS PASSAGE.

I believe that there is extraterrestrial life—probably in some other galaxy. It is particularly human to believe that our solar system is the only one that can support intelligent life. But our solar system is only an infinitesimal dot in the infinity of the cosmos and it is just not believable that there is not life out there—somewhere.

39. What is the author of this passage proposing?

    (A) That there is other life in the universe

    (B) That there is no life on Earth

    (C) That humans live on other planets

    (D) That the sun is a very small star

    (E) That we should explore other galaxies

40. The words *infinitesimal* and *infinite* are best characterized by which pair of words below?

    (A) Small and large

    (B) Very small and very large

    (C) Very small and limitless

    (D) Large and limitless

    (E) Small and very large

QUESTIONS 41–44 ARE BASED ON THIS PASSAGE.

(The following passage was excerpted from *The Colored Cadet at West Point, Autobiography of Lieut. Henry Ossian Flipper,* published in 1878. It discusses Flipper's experiences as the first African American graduate from the U.S. Military Academy.)

"It is just possible that some of our readers may not know who Flipper is. For their benefit we make haste to explain that Flipper is the solitary colored cadet now at West Point . . . Flipper's friends declare that he is getting along finely in his
Line studies, and that he is quite up to the standard of the average West Point student.
(5) Nevertheless they intimate that he will never graduate. Flipper, they say, may get as far as first class when he will be 'slaughtered.'

"A correspondent of the *New York Times* takes issue with this opinion. He says there are many 'old heads' who believe Flipper will graduate with honor, and he thinks so too . . .

(10) "The *Chicago Tribune* seems to find it difficult to come to any conclusion concerning Flipper's chances for graduating. It says: 'It is freely asserted that Flipper will never be allowed to graduate; that the prejudice of the regular army instructors against the colored race is insurmountable, and that they will drive away from the Academy by persecution of some petty sort any colored boy who may obtain admittance there. The story
(15) does not seem to have any substantial basis; still, it possesses considerable vitality.'"

41. The main focus of this passage is

    (A) race relations at West Point.

    (B) Flipper's future at West Point.

    (C) the hypocrisy of race prejudice.

    (D) disagreements between rival papers.

    (E) unfairness in the military.

42. Which of the statements below is the author most likely to agree with?

    (A) Flipper's friends do not think he deserves to graduate.

    (B) The *Chicago Tribune* story is false.

    (C) Flippers biggest problem is the high-ranking officers at West Point.

    (D) Flipper deserves a fair chance to graduate.

    (E) Flipper will be killed before he is allowed to graduate.

43. In line 5 the author uses the word *intimate* to mean

Ⓐ to show a relationship.
Ⓑ imply.
Ⓒ declare.
Ⓓ forswear.
Ⓔ emotional awareness.

44. Based on the passage, which of the following questions have regular army instructors asked themselves about Flipper's graduation?

Ⓐ Why should we pass someone who is obviously inferior?
Ⓑ Why not let him pass, and the whole world would see what a poor officer he is?
Ⓒ Why should we be worried about what the newspapers write?
Ⓓ What is the point in failing him?
Ⓔ Where does it say that we have to pass anybody?

Albert Payson Terhune (1872–1942) was a famous author about dogs. He lived on an estate called "The Place" in suburban New Jersey. The Place was filled with collies. Terhune wrote over thirty books about dogs that were popular mainly with younger audiences. Terhune never became the great writer that he wanted to become. Many of his plots were called stilted and overly optimistic. But his unique ability to write about the relationship between dogs and human beings has never been matched in American literature.

45. The author of this passage suggests that despite the criticism and the lack of an adult audience for his books, Terhune's books are timeless because they

Ⓐ focus on dogs.
Ⓑ are set in a suburban setting.
Ⓒ appeal to a largely young audience.
Ⓓ show kinship.
Ⓔ show optimism.

QUESTION 46 IS BASED ON THIS PASSAGE.

Security among aircraft has become a central aspect of American life. Passengers are regularly screened before they enter an aircraft. But much of the cargo that is transported by air goes uninspected. Most of the explosive materials found in air shipments have been uncovered from tips from foreign governments. All of this leads me to the inescapable conclusion that we should divert a lot of our efforts screening airline passengers to screening airline cargo.

46. Which of the following statements, if true, is MOST likely to weaken the author's position about screening airline passengers?

    (A) Airline passengers can hide explosives in body cavities, which makes it much harder to detect them.

    (B) There are many more pieces of air cargo than there are air passengers, making it more difficult to screen packages than passengers.

    (C) Increased screening of packages does not mean that there has to be decreased screening of air passengers.

    (D) Tips from foreign governments may not always be available and not always accurate and we cannot rely on those tips to find troublesome packages.

    (E) The chances of being killed on a plane that blows up because of a bomb are a lot less than the chances of being killed on the highways of America.

QUESTIONS 47–52 ARE BASED ON THE FOLLOWING PASSAGES.

I

Abraham Lincoln is usually rated among the top three presidents of the United States. Some point to his role as president during the Civil War, while others remark on his famous, brief Gettysburg Address.

Line
(5) Lincoln is often cast as antislavery, but the record paints a different picture. He wanted to win the Civil War and preserve the Union, but ending slavery was not his main objective. His much praised Emancipation Proclamation freed only the slaves in rebellious states. While he felt that slavery was morally wrong, he admitted that he was not quite sure how to solve the problem. He was opposed to giving blacks the right to vote and stated in the famous Lincoln-Douglas debates that, "I will say then
(10) that I am not, nor ever have been, in favor of bringing about in any way the social and political equality of the white and black races."

II

Abraham Lincoln was a brilliant president, and he is ranked first in more polls and expert surveys. Lincoln is most associated with the end of slavery in the United States. He often expressed the view that slavery was morally wrong but often noted that he
(15) was at a loss to find a way to end it under the current Constitution.

He was a politician running for office, and he frequently found himself in elections in which being antislavery would have cost him the election. In those circumstances, probably most famously in the Lincoln-Douglas debates, he made statements to counter the charge that he was in favor of negro equality, knowing that to say
(20) otherwise would have cost him the election. Lincoln's statements were a means to an end, but they must be judged by the Thirteenth Amendment abolishing slavery in the United States, which was passed before his assassination.

47. The authors of these passages agree that

    (A) Lincoln was a brilliant president.

    (B) Lincoln was the best president of the United States.

    (C) Lincoln is most associated with ending slavery in the United States.

    (D) Lincoln was a politician.

    (E) The Thirteenth Amendment, known as the Emancipation Proclamation, was associated with Lincoln.

48. Reviewing the passages, we can see that the author of passage II mentions which of the following not mentioned in passage I?

   (A) Lincoln-Douglas debates
   (B) Lincoln's assassination
   (C) Lincoln felt slavery was morally wrong
   (D) The Emancipation Proclamation
   (E) Lincoln's roots in Illinois

49. Which of the following statements best describes the relationship among the passages?

   (A) The passages each mention the Lincoln-Douglas debates.
   (B) Each passage consistently emphasizes Lincoln's antislavery stance.
   (C) The first passage gives Lincoln more credit for ending the Civil War than the second passage.
   (D) Each passage points out that Lincoln did not think slavery was morally wrong.
   (E) The first passage is less forgiving of Lincoln's views of slavery than the second passage.

50. Which of the following extends an action mentioned in the first passage?

   (A) The Thirteenth Amendment
   (B) The Lincoln-Douglas debates
   (C) Freeing slaves in confederate states
   (D) Lincoln's statements as a means to an end
   (E) The Union is preserved

51. Which of the following, if added as the last sentence in the first passage, would weaken the author's stance in that paragraph?

   (A) This just reinforced his pro-slavery views.
   (B) Most observers saw this as a purely political statement.
   (C) Observers were not surprised by this comment.
   (D) He inadvertently omitted "economic."
   (E) This statement just agreed with previous comments.

52. In line 4 of the first passage, the word *cast* most nearly means

   (A) embedded.
   (B) portrayed.
   (C) shadowed.
   (D) molded.
   (E) thrown.

Sun	Mon	Tue	Wed	Thu	Fri	Sat
	1 8:00 A.M. Aerobics A 10:00 A.M. Pilates A 2:00 P.M. Bicycle A	2 8:00 A.M. Aerobics B 10:00 A.M. Pilates B 2:00 P.M. Bicycle B	3 8:00 A.M. Aerobics A 10:00 A.M. Pilates B 2:00 P.M. Bicycle A	4 8:00 A.M. Aerobics C 10:00 A.M. Pilates A 2:00 P.M. Bicycle C	5 8:00 A.M. Aerobics B 10:00 A.M. Pilates C 2:00 P.M. Bicycle A	6 2:00 P.M. Swimming 1
7 OFF	8 8:00 A.M. Aerobics D 10:00 A.M. Pilates D 2:00 P.M. Bicycle D	9 10:00 A.M. Aerobics A 1:00 P.M. Pilates A 4:00 P.M. Bicycle A	10 OFF	11 8:00 A.M. Aerobics E 10:00 A.M. Pilates D 2:00 P.M. Bicycle E	12 6:00 P.M. Swimming 1	13 10:00 A.M. Swimming 3
14 OFF	15 8:00 A.M. Aerobics D 10:00 A.M. Pilates E 2:00 P.M. Bicycle D	16 OFF	17 8:00 A.M. Aerobics G 10:00 A.M. Pilates G 2:00 P.M. Bicycle G	18 6:00 P.M. Swimming 3	19 8:00 A.M. Aerobics A 10:00 A.M. Pilates B 2:00 P.M. Bicycle C	20 OFF
21 10:00 A.M. Swimming 2	22 OFF	23 8:00 A.M. Aerobics D 10:00 A.M. Pilates E 2:00 P.M. Bicycle F	24 8:00 A.M. Aerobics G 10:00 A.M. Pilates G 2:00 P.M. Bicycle G	25 OFF	26 8:00 A.M. Aerobics E 10:00 A.M. Pilates E 2:00 P.M. Bicycle E	27 2:00 P.M. Swimming 4

53. Quinn's college training program requires him to participate in a certain number of activities. He must participate once in each of the lettered and numbered activities for aerobics, pilates, bicycling, and swimming. Because of his schedule, he cannot participate in activities on Mondays and Thursdays.

Which of the following is the best strategy for Quinn to follow to complete the Pilates E activity as early in the month as possible?

Ⓐ Quinn should complete the Pilates E activity on the third day of the month.
Ⓑ Quinn should complete the Pilates E activity on the ninth day of the month.
Ⓒ Quinn should complete the Pilates E activity on the fifteenth day of the month.
Ⓓ Quinn should complete the Pilates E activity on the twenty-third day of the month.
Ⓔ Quinn should complete the Pilates E activity on the twenty-sixth day of the month.

54. Which of the following is the best explanation of why Quinn would take Aerobics A on the ninth of the month?

Ⓐ Aerobics A was offered later that day than on any other day.

Ⓑ There were three hours to rest between aerobics and pilates, not the two hours on other days.

Ⓒ This was the first time Aerobics A was not offered on a Monday or Thursday.

Ⓓ Bicycle A was offered on Friday the fifth and he wanted to avoid a conflict.

Ⓔ There were no activities scheduled for Wednesday the ninth of the month.

55. Based on the calendar, which of the following activities could Quinn have participated in *just one* single time?

Select all that apply.

A Swimming 3

B Aerobics A

C Aerobics D

Even with the glacier covering Alaska, the Aleuts had established a culture on the Aleutian Islands off southern Alaska by 5000 B.C.E. Once glaciers melted in the area, the Eskimo and Intuit tribes established a culture in northern Alaska about 1800 B.C.E. This hunting fishing society has retained much of its ancient character. Navajo peoples lived in these same northern locales before migrating to the Southwest sometime between 1200 C.E. and 1500 C.E. Primitive woodland cultures developed in the northeastern United States about 3000 B.C.E. These cultures included Algonquin tribes such as the Shawnee and the Iroquois Federation. There is evidence that northern woodland tribes may have been exposed to outside contact five hundred years before the arrival of Europeans after Columbus. [Dates labeled B.C.E were previously labeled B.C., and dates labeled C.E. were previously labeled A.D.]

56. What Native American group established a culture in about 5000 years ago?

Ⓐ Aleut

Ⓑ Algonquin

Ⓒ Eskimo

Ⓓ Intuit

Ⓔ Navajo

WRITING TEST (5722)

40 ITEMS **40 MINUTES**

2 CONSTRUCTED RESPONSES **60 MINUTES**

Usage

> **Directions:** You will read sentences with four parts underlined and lettered. Determine whether one of the underlined parts contains grammatical, word use, or punctuation errors. If so, mark that letter. If there are no errors, mark E.

1. A professional golfer told the <u>new golfer</u> that <u>professional instruction</u> or more
   (A)   (B)

   practice <u>improve</u> most golfers' <u>scores</u>. <u>No error</u>.
   (C)   (D)   (E)

2. It was <u>difficult for</u> the farmer <u>to comprehend</u> the unhappiness he
   (A)   (B)

   <u>encountered among</u> so many of the rich <u>produce buyers</u> in the city. <u>No error</u>.
   (C)   (D)   (E)

3. No goal is <u>more noble</u>—no feat more <u>revealing</u>—<u>as the</u> exploration <u>of space</u>.
   (A)   (B)   (C)   (D)

   <u>No error</u>.
   (E)

4. The soccer player's <u>slight</u> strain from the <u>shot</u> on goal led to a <u>pulled</u> muscle,
   (A)   (B)   (C)

   <u>resulted</u> in the player's removal from the game. <u>No error</u>.
   (D)   (E)

5. The <u>young college graduate</u> had no family to help her but <u>she was fortunate</u>
   (A)   (B)

   to get a job with a <u>promising school district superintendent</u> and
   (C)

   <u>eventually became a superintendent</u> herself. <u>No error</u>.
   (D)   (E)

6. He <u>was concerned</u> about crossing the bridge, <u>but the officer</u> said <u>that it</u> was
   (A)   (B)   (C)

   <u>all right</u> to cross. <u>No error</u>.
   (D)   (E)

7. As the students <u>prepared to take</u> the test, they <u>came to realize</u> that it was not
   (A)   (B)

   only what they knew <u>and also</u> how well they <u>knew how</u> to take tests. <u>No error</u>.
   (C)   (D)   (E)

8. As many as a ton of bananas may have spoiled when the ship was stuck in the
  Ⓐ   Ⓑ   Ⓒ   Ⓓ
   Panama Canal. No error.
                 Ⓔ

9. Employment agencies often place newspaper advertisements when no
                       Ⓐ   Ⓑ
   jobs exist to get the names of potential employees on file. No error.
        Ⓒ   Ⓓ   Ⓔ

10. Visitors to New York can expect to encounter people, noise, and
               Ⓐ   Ⓑ
   finding themselves in traffic just about any day of the week. No error.
                Ⓒ   Ⓓ   Ⓔ

11. It was obvious to Kim that neither her family or her friends could
         Ⓐ   Ⓑ
   understand why the study of science was so important to her. No error.
              Ⓒ   Ⓓ   Ⓔ

12. While past safaris had entered the jungle to hunt elephants with rifles, this safari
           Ⓐ   Ⓑ
   had only a single armed guard to protect the tourists as they took photographs.
               Ⓒ   Ⓓ
   No errors.
        Ⓔ

13. Buddhism is an interesting religion because Confucius was born in India,
         Ⓐ   Ⓑ   Ⓒ
   but the religion never gained lasting popularity there. No error.
                       Ⓓ   Ⓔ

14. John Dewey's progressive philosophy influenced thousands of teachers;
                 Ⓐ   Ⓑ
   however, Dewey was often displeased with there teaching methods. No error.
                        Ⓒ   Ⓓ   Ⓔ

15. While only in the school for a few weeks, the gym teacher was starting to
         Ⓐ   Ⓑ   Ⓒ
   felt comfortable with the principal. No error.
        Ⓓ   Ⓔ

16. The carnival, which featured a wild animal act was due to arrive in town
          Ⓐ   Ⓑ   Ⓒ   Ⓓ
   next week. No error.
                 Ⓔ

17. While the bus driver waited, the motor runs and uses expensive gasoline.
    Ⓐ   Ⓑ   Ⓒ   Ⓓ

    No error.
    Ⓔ

18. Having needed to eat and earn money, the college graduate decided it was
    Ⓐ   Ⓑ   Ⓒ

    time to look for a job. No error.
    Ⓓ   Ⓔ

Sentence Correction

> **Directions:** You will read sentences with some or all of the sentence underlined, followed by five answer choices. The first answer choice repeats the underlined portion and the other four present possible replacements. Select the answer choice that best represents standard English without altering the meaning of the original sentence. Mark that letter on the test or answer sheet.

19. The dean was famous for delivering grand sounding but otherwise unintelligible speeches.

    Ⓐ but otherwise unintelligible speeches.
    Ⓑ but in every other way speeches that could not be intelligible.
    Ⓒ but speeches which were not that intelligent.
    Ⓓ but otherwise speeches that could be understood.
    Ⓔ but speeches that could be unintelligible.

20. The hiker grew tired greater as the day wore on.

    Ⓐ The hiker grew tired greater
    Ⓑ The hiker grew tired more
    Ⓒ The hiker grew greater tired
    Ⓓ The hiker's tired grew greater
    Ⓔ The hiker grew more tired

21. The man knew that to solve the problem now can be easier than putting it off for another day.

    Ⓐ to solve the problem now can be easier
    Ⓑ to solve the problem now is easier
    Ⓒ to solve the problem now can be less difficult
    Ⓓ solving the problem now can be easier
    Ⓔ to try to solve the problem now

22. Lee's <u>mother and father insists that</u> he call if he is going to be out after 8:00 P.M.

    Ⓐ mother and father insists that
    Ⓑ mother and father insist that
    Ⓒ mother and father insists
    Ⓓ mother and father that insist
    Ⓔ mother and father that insists

23. The weather forecaster said that people living near the shore should be prepared <u>in the event that</u> the storm headed for land.

    Ⓐ in the event that
    Ⓑ if the event happened and
    Ⓒ the event
    Ⓓ if
    Ⓔ and

24. After years of observation, the soccer coach concluded that women soccer players were more aggressive than <u>men who played soccer.</u>

    Ⓐ men who played soccer.
    Ⓑ men soccer players.
    Ⓒ soccer playing men.
    Ⓓ those men who played soccer.
    Ⓔ men.

25. The stockbroker advised her client to sell the stock before it <u>could no longer be popular.</u>

    Ⓐ could no longer be popular.
    Ⓑ could be popular no longer.
    Ⓒ may be popular no longer.
    Ⓓ could become unpopular.
    Ⓔ was no longer popular.

26. Bringing in an outside consultant usually means that it will take too long for the consultant to understand what's going on, <u>the functioning of the office will be impaired</u>, and because a new person has been introduced into the company, it will create dissension.

    Ⓐ the functioning of the office will be impaired
    Ⓑ the impairment of office functioning will follow
    Ⓒ caused impairment in office functioning
    Ⓓ office functioning impairment will occur
    Ⓔ it will impair the functioning of the office

27. The primary election was very <u>important because winning could give the candidate a much more</u> clearer mandate.

    Ⓐ important because winning could give the candidate a much more
    Ⓑ important because winning there could give the candidate a much more
    Ⓒ important because a win there could give the candidate a
    Ⓓ important because winning could give the candidate a
    Ⓔ important because a loss there would be devastating

28. She had become a doctor with the noble purpose of saving lives; however, <u>the process of applying for medical benefits and the responsibilities for managing the office had become her primary and overriding concern.</u>

    Ⓐ the process of applying for medical benefits and the responsibilities for managing the office had become her primary and overriding concern.
    Ⓑ applying for medical benefits and managing the office had become her main concerns.
    Ⓒ applying for medical benefits, and the responsibilities for managing the office had become her primary and overriding concern.
    Ⓓ applying for medical benefits and office work had become her main concern.
    Ⓔ she soon found out that being a doctor was not noble.

29. Among the most popular television programs are those that critics classify <u>is soap operas.</u>

    Ⓐ is soap operas.
    Ⓑ are soap operas.
    Ⓒ as soap operas.
    Ⓓ in soap operas.
    Ⓔ with soap operas.

30. If a person <u>has the ability in music</u>, then he should try to develop this ability by taking music lessons.

    Ⓐ has the ability in music
    Ⓑ has musical ability
    Ⓒ can play an instrument
    Ⓓ is a talented musician
    Ⓔ is interested in music

31. The players on the national team were supposed by some of their countrymen to have almost superhuman ability.

    Ⓐ The players on the national team were supposed by some of their countrymen to have almost superhuman ability.

    Ⓑ The players on the national team had superhuman ability, according to some of their countrymen.

    Ⓒ The players in the national team were better at the sport than most of their countryman.

    Ⓓ Suppose the players on the national team were not good enough, thought some of their countrymen.

    Ⓔ Some of their countrymen thought that the players on the national team had almost superhuman ability.

Revision in Context

Select the best answer.

QUESTIONS 32–36 ARE BASED ON THE FOLLOWING PASSAGE.

Gettysburg Address

(1) At the end of the Battle of Gettysburg, more than 51,000 Confederate and Union soldiers were wounded, missing, or dead. (2) Pennsylvania governor Andrew Curtin commissioned David Wills, an attorney, to purchase land for a proper burial site for the deceased Union soldiers. (3) Wills acquired 17 acres for the cemetery, which was planned and designed by landscape architect William Saunders.

(4) The cemetery was dedicated on November 19, 1863. (5) The main speaker for the event Edward Everett, was one of the nation's foremost orators. (6) President Lincoln was also invited to speak "as Chief Executive of the nation, formally to set apart these grounds to their sacred use by a few appropriate remarks." (7) At the ceremony, Everett spoke for more than two hours; Lincoln spoke for two minutes.

(8) President Lincoln had given his brief speech a lot of thought. (9) He saw meaning in the fact that the Union victory at Gettysburg coincided with the nation's birthday; but rather than focus on the specific battle in his remarks, he wanted to present a broad statement about the larger significance of the war. (10) He invoked the Declaration of Independence and its principles of liberty and equality, and he spoke of "a new birth of freedom" for the nation. (11) In his brief address, he continued to reshape the aims of the war for the American people—transforming it from a war for Union to a war for Union and freedom. (12) Lincoln expressed disappointment in the speech initially.

32. Which of the following sentences, added after sentence 12, would provide the most fitting conclusion to this paragraph?

    Ⓐ But it has come to be regarded as one of the most elegant and eloquent speeches in U.S. history.

    Ⓑ He eventually realized he was no match for a great orator.

    Ⓒ The continuation of the Civil War made the initial reaction final.

    Ⓓ It became clear to him that he had been somewhat successful in rewriting history.

    Ⓔ But on the train trip back to Washington he completely dismissed the matter.

33. In the context of this passage, what is the best replacement for the underlined portion of sentence 3, shown below?

Wills acquired 17 acres for the cemetery, which was planned and designed by landscape architect William Saunders.

Ⓐ Leave as is.
Ⓑ Delete it.
Ⓒ The 17-acre cemetery was designed by William Saunders.
Ⓓ William Saunders designed the cemetery
Ⓔ Wills acquired the land for the cemetery, which was designed by William Saunders.

34. In the context of this passage, which of the following is the best addition to the end of sentence 4?

Ⓐ , after the battle.
Ⓑ , in Pennsylvania.
Ⓒ , with the battle still raging.
Ⓓ , near Gettysburg.
Ⓔ , before the war ended.

35. In the context of this passage, which of the choices below is the best suggestion to revise the underlined portion of sentence 9, shown below?

He saw meaning in the fact that the Union victory

Ⓐ He saw meaning in the fact that the North's victory
Ⓑ He saw special meaning in Union victory
Ⓒ He saw meaning in the very fact that the Union victory
Ⓓ He saw meaning because the Union victory
Ⓔ He saw meaning in the Union victory

36. In the context of this passage, which choice below is the best revision of Sentence 5 shown below?

The main speaker for the event Edward Everett, was one of the nation's foremost orators.

Ⓐ Leave as is.
Ⓑ The primary speaker for the event Edward Everett, one of the nation's foremost orators.
Ⓒ The main speaker for the event Edward Everett, as the nation's foremost orator.
Ⓓ The main speaker for the event, Edward Everett, was one of the nation's foremost orators.
Ⓔ The first speaker for the event Edward Everett, as one of the nation's outstanding orators.

Research Skills

Select the best answer.

37. Robert Dereko, "The Key to a Successful Relationship Is Often in the Differences," *New Square News* February 18, 2014, accessed March 23, 2014.

    The citation above is from which of the following types of sources?

    Ⓐ An online article
    Ⓑ A newspaper article
    Ⓒ A blog
    Ⓓ A book
    Ⓔ An interview

38. A friend is writing a paper about the Holocaust. Which of the following could be a primary source for this paper?

    Ⓐ Notes from a guard about the Holocaust prison camp
    Ⓑ A book about the Holocaust by the daughter of a Holocaust survivor
    Ⓒ Handwritten notes from a Holocaust survivor about her life after the Holocaust
    Ⓓ A list of names of those killed in concentration camps provided by a government
    Ⓔ A visit to the site of the Auschwitz Concentration Camp

39. Which of the following would be correctly cited as a secondary source about the first moon landing?

    Ⓐ A video of that moon landing
    Ⓑ A book about the moon landing by an astronaut on that original lander
    Ⓒ A book about space travel by an astronaut
    Ⓓ A sample of rocks collected on the moon after the lunar lander touched down
    Ⓔ A recording of an astronaut on that first lander as it touched down on the moon

40. In a paper about the origins of the term *Uncle Sam* to personify the U.S. government during the War of 1812, which of the following pieces of information is directly relevant to the paper?

    Ⓐ It is believed that during the War of 1812, soldiers used the initials U.S. to arrive at "Uncle Sam."
    Ⓑ During the War of 1812 British troops sacked the Capitol Building in Washington, D.C.
    Ⓒ During the War of 1812 Frances Scott Key is reputed to have written the "Star Spangled Banner" while a prisoner on a ship in Baltimore Harbor but did not include a reference to Uncle Sam.
    Ⓓ The author of the paper has an uncle named Sam and so is familiar with Uncle Sam.
    Ⓔ In 1989, the U.S. Congress officially recognized "Uncle Sam Day."

ARGUMENTATIVE CONSTRUCTED RESPONSE

30 MINUTES

> **Directions:** You have 30 minutes to complete this essay question. Use a computer, but not the spell or grammar check, to type a brief essay based on this topic.

A college student who received a poor grade in a class should be able to have any record of the class and the grade removed from his or her transcript.

Describe the extent to which you agree or disagree with this statement. Support your response with specific details, examples, and experiences.

Write a brief outline here.

INFORMATIVE/EXPLANATORY (SOURCE-BASED) CONSTRUCTED RESPONSE

30 MINUTES

> **Directions:** You have 30 minutes to read two position papers on a topic and then type an essay based on the topic. Use a computer, but not the spell or grammar check. The essay should discuss the important points in the topic.
>
> Read the topic and sources below. It is good to spend time organizing your thoughts and planning your essay before you start to write. You MUST write on the given topic, and you MUST include references to the sources.
>
> This essay gives you a chance to demonstrate how well you can write and include sources in your writing. That means you should focus on writing well and using examples and references, all while being sure to cover the topic presented. While how much you write is not a specific scoring criteria, you will certainly want to write several meaningful paragraphs.

Topic

Pumping gas is one of the most common of daily experiences. You drive up to the pump, swipe your credit card, select the grade, put the nozzle in the gas filler tube, and depress the lever. You may even be able to set the pump to operate "automatically," and the pump stops when the pump's sensors indicate that the tank is full. There are signs that tell you to turn off your engine and not to introduce any flammable items into the situation but no one to check to see that you follow the rules. At this writing, that cannot happen in New Jersey, Oregon, and some localities. In those states and localities a station employee must operate the pump.

Read the two source passages below. Then type an essay that highlights the most important aspects of the positions and explain why they are important. Your essay should refer to EACH of the sources and must CITE the sources as you refer to them or provide direct quotations. You may also use your own experiences and readings.

Self-Service—Even if You Can—Service Yourself Is Dangerous and Costs Jobs
(Andrews, web access 10/17/2017)

In all but two states a person can fill his or her own gas tank with fuel. Those states are New Jersey and Oregon. So a reasonable question is why these two states still have decades-old laws against fueling self-service. Before the discussion let me point out that the "traditional" gas stations in New Jersey and Oregon employ over 20,000 people. A little simple math indicates that we would add over 500,000 employees by eliminating self-service stations.

There are two clear reasons for a ban on self-service stations. The first is that these stations discriminate against the disabled. A disabled person is always discriminated against at self-service stations. The only issue is the extent of that discrimination, and since many self-service stations combine fuel dispensing with a convenience store, there is often only one employee present. That person cannot leave the store and the disabled person is just out of luck. The typical self-service station always violates federal law, and why that practice is allowed to continue is unclear to me.

Some think that the absence of employees at non-self-service stations would lower costs. But this is not true. Self-service stations pay much more for liability insurance, at least equal to the cost of actual employees, than non-self-service.

First, that makes the point that self-service stations are inherently less safe than non self-service stations. That is what all the statistics show as well, so the safety reason for banning self-service stations is hard to argue with. It also sharpens the issue of paying employees to pump gas. That seems a much better choice than paying an insurance company.

What may seem a "no-brainer" in favor of self-service stations turns out to be a no-brainer against them.

Self-Service—Can 48 States Really Be Wrong
(Callman, web access 9/28/2017)

You can make lots of arguments in favor of or against self-service filling stations. But I will start with the most obvious one. You can refuel your car, yourself, in all but 2 states, New Jersey and Oregon. In each one of those states the laws forbidding self-service gas stations are many decades old. It is simple: most people prefer to pump gas themselves and not hand over a credit card to a gas station employee.

So, yes, when you look at the big picture, you have to understand that 48 states really cannot be wrong. The citizens of these states have looked at all the issues, looked at all the pros and cons, and have reached a conclusion—self-serve stations are better than non-self-serve stations. There are undoubtedly many reasons, besides convenience, for their decisions. They have looked at them all.

The primary reason given for opposition to self-service stations is safety. But self-service opponents know that the safety requirements for self-service gas are more stringent than the requirements for employee-operated pumps. Besides that, it is just as easy for a poorly-paid gas station employee to cause an accident as it is for the self-service pump operator. There are some legitimate concerns about the very few disabled people who cannot get out of a car to fuel his or her vehicles. The truth is that very few of these people are driving and there is always a way to get help. The other day I was at a self-service station and a person who seemed to require a wheelchair just rolled down the window and asked another person to fuel the car. It worked great.

This is one of those times when the vast majority has it right. It is better to be able to fuel your vehicle yourself than to have to rely on an attendant, some of whom are not that attendant.

Write a brief outline here.

MATHEMATICS TEST (5732)

56 ITEMS   85 MINUTES

> **Directions:** Choose the correct answer(s) or write the answer in the box(es).

1. The triangle on the coordinate grid below was translated down 3 units and left 2 units. What is the coordinate of point *C* after these translations?

    Ⓐ (–1, 1)
    Ⓑ (0, –4)
    Ⓒ (0, 3)
    Ⓓ (5, –3)
    Ⓔ (5, 0)

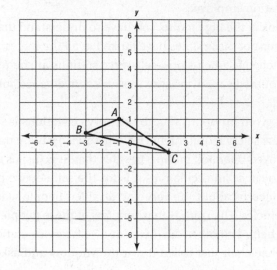

2. A machine used to flatten asphalt has two cylindrical rollers. The larger cylinder has a diameter of 5 feet. The smaller cylinder has a diameter of 3 feet. In one job, the machine travels once along a stretch of asphalt 320 feet long. What is the combined distance traveled by both cylindrical rollers during that job?

    Ⓐ 203π feet
    Ⓑ $32\pi/320$ feet
    Ⓒ 8π (320) feet
    Ⓓ 640π feet
    Ⓔ 640 feet

3. The heights of seven cell phone towers are 280 feet, 270 feet, 320 feet, 90 feet, 130 feet, and 105 feet, while the height of the seventh tower is unknown. However, the height of the seventh tower is different from any of the other heights, and is the median height of the seven towers. Which of the following could NOT be the height of the seventh tower?

    Ⓐ 91
    Ⓑ 135
    Ⓒ 167
    Ⓓ 200
    Ⓔ 269

4. The graph below shows part of a linear equation plotted on the coordinate plane. The graph actually extends infinitely in both directions. What would the *y* value be if the graph was extended to *x* value equals −190? Write your answer in the box below.

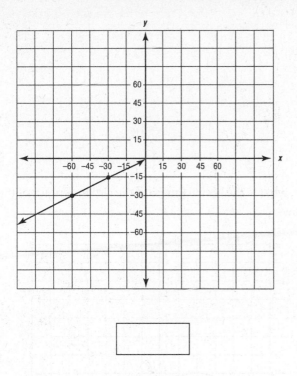

5. The figure below shows the lower portion of a right circular cone. If the height of the entire cone is 16, what is the volume of the missing top part of the cone?

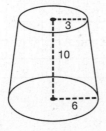

Note that the volume of a right circular cone with the base radius *r* and height *h* is $\frac{1}{3}\pi r^2 h$.

Ⓐ 6π

Ⓑ 18π

Ⓒ 72π

Ⓓ 96π

Ⓔ 192π

6. Which of the following addition examples is equivalent to $\frac{3x+6y}{12}$?

Ⓐ $\frac{3x}{4} + \frac{2y}{3}$

Ⓑ $\frac{2x}{4} + \frac{2y}{2}$

Ⓒ $\frac{x}{2} + \frac{y}{4}$

Ⓓ $\frac{4}{x} + \frac{3}{y}$

Ⓔ $\frac{x}{4} + \frac{y}{2}$

7. Using 3.14 for π, what is the best estimate of the circumference of the circle on the coordinate below?

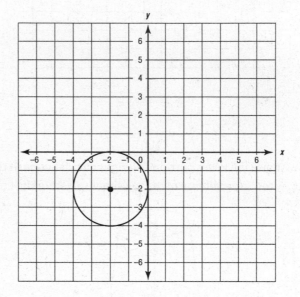

Ⓐ 6.28
Ⓑ 12.56
Ⓒ 24.02
Ⓓ 25.12
Ⓔ 50,24

8. A triangle has three sides of different lengths. The length of *a* < length of *b* < length of *c*. It also has three different angles. The measure of angle *x* is < the measure of angle *y* < the measure of angle *z*. Indicate all the angles that could NOT be opposite side *c*.

Ⓐ Angle *x*

Ⓑ Angle *y*

Ⓒ Angle *z*

Ⓓ One of the angles that measures 180°

Ⓔ None of the angles

9. At sea level, sound travels about 34,000 cm per second, while light travels almost instantaneously. You see a lightning bolt, and 5 seconds later you hear the thunderclap associated with that lightning bolt. Which of the following is the best estimate of how far away the lightning bolt was using scientific notation?

Ⓐ 17.0×10^4

Ⓑ 1.7×10^5

Ⓒ 1.7×10^6

Ⓓ 0.17×10^6

Ⓔ $170,000$

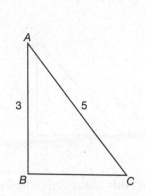

10. Which of the statements below is true about the triangle above?

The triangle is not drawn to scale.

Ⓐ The measure of angles A and B total more than 180°.

Ⓑ The area of the triangle is 6 square units.

Ⓒ The perimeter of the triangle is 15 units.

Ⓓ The area of the triangle is $7\frac{1}{2}$ square units.

Ⓔ The perimeter of the triangle is 11 units.

x	y
0	−5
3	4
6	13
9	22
12	31

11. Which of the following equations creates the pattern in the table above?

Ⓐ $y = 4x - 5$

Ⓑ $y = 2x - 2$

Ⓒ $y = 3x + 5$

Ⓓ $y = 3x - 5$

Ⓔ $y = 3x + 13$

12. A representative of the magazine advertising department is responsible for 9 to 10 full-page ads, 12 to 14 half-page ads, and 15 to 20 quarter-page ads per issue. The minimum and maximum numbers of ads that each representative is responsible for are

Ⓐ 9 and 20
Ⓑ 9 and 15
Ⓒ 15 and 20
Ⓓ 36 and 44
Ⓔ 10 and 20

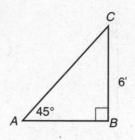

13. Construction workers laid out this triangular plot of land. What is the area of land inside the triangle?

Ⓐ $3\sqrt{3}$ square feet
Ⓑ $6\sqrt{3}$ square feet
Ⓒ 6 square feet
Ⓓ 18 square feet
Ⓔ 36 square feet

14. Which of the following expresses the relationship between x and y shown in the table?

x	y
0	1
3	7
6	13
7	15
9	19

Ⓐ $y = 3x - 2$
Ⓑ $y = 2x + 1$
Ⓒ $y = x + 3$
Ⓓ $y = 2x - 2$
Ⓔ $y = 2x + 3$

15. It took Liz 12 hours to travel by train from New York to North Carolina at an average speed of 55 miles per hour. On the return trip from North Carolina to New York, Liz traveled by bus and averaged 45 miles per hour. How much longer was her return trip?

Ⓐ $2\frac{2}{3}$ hours

Ⓑ $3\frac{2}{3}$ hours

Ⓒ $4\frac{2}{3}$ hours

Ⓓ 5 hours

Ⓔ $6\frac{2}{3}$ hours

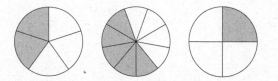

16. In the figure above, about what percent of the combined regions are shaded?

Ⓐ $66\frac{2}{3}$ %

Ⓑ 40%

Ⓒ 25%

Ⓓ 60%

Ⓔ $33\frac{1}{3}$ %

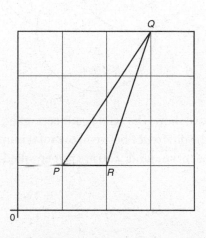

17. The graph is drawn on the coordinate plane, the vertex of angle R is at (6, 3). The vertex at angle Q is reflected across the y-axis. What are the new coordinates of the vertex of the reflected angle Q?

Ⓐ (12, –9)

Ⓑ (–9, +12)

Ⓒ (16, 3)

Ⓓ (6, –3)

Ⓔ (–6, –9)

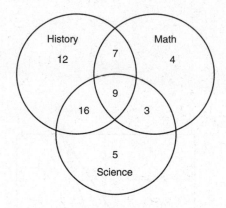

18. Three points P, Q, and R, are on this number line. The sum of the coordinates of points P and Q is 6. Point R is between points P and Q. Which of the following could be the coordinates for point R?

Ⓐ +1

Ⓑ −1

Ⓒ −5

Ⓓ −6

Ⓔ +6

19. C is 5 more than half of B. Which of the following expressions states this relationship?

Ⓐ $C + 5 = B/2$

Ⓑ $C = \frac{1}{2}B + 5$

Ⓒ $C + 5 = 2B$

Ⓓ $C + 5 > B/2$

Ⓔ $C + 5 < B/2$

20. The Venn diagram above shows the school subjects taken by members of the school's sport teams. What is the difference between the total number of students enrolled in history and the number of students who are just enrolled in history?

Ⓐ 56

Ⓑ 42

Ⓒ 32

Ⓓ 23

Ⓔ 9

21. $\sqrt{300 \times 3} =$

Ⓐ $10\sqrt{3}$

Ⓑ $3\sqrt{30}$

Ⓒ 90

Ⓓ $9\sqrt{10}$

Ⓔ 30

Time	8 A.M.	9 A.M.	10 A.M.	11 A.M.	12 NOON
Temp	50°	55°	60°	65°	70°
Time	1 P.M.	2 P.M.	3 P.M.	4 P.M.	
Temp	75°	80°	70°	65°	
Time	5 P.M.	6 P.M.	7 P.M.	8 P.M.	
Temp	55°	50°	47°	45°	

22. The table above shows the temperature tracked for a 12-hour period of time. Which graph best illustrates this information?

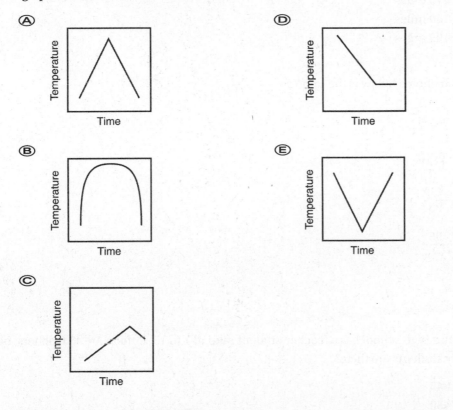

23. A rectangular garden measures 23 feet by 63 feet. What is the greatest number of nonoverlapping 5-foot square plots that can be ruled off in this garden?

Ⓐ 48

Ⓑ 57

Ⓒ 58

Ⓓ 289

Ⓔ 290

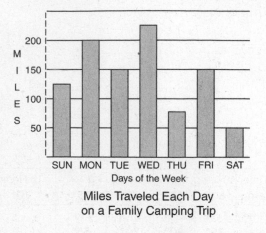

Miles Traveled Each Day
on a Family Camping Trip

24. The bar graph shows the number of miles a family traveled each day on a camping trip. Approximately how many miles did the family travel on average each day?

Ⓐ 125 miles
Ⓑ 200 miles
Ⓒ 175 miles
Ⓓ 140 miles
Ⓔ 100 miles

25. Which choice below is the same as $\dfrac{7}{xy} \div \dfrac{x}{14}$?

Ⓐ $98x^2y$

Ⓑ $\dfrac{7}{14xy}$

Ⓒ $\dfrac{x^2y}{98}$

Ⓓ $\dfrac{98}{x^2y}$

Ⓔ $\dfrac{1}{2}y$

26. A junior high school has a teacher-student ratio of 1 to 15. If there are 43 teachers, how many students are there?

Ⓐ 645
Ⓑ 430
Ⓒ 215
Ⓓ 630
Ⓔ 600

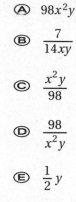

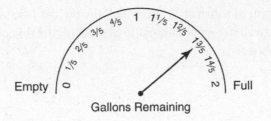

Empty | 0 1/5 2/5 3/5 4/5 1 1 1/5 1 2/5 1 3/5 1 4/5 2 | Full

Gallons Remaining

27. The gauge above shows the amount of gas in the tank after mowing the lawn. If the tank was full at the start of mowing, which of the following is the best estimate of how many "mows" are left?

Ⓐ 2
Ⓑ 3
Ⓒ 4
Ⓓ 5
Ⓔ 6

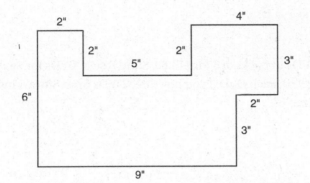

28. A floor plan is drawn with a scale of 5 feet per inch. If the diagram represents the floor plan, what is the actual perimeter of the house?

Ⓐ 38 inches
Ⓑ 38 feet
Ⓒ 200 feet
Ⓓ $7\frac{2}{5}$ feet
Ⓔ 190 feet

29. Mary must make tablecloths for 12 banquet tables. She needs a piece of cloth 5 ft. by 8 ft. for each tablecloth. Each cloth must be made from the same bolt and cannot be sewn. Of the five bolts listed here, which one must be eliminated due to insufficient material?

Ⓐ 34 yd. remaining on an 8-ft. wide bolt
Ⓑ 33 yd. remaining on a 6-ft. wide bolt
Ⓒ 25 yd. remaining on a 5-ft. wide bolt
Ⓓ 35 yd. remaining on an 8-ft. wide bolt
Ⓔ 36 yd. remaining on a 7-ft. wide bolt

30. Blaire bought a pair of shoes at 25 percent off the regular price of $40.00. She had a coupon, which saved her an additional 15 percent off the sale price. What price did she pay for the shoes?

Ⓐ $24.00
Ⓑ $15.00
Ⓒ $25.50
Ⓓ $11.25
Ⓔ $27.50

31. Points L, M, N, and O are on the same line. The ratio of LM to NO is $3 : 2$. Which could NOT be values for LM and NO?

Ⓐ $LM = 15$; $NO = 10$
Ⓑ $LM = 12$; $NO = 9$
Ⓒ $LM = 3$; $NO = 2$
Ⓓ $LM = 0.75$; $NO = 0.5$
Ⓔ $LM = 1$; $NO = \frac{2}{3}$

32. Store A has DVDs in packs of 3 for $15.60. Store B sells DVDs for $6.00 each. How much is saved (if any) on each DVD if you buy three DVDs from Store A instead of three DVDs from Store B?

Ⓐ $3.40
Ⓑ $0.80
Ⓒ $1.80
Ⓓ $2.40
Ⓔ There is no saving.

33. Two different whole numbers are multiplied. Which of the following could not result?

Ⓐ 0
Ⓑ 1
Ⓒ 7
Ⓓ 19
Ⓔ 319

34. Which of the following does not have the same value as the others?

Ⓐ $(0.9 + 0.2) \times 3.2$
Ⓑ $(0.9 \times 3.2) + (0.2 \times 3.2)$
Ⓒ $0.9 + (0.2 \times 3.2)$
Ⓓ $3.2 \times (0.2 + 0.9)$
Ⓔ $3.2 \times (1.1)$

35. Each of the following is $66\frac{2}{3}$ percent of 50 EXCEPT

Ⓐ $0.66\overline{6} \times 50$

Ⓑ 0.66×50

Ⓒ $\frac{2}{3} \times 50$

Ⓓ $.66\frac{2}{3} \times 50$

Ⓔ $\frac{26}{39} \times 50$

36. A calculator displays a multiple-digit whole number ending in 0. All the following statements must be true about the number EXCEPT:

Ⓐ it is an even number.
Ⓑ it is a multiple of 5.
Ⓒ it is a power of 10.
Ⓓ it is a multiple of 10.
Ⓔ it is a multiple of 1.

37. Some values of Y are more than 50. Which of the following could NOT be true?

Ⓐ 60 is not a value of Y.
Ⓑ 45 is not a value of Y.
Ⓒ There are Y values more than 50.
Ⓓ All values of Y are 50 or less.
Ⓔ Some values of Y are less than 50.

38. A pedometer shows distance in meters. A distance of 0.5 kilometers would have a numerical display that is

Ⓐ 100 times as great.
Ⓑ twice as great.
Ⓒ half as great.
Ⓓ 1,000 times as great.
Ⓔ $\frac{1}{10}$ times as great.

39. Which of the following shows the least to greatest ordering of the fractions?

Ⓐ $\frac{12}{13}, \frac{99}{100}, \frac{25}{24}, \frac{17}{16}, \frac{5}{4}$

Ⓑ $\frac{99}{100}, \frac{25}{24}, \frac{17}{16}, \frac{5}{4}, \frac{12}{13}$

Ⓒ $\frac{25}{24}, \frac{12}{13}, \frac{99}{100}, \frac{5}{4}, \frac{17}{16}$

Ⓓ $\frac{17}{16}, \frac{5}{4}, \frac{25}{24}, \frac{12}{13}, \frac{99}{100}$

Ⓔ $\frac{5}{4}, \frac{12}{13}, \frac{17}{16}, \frac{99}{100}, \frac{25}{24}$

40. Two dice are rolled. What is the probability that the sum of the numbers is even?

    Ⓐ $\frac{1}{2}$

    Ⓑ $\frac{16}{36}$

    Ⓒ $\frac{3}{4}$

    Ⓓ $\frac{1}{12}$

    Ⓔ $\frac{5}{6}$

41. If the product of P and 6 is R, then the product of P and 3 is

    Ⓐ $2R$

    Ⓑ $R/2$

    Ⓒ $\frac{1}{2}P$

    Ⓓ $2P$

    Ⓔ $P/6$

42. The multiplication and division buttons on a calculator are reversed. A person presses $\div$ 5 $=$ and the calculator displays 625. What answer should have been displayed?

    Ⓐ 125

    Ⓑ 625

    Ⓒ 25

    Ⓓ 50

    Ⓔ 250

43. If $V, l, w,$ and h are positive numbers and $V = l \times w \times h$, then $l =$

    Ⓐ $\frac{1}{3}whV$

    Ⓑ $\frac{v}{wh}$

    Ⓒ $\frac{lw}{v}$

    Ⓓ Vlw

    Ⓔ $w(V + h)$

44. If 0.00005 divided by $X = 0.005$, then $X =$

    Ⓐ 0.1

    Ⓑ 0.01

    Ⓒ 0.001

    Ⓓ 0.0001

    Ⓔ 0.00001

45. The product of two numbers is 900. One number is tripled. In order for the product to remain the same, the other number must be

 (A) multiplied by 3.

 (B) divided by $\frac{1}{3}$.

 (C) multiplied by $\frac{1}{3}$.

 (D) subtracted from 900.

 (E) quadrupled.

46. Which of the following could be the face of the cross section of a cylinder?

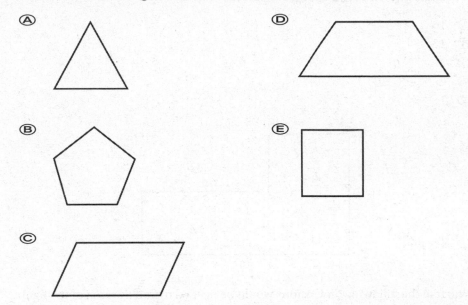

47. Quinn needs to buy enough fencing to enclose a 3 foot by 4 foot piece of land and to build a diagonal fence from one corner to the other. How much fencing is needed?

 (A) 12 feet

 (B) 14 feet

 (C) 17 feet

 (D) 19 feet

 (E) 20 feet

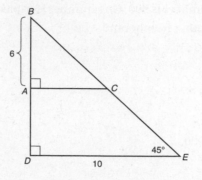

48. In triangle *BDE* what is the length of side *AD*?

    Ⓐ 16
    Ⓑ 10
    Ⓒ 4
    Ⓓ 2
    Ⓔ 1

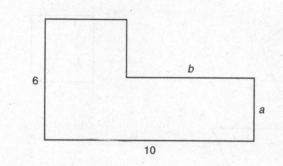

49. Which of the following dimensions would be needed to find the area of the figure?

    Ⓐ *a* only
    Ⓑ *b* only
    Ⓒ neither *a* nor *b*
    Ⓓ both *a* and *b*
    Ⓔ either *a* or *b*

50. Deena finished the school run in 52.8 seconds. Lisa's time was 1.3 seconds faster. What was Lisa's time?

    Ⓐ 51.5 seconds
    Ⓑ 54.1 seconds
    Ⓒ 53.11 seconds
    Ⓓ 65.8 seconds
    Ⓔ 52.93 seconds

51. Quinn had 5 weeks to practice the violin before the concert. He practiced an average of 7 hours a week. In one of the weeks he practiced 7 hours. He practiced 2 hours more than that during each of two other weeks. In one other week he practiced 10 hours. To the nearest whole number how many hours did he practice in the remaining week?

Ⓐ 0

Ⓑ 5

Ⓒ 7

Ⓓ 9

Ⓔ 35

52. Manuel and Ellen are conducting a probability experiment. The auditorium is emptying out of students after a play and more than a hundred students are walking single file down the hall. Starting at one, Manuel writes down the number of each third student (the first number he writes down is 3). Also starting at one, Ellen writes the number for each fourth student. Counting stops when they reach the hundredth student. When the experiment is over, how many numbers are written twice?

Ⓐ 6

Ⓑ 8

Ⓒ 10

Ⓓ 12

Ⓔ 16

53. There are a total of 28 vehicles in the parking lot. Some are cars, while some are SUVs. Which of the following could be the ratio of cars to SUVs?

Ⓐ 2 to 3

Ⓑ 3 to 4

Ⓒ 4 to 7

Ⓓ 5 to 7

Ⓔ 6 to 10

54. A store offers merchandise for half off the listed price (L). Each of the following choices represents this result EXCEPT

Ⓐ $0.50 \times L$

Ⓑ $L - .50L$

Ⓒ $\dfrac{L}{2}$

Ⓓ $\dfrac{5L}{10}$

Ⓔ $\dfrac{L}{0.50}$

55. A car travels 40 miles per hour. Which of the following gives the approximate speed of the car in kilometers per hour?

Ⓐ $\dfrac{16}{100} \times 40$

Ⓑ 0.6×40

Ⓒ $32 \div 2 \times \dfrac{1}{10} \times 40$

Ⓓ $0.6 \times 10 \times 40 \times \dfrac{1}{10}$

Ⓔ $\dfrac{60}{10} \div (\dfrac{1}{40} \times 30 \times 2)$

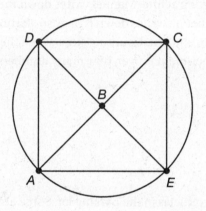

56. Point B is at the center of the circle shown above. Which of the following must be true?

Select all that apply.

Ⓐ $\overline{AC}$ is a chord.

Ⓑ $\overline{AE}$ is a radius.

Ⓒ $\overline{BE}$ is a radius.

Ⓓ $\overline{AB}$ is a diameter.

Ⓔ $\overline{BD}$ is a chord.

> Now that you've completed both practice tests in this book, be sure to take the online test at *barronsbooks.com/tp/praxis/core* for additional practice.

READING TEST

1. **C**	11. **C**	21. **C**	31. **A**	41. **B**	51. **B**
2. **D**	12. **E**	22. **A**	32. **C**	42. **D**	52. **B**
3. **A**	13. **C**	23. **E**	33. **B**	43. **B**	53. **D**
4. **E**	14. **B**	24. **B**	34. **D**	44. **A**	54. **C**
5. **D**	15. **B**	25. **D**	35. **D**	45. **D**	55. **A, C**
6. **B**	16. **C**	26. **D**	36. **C**	46. **C**	56. **B**
7. **B**	17. **E**	27. **B**	37. **C**	47. **D**	
8. **B**	18. **D**	28. **D**	38. **D**	48. **B**	
9. **A**	19. **B**	29. **C**	39. **A**	49. **E**	
10. **D**	20. **B**	30. **D**	40. **C**	50. **A**	

WRITING TEST

Usage

1. **C**	4. **D**	7. **C**	10. **C**	13. **E**	16. **C**
2. **E**	5. **C**	8. **A**	11. **B**	14. **D**	17. **C**
3. **C**	6. **E**	9. **E**	12. **B**	15. **D**	18. **A**

Sentence Correction

19. **A**	22. **B**	25. **E**	28. **B**	31. **E**
20. **E**	23. **D**	26. **E**	29. **C**	
21. **D**	24. **B**	27. **D**	30. **B**	

Revision in Context

32. **A**	33. **B**	34. **E**	35. **D**	36. **D**

Research Skills

37. **B**	38. **A**	39. **B**	40. **A**

See pages 334–336 for sample responses for the Argumentative and Informative/Explanatory (Source-Based) essays.

MATHEMATICS TEST

1. **B**	10. **B**	20. **C**	30. **C**	40. **A**	50. **A**
2. **E**	11. **D**	21. **E**	31. **B**	41. **B**	51. **A**
3. **A**	12. **D**	22. **A**	32. **B**	42. **C**	52. **B**
4. **−95**	13. **D**	23. **A**	33. **B**	43. **B**	53. **B**
5. **B**	14. **B**	24. **D**	34. **C**	44. **B**	54. **E**
6. **E**	15. **A**	25. **D**	35. **B**	45. **C**	55. **C**
7. **B**	16. **B**	26. **A**	36. **C**	46. **E**	56. **A, C**
8. **A, B, D, E**	17. **B**	27. **C**	37. **D**	47. **D**	
9. **B**	18. **A**	28. **E**	38. **D**	48. **C**	
	19. **B**	29. **C**	39. **A**	49. **D**	

ANSWERS EXPLAINED

Reading Test

1. **(C)** This choice paraphrases the last sentence of the passage.

2. **(D)** The author includes details about the moon's cycle and Earth's revolution as factors contributing to the development of the current calendar.

3. **(A)** The author explains the difference with the description and an example.

4. **(E)** The passage constantly refers to what youth do not know about AIDS.

5. **(D)** This choice paraphrases the third sentence in the paragraph.

6. **(B)** The passage uses many synonyms of this word to describe young people's knowledge of AIDS.

7. **(B)** This choice paraphrases the first sentence in the passage.

8. **(B)** The author says, and then gives an example to show, that men are discriminated against just as much as women.

9. **(A)** *Drafted*, in the sense used here, means to be *inducted* into the armed forces *against one's will*.

10. **(D)** *Alice in Wonderland*, a fanciful story about a young girl's adventures underground, has underlying figurative meanings.

11. **(C)** The passage states that *Understanding Alice* contains original text with marginal notes, indicating that the marginal notes are written next to the main text.

12. **(E)** Music is more than notes and varies with the mood of the performer.

13. **(C)** The passage refers to rockets as ordnance or weapons used by the British.

14. **(B)** *Ravished* is the best choice and describes what happens when a town is *sacked*.

15. **(B)** The last sentence of the first paragraph says that most Americans remember Perry, but not where he served.

16. **(C)** Francis Scott Key must have been able to distribute his "Star Spangled Banner" in America, so he must have been released by or escaped from the British.

17. **(E)** The second sentence in the paragraph identifies the United States as the aggressor.

18. **(D)** The answer to this question is in the first sentence of the passage.

19. **(B)** The next to the last sentence in the first paragraph indicates that these programs do not teach about spelling or word meanings.

20. **(B)** The type of computer used and teaching methods are not mentioned in the passage.

21. **(C)** The fourth sentence in the first paragraph explains that the author likes having a program to perform the mechanical aspects.

22. **(A)** This question can be answered from information in the passage's last paragraph.

23. **(E)** This choice paraphrases the first sentence in the last paragraph.

24. **(B)** This information is found in the first sentence of the first paragraph.

25. **(D)** The author wants to share what he or she learned about the *Hardy Boys* books.

26. **(D)** The author is more disappointed than anything else upon learning that a favorite childhood author did not really exist.

27. **(B)** A ghost writer is someone who writes books but does not receive credit.

28. **(D)** Every other choice is an acceptable replacement for the word *awe*.

29. **(C)** The word "dominant" is subjective and open to interpretation, which makes this choice an opinion and not a fact. Recall that an opinion can be true.

30. **(D)** This information is contained in the first sentence of the first paragraph.

31. **(A)** This choice is supported by the last sentence in the first paragraph.

32. **(C)** The first sentence of the second paragraph provides this information.

33. **(B)** This paragraph is about Pasteur's scientific discoveries, not about Pasteur the person.

34. **(D)** This answer can be found in lines 5–6 of the passage.

35. **(D)** The passage contains examples of scientists who opposed Pasteur's theories even though Pasteur had proven his theories scientifically.

36. **(C)** The first sentence indicates that Europeans had already started to devote resources to medicine when Pasteur was born, and theories about germs existed when Pasteur began his work.

37. **(C)** The passage mentions that his early work was at a university dedicated to supporting an important product of the French economy.

38. **(D)** The third from last sentence in the passage mentions that Pasteur developed vaccines for many diseases.

39. **(A)** This choice paraphrases the first sentence in the paragraph.

40. **(C)** *Infinitesimal* means very small, and *infinite* means without limit.

41. **(B)** Each paragraph in the passage discusses the likelihood that Flipper will graduate from West Point. The main focus of the passage is on his future at West Point.

42. **(D)** The author wrote the article as an objective story, but includes information about support for Flipper and never indicates the author's personal view that Flipper does not deserve to graduate. One is left with the feeling that the absence of this negative view of Flipper indicates that the author believes Flipper deserves a fair chance.

43. **(B)** In this context, the word *intimate* means *to imply* or *to indicate indirectly*.

44. **(A)** The passage states that "the prejudice of the regular army instructors against the colored race is insurmountable." It would follow that these instructors would question why they should pass an obviously inferior person.

45. **(D)** The final paragraph indicates that of all the qualities of Terhune's books it is the relationship, or kinship, between humans and dogs that has never been matched in American literature. This accounts for Terhune's books timelessness.

46. **(C)** The author's message about less need for screening passengers as opposed to screening cargo is weakened by a statement that more screening of cargo does not mean there has to be less screening of passengers.

47. **(D)** Both passages note that Lincoln was president of the United States, a political office. That means he was a politician. While only stated directly in the second passage it is a common thread in both passages. The other choices are found in only one of the two passages.

48. **(B)** Only the second passage mentions that Lincoln was assassinated.

49. **(E)** The first passage points out more examples of Lincoln's pro-slavery views than the second passage. For choice (A), both passages mention the Lincoln-Douglas debates, but this fact does not describe the relationship between the passages.

50. **(A)** The Thirteenth Amendment abolishing slavery extended freedom to slaves in Confederate states, not found in the Emancipation Proclamation.

51. **(B)** Passage I is most direct in pointing out Lincoln's pro-slavery statements. To say these statements were made for purely political reasons implies that the statements were not deeply held personal views and diminishes their impact.

52. **(B)** *Cast* is a word with many meanings. In this context, it means *portrayed*. Lincoln is often portrayed as antislavery.

53. **(D)** The twenty-third day of the month is the first day that Pilates E is not scheduled on a Monday or a Thursday.

54. **(C)** The best explanation is that this was not the first time during the month that Quinn could take Aerobics A.

55. **(A, C)** Quinn cannot attend classes on Mondays and Thursdays, and Swimming 3 is only on a Thursday and a Saturday. Quinn can only attend the Saturday session. Aerobics A is available on a number of days when Quinn can attend. Quinn can only attend the Aerobics D session on Tuesday. Note that there are other activities not listed as an answer choice that Quinn could choose to attend one single time.

56. **(B)** Civilization is about 2000 years into the Common Era (c.e.), so a civilization 5,000 years old would have been established about 3,000 years Before the Common Era (b.c.e.). Scanning the passage you see that there is only one date 3,000 b.c.e., the date of the Algonquin culture in the northeastern United States. The most common error is selecting A because those settlements were established 5,000 b.c.e., or 7,000 years ago.

Writing Test

USAGE

1. **(C)** This singular verb should end in *s*.

2. **(E)** This sentence contains no errors.

3. **(C)** The phrase *as the* should be replaced by *than the*.

4. **(D)** *Resulted* should be replaced by *resulting*.

5. **(C)** It is not possible to tell whether the school district or the superintendent is promising. Delete either *school district* or *superintendent*.

6. **(E)** This sentence contains no errors.

7. **(C)** Replace *and also* with *but also*.

8. **(A)** Replace *many* with *much*.

9. **(E)** This sentence contains no errors.

10. **(C)** Remove *finding themselves in* to maintain the parallel development of this sentence.

11. **(B)** Replace *or* with *nor*.

12. **(B)** This phrase makes it seem that elephants are armed with rifles. Delete *with rifles*.

13. **(E)** This sentence contains no errors.

14. **(D)** Replace *there* with *their*.

15. **(D)** Replace *felt* with *feel*.

16. **(C)** A comma is missing following the word *act*.

17. **(C)** Replace *waited* with *waits*.

18. **(A)** Replace *having needed* with *needing*.

SENTENCE CORRECTION

19. **(A)** The underlined portion is acceptable as written.

20. **(E)** Use this replacement for the awkward wording in the original sentence.

21. **(D)** Use this replacement for the awkward wording in the original sentence.

22. **(B)** The plural verb does not end in *s*.

23. **(D)** Use the word *if* in place of the wordy underlined phrase.

24. **(B)** This wording is clearer and more understandable than the original wording in the sentence.

25. **(E)** The correct verb is *was*, rather than *could . . . be*.

26. **(E)** Use this replacement to maintain the parallel structure of the sentence.

27. **(D)** The words *much more* in the original sentence are not needed. Choice (C) Is not correct because it unnecessarily changes the sentence.

28. **(B)** Use this more direct wording to replace the underlined portion of the sentence.

29. **(C)** Replace *is* with *as*.

30. **(B)** Use this more direct wording to replace the underlined portion of the sentence.

31. **(E)** Use this more direct wording to replace the underlined portion of the sentence.

REVISION IN CONTEXT

32. **(A)** This choice best reflects the tone of the passage and does provide the most fitting conclusion.

33. **(B)** This sentence adds nothing to the passage, which is about the Gettysburg Address. Deleting the sentence takes nothing away from the meaning of the passage.

34. **(E)** This choice, alone, would remind the reader that Lincoln's Gettysburg Address came before the war's end.

35. **(D)** You should always edit out "the fact that" from any written work. Choices (B), (D), and (E) accomplish that task. However, choices (B) and (E) do not make sense in context, leaving choice (D) as the only correct choice.

36. **(D)** The word *as* can be an adverb, a conjunction, a preposition, or even a noun. What it cannot be is a verb. This sentence does not have a verb, and choice (D) solves that problem by including the verb "was."

RESEARCH SKILLS

37. **(B)** It is an article from a newspaper. The article was accessed online, as is the case for many newspaper articles, but there is no evidence that it is an online article.

38. **(A)** A primary source is firsthand information. The only primary source on this list is the notes from a concentration camp guard.

39. **(B)** The book by a participating astronaut in that original lander is a secondary source because the events were recalled after the fact. Choices (A), (D), and (E) are primary sources. Choice (C) is a general reference and neither a primary nor a secondary source.

40. **(A)** This is the only choice, correct or not, that refers to the origins of the name "Uncle Sam." None of the other choices directly address the origin of the name "Uncle Sam."

Argumentative Essay

Compare your essay to the sample essay that follows. You may want to show your essay to an English expert for further evaluation.

This essay would likely receive a rating of 5 or 6 out of 6 points.

I think that the idea of removing any record of a poor grade in a class and any record of the class from a transcript is one of the worst ideas I've ever heard of. A transcript is a record of work in college and that record should not be tampered with. I am going to explain why and try to explain why people might think it is a good idea for them and why that does not make it right.

A class and a grade on a final transcript is a record of what has happened in a college classroom. It is a reflection of what happens between a professor and a student. If a students got a poor grade there is certainly a good reason for it. Not only would this practice strike at the very basis of academic it would encourage students to pay less attention to their studies, knoing that they could just have any grade they wanted to have removed. Besides that there are many ways besides their performance in class that a student can stop a grade from appearing on their final record. The first is to withdraw. Every college has withdrawal policies that allow a students to leave a class and have no grade recorded. Often students can withdraw very late from a class, even after they know what their grade will be. The second thins is grade appeal. Every college has a grade appeal process. In what I see at the college I attend if a student really did not deserve a grade the grade will be overturned on appeal. Most colleges also have hardship provisions. That means say you were in a hospital, or something else tragic happeed in your life, a college committee can decide not to record your grade on a transcript. But once the grade is there after all the things to protect students then it belongs there.

There will be some people who write in favor of this statement because they apply it to themselves. They say "wow" it would be great if I could just go through my transcript and remove every grade and course I did not like. Of course that is what they are going to write. But it is so serving of themselves that we just can't pay attention to them. It would be giving the wrong people a say over what is happening in our college where there are already enough questions about the quality of what goes on there. Why not just take the tuition money and let the students write their own grades.

To summarize my position I disagree with the statement about a college student being able to have any grade and class removed from their transcript. There are already many, many safeguards for students to stop the grade from appearing or to challenge a grade if it is incorrect or was because of some hardship. Things are bad enough as they are without removing this one last tiny bit of honesty in colleges and universities throughout the country.

Informative/Explanatory (Source-Based) Essay

Compare your essay with the sample essays that follow. You may want to show your essay to an English expert for further evaluation.

This essay would receive a rating of 5, but probably not a 6.

I never thought of self-serve gas stations as an issue that could lead to a useful analysis, but I see that's not true. The issue raises a number of fundamental questions. Both authors seem to agree that safety and dealing with disabled drivers, while Andrews alone raises the issue of jobs and Callman alone raises the issue of popular support.

I want to say immediately that Andrews point that requiring attendants would create about 500,000 jobs carries the day for me. Entry level jobs are hard to come by, and I believe his point that the extra liability premiums are certainly no more than the cost of the new jobs.

Pumps operated by station employees eliminates the issue of servicing disabled people. I am suspicious of Callman's statement about a disabled person getting another driver to refuel the car. It just seems too convenient, and I would not want to give my credit card to someone I did not know. Besides, and if an employee was present this arrangement would not be necessary. Besides, from what I know, it's legal to only refuel your own car.

The safety issue seems to be a little less clear. Andrews makes the issue of higher liability costs, while Callman mentions increased safety requirements for self-service stations. It seems to make sense that stations with pumps operated by employees would be safer for patrons than self-pumped gas. But neither author gives us any information about comparative safety of either type of station.

Callman's populous argument about the majority being correct reads like an example of an faulty argument. That the practice is widespread is interesting, but it does not prove that self-service stations are the best approach.

Andrew's argument for jobs, and Callman's silence on this issue, convinces me that requiring that attendants dispense all gasoline is a strong enough point on its own. It is clear to me that the extra cost of employees would be offset by the reduction in insurance costs.

Discussion

This essay clearly defines the main issues and points out which position papers refer to which issues. The essay quickly identifies the main issue and then fully reviews the other issues, bringing in the author's own perspective. The essay is long enough, well developed, and is free of meaningful errors in usage and grammar. The essay uses information from the two position papers but only by paraphrase and somewhat casually cites the appropriate position paper. It would be easy for a rater to place this essay in the upper third; however, the lack of any direct quotations and the somewhat casual citing would likely limit the highest possible rating on this essay to a 5.

This essay would receive a rating of 3, but probably not a 4.

It jumps right out on top of you. We need jobs, and having people working in gas stations would create jobs, so let us have a law that says only employees can pump gas. That is the point made by Anderson, "We would add over 500,000 employees by eliminating self-service stations." Half a million jobs. Do we really need more discussion. The discussion is over.

All the rest of the arguments don't amount to much compared to jobs. Anderson says you can tell self-service stations are more dangerous because the liability insurance is higher. Callman write "it's just as easy for poorly-paid gas station employee to cause an accident as it is for the self-service pump operator. Neither argument is a real winner.

Callman claims to have witnessed disabled drivers getting help from other drivers at self-service stations. Anderson says in a response that "The typical self-service station always violates federal law. They each make a point and it's hard to tell who is really correct. I guess there should be some way of a disabled driver to get help at a self-serve.

So this brings us back to the issue of jobs. The unemployment rate in the country is high, and it is very high for those without a college degree. A gas station job would provide an opportunity for unskilled workers. These workers would make money, be able to support themselves, and be able to contribute to society. When I first began to read these position papers it seemed it was about gas stations, but it's really about people and providing work for them. How can we turn our backs on a plan that will add so many jobs?

Discussion

This essay is fairly well developed, although there are errors, including sentence fragments. The writer refers to the position papers and associates the sources with information drawn from the papers. However, the essay is not developed enough to earn a rating in the upper third, and this lack of development also means that the typical grader would not assign a rating of 4.

This essay would likely earn a rating of 2.

One of these essays mentions job growth from non-self-serve stations. The other person doesn't mention job growth at all. One essays says that self-service stations are more dangerous than regular stations, and the other person says they are really not more dangerous.

When it comes to disabled people, one essay says that self-service stations break the law because there is no one to pump gas for the disabled, but the other person says that other customers are there to help the disabled. Personally I think people probably are discriminated against.

The conclusion I reach from all this is that the jobs issue is the only issue the second essay dos not have a response to. To me, that means that the jobs issue is the main point and the one we should pay the most attention to.

Discussion

An essay this short with some citations could never earn a rating above 3. The absence of any citations and poor development mean that the highest rating possible is a 2. The rating could not be higher unless both the development and the citations were significantly improved.

Mathematics Test

1. **(B)** Point C begins at coordinates $(2, -1)$.

   Shift down 3 units: $y = -1$. Subtract 3: $(-1) - 3 = -4$. The new y value is -4.

   Shift left 2 units: $x = 2$. Subtract 2: $(2) - 2 = 0$. The new x value is 0.

   After the shift, the coordinates of point C are $(0, -4)$.

2. **(E)** Each roller must travel 320 feet so the combined distance traveled by both rollers must be 640 feet, even though each roller will have a different number of rotations.

3. **(A)** The median will be some number between 130 and 270, although we will not know exactly what that is. Any number NOT between 130 and 270 could not be the median. Choice (A), 91, is the only number that meets that criteria. All the other choices could be the median, even though you do not know if any of them is the actual median.

4. **(−95)** The y value changes -15 for every change of -30 on the x-axis. So the y value changes at half the rate of the x-axis. At that rate, a point with a value of $x = -190$ would have a y value of -95.

5. **(B)** The "trick" to solving the problem is to notice that the missing part is also a cone. You can see that the radius of this cone is 3 from the diagram. Subtract $16 - 10 = 6$ to find the height of the missing cone. You have the dimensions you need to solve the problem: $r = 3$, $h = 6$

   Substitute the values in the formula: $\frac{1}{3}\pi r^2 h$

   $$\frac{1}{3}\pi(3)^2\, 6 = \frac{1}{3}\pi(9)(6) = \pi(\frac{1}{3})(9)(6) = \pi(3)(6) = 18\pi$$

   Leave the answer in π form.

6. **(E)** Rewrite the fraction as two fractions: $\dfrac{3x}{12} + \dfrac{6y}{12}$

   Write in simplest form: $\dfrac{x}{4} + \dfrac{y}{2}$

7. **(B)** You have to know the formula for the circumference of a circle is πd $(2\pi r)$. Use 3.14 for π. The diameter of the circle is 4. It does not matter that the x-and y-coordinates are negative because that has nothing to do with the diameter of the circle.

   Let's calculate $\pi d = 3.14 \times d = 3.14 \times 4 = 12.56$

8. **(A, B, D, E)** In a triangle, the longest side is opposite the largest angle. Side c is the longest side, and angle z is the largest angle. This means that side c and that angle z must be opposite each other. Recognize that this is a "NOT" question. All the answer choices, other than choice (C), are the correct answers.

9. **(B)** Start by multiplying $5 \times 34{,}000 \text{ cm} = 170{,}000 \text{ cm}$.

   Write the answer using scientific notation, which has a digit in the one's place multiplied by a power of 10. That is 1.7×10^5. Note that choices (A), (D), and (E) are mathematically correct but do not correctly represent the number using scientific notation.

10. **(B)** The triangle is a right triangle, and the best approach to answering this question is to see that the sides of the triangle form the Pythagorean triple: 3, 4, 5. Now find the area of $A = \frac{(3 \times 4)}{2} = 6$.

11. **(D)** Keep in mind that each x pair in the table must work in the equation. Some answers just work for one pair. It is best to follow a step-by-step approach. The pair $(0, -5)$ is a hint that subtraction by 5 may be involved. Only choice (D) works for every (x, y) pair.

12. **(D)** Add the three smaller numbers and then the three larger numbers to find this answer.

13. **(D)** Recognize this triangle as a 45°–45°–90° triangle. That means both legs have the same length of 6 feet. Use the formula for the area of a triangle: $A = \frac{1}{2} bh$.

$$A = \frac{1}{2}(6)(6) = \frac{1}{2} \times 36 = 18$$

The area is 18 square feet.

14. **(B)** Multiply x by 2 and then add 1 to find y.

15. **(A)** Take 12 times $55 = 660$ to find the total length of the trip. Divide 660 by $45 = 14\frac{2}{3}$ to find the number of hours for the return trip. Subtract $14\frac{2}{3} - 12 = 2\frac{2}{3}$.

16. **(B)** The shaded parts of 3 circles total $\frac{2}{5} + \frac{5}{9} + \frac{1}{4} = \frac{72}{180} + \frac{100}{180} + \frac{45}{180} = \frac{217}{180}$.

Because there are three circles, divide by 3. That's like multiplying by $\frac{1}{3}$.

$\left(\frac{1}{3} \times \frac{217}{180}\right) = \frac{217}{540}$ = about 40 percent. The trick to finding the total shaded part is to consider the 3 circles as 1 circle.

17. **(B)** Each line on the grid represents 3 units. That means point Q is at (9, 12). As a point is reflected across the y-axis, the new point has the same y-coordinate but the opposite of the x-coordinate. The coordinate of the new point Q is (–9, +12).

18. **(A)** Points P and Q could be +6 and 0, +5 and +1, +4 and +2, +2 and +4, +1 and +5, or 0 and +6. That means point R must be between +6 and 0. The only choice that meets this requirement is choice (A). Choice (E), +6, is incorrect because point R would have to be less than +6 to be between +6 and 0.

19. **(B)** This equation correctly expresses the relationship.

20. **(C)** There are $16 + 12 + 9 + 7 = 44$ students enrolled in history. Twelve of these students are enrolled only in history. The difference between all the students enrolled in history and the number of students just enrolled in history is $44 - 12 = 32$.

21. **(E)** $\sqrt{300 \times 3} = \sqrt{900} = 30$ or $\sqrt{300 \times 3} = \sqrt{3 \times 3 \times 100} = \sqrt{3} \times \sqrt{3} \times \sqrt{100} = \sqrt{9} \times 10 = 3 \times 10 = 30$

22. **(A)** This graph best represents the steady movement up and then down of the temperatures.

23. **(A)** $5\overline{)23} = 4$ R3; $5\overline{)63} = 12$ R3; $4 \times 12 = 48$

24. **(D)** $(125 + 200 + 150 + 225 + 75 + 150 + 50) \div 7 =$ the average (139.3) miles per day. 140 is closest.

25. **(D)** Invert the divisor and then multiply.

$$\frac{7}{xy} \div \frac{x}{14} = \frac{7}{xy} \times \frac{14}{x} = \frac{98}{x^2 y}$$

26. **(A)** Write the proportion $\frac{1}{15} = \frac{43}{x}$, cross multiply to get $x = 645$.

27. **(C)** The lawnmower tank total capacity equals 2g. The amount left in the tank is $1\frac{3}{5}$ g. $2 - 1\frac{3}{5} = \frac{2}{5}$ g. The amount used for 1 mowing is $1\frac{3}{5} \div \frac{2}{5} = 4$.
This is the number of "mows" still possible.

28. **(E)** Add the perimeters to find the total of 38 inches; $5 \times 38 = 190$.

29. **(C)** Choice (C) yields a piece 75 feet by 5 feet. Mary needs a piece 96 feet by 5 feet.

30. **(C)** $0.25 \times \$40 = \$10$; $\$40 - \$10 = \$30$; $0.15 \times \$30 = \$4.50$; $\$30 - \$4.50 = \$25.50$.

31. **(B)** The ratio of *LM* to *NO* is 3:2. Choice (B) does not reflect this ratio.

32. **(B)** Three DVDs cost $15.60 at Store A and $18.00 at Store B. The saving for all three DVDs is $2.40. The saving on one DVD is $0.80.

33. **(B)** The product of two whole numbers is 1 only if both whole numbers are 1.

34. **(C)** The value of choice (C) is 1.54. The value of each of the other choices is 3.52.

35. **(B)** $66\frac{2}{3}$ percent is written as $\frac{2}{3}$ or in decimal form as $0.66\overline{6}$ where the line over the last 6 shows that the 6 repeats endlessly. $0.66\overline{6}$ is not equal to 0.66. Choice (B) is the only choice that does not represent $66\frac{2}{3}$ percent correctly.

36. **(C)** Powers of 10 are 1 (10^0), 10 (10^1), 100 (10^2), 1000 (10^3). The calculator could be displaying 20, which is not a power of 10.

37. **(D)** If some of the values of *Y* are more than 50, then all of the values of *Y* could NOT be less than 50.

38. **(D)** The display would show 500, which is 1,000 times (0.5).

39. **(A)** Find the fractions smaller than 1. That is $\frac{12}{13}$ and $\frac{99}{100}$. Cross multiply

$\frac{12}{13} \diagdown \frac{99}{100} = \frac{1,283}{1,200}$. The bottom product is smaller, so the first fraction is smaller.

40. **(A)** There are 36 possible outcomes. Half of these outcomes are even and half are odd.

41. **(B)** $6 \cdot P = R$. Divide both sides by 2 to get $3 \cdot P = R/2$.

42. **(C)** When the $\div$ key was pressed, the calculator multiplied: $125 \times 5 = 625$. The correct answer is $125 \div 5 = 25$.

43. **(B)** $V = l \times w \times h$. Divide both sides by $w \times h$ to get $\dfrac{V}{wh} = l$.

44. **(B)** Dividing by 0.01 is the same as multiplying by 100.

45. **(C)** Divide by 3 to reverse tripling the other number. Multiplying by $\dfrac{1}{3}$ is the same as dividing by 3.

46. **(E)** Imagine a cylinder with a height equal to its diameter. The vertical cross section of this cylinder is a square.

47. **(D)** Use the Pythagorean formula to find the length of the diagonal.
$3^2 + 4^2 = x^2 \qquad 25 = x^2 \qquad x = 5$ feet
Find the perimeter $3 + 3 + 4 + 4 = 14$ feet
Add the perimeter and the length of the diagonal $14 + 5 = 19$ feet

48. **(C)** Recognize this as a 45°–45°–90° triangle. This means that sides $\overline{BD}$ and $\overline{DE}$ are the same length. The length of $\overline{DE}$ is 10. The length of $\overline{AB}$ is 6. The length of $\overline{AD}$ is $10 - 6 = 4$.

49. **(D)** Neither a nor b can be determined from the information on the figure. Both dimensions are needed to find the area.

50. **(A)** Faster times are represented by smaller numbers. Subtract $52.8 - 1.3$ to find Lisa's time.

51. **(A)** Quinn practiced an average of 7 hours a week for 5 weeks. That is 35 hours in all. Use addition to solve this problem. He practiced 7 hours in one week, $7 + 2 = 9$ hours in each of two weeks, and 10 hours in the fourth week. Add to find the total number of hours: $7 + 9 + 9 + 10 = 35$. That equals the total number of hours he practiced. That means he did not practice at all in one of the weeks. That means the correct answer is 0. It is incorrect to divide 35 by 5 and get 7, and it is incorrect to divide 35 by 4, which is 8.75, or 9 to the nearest whole number.

52. **(B)** The first number written twice is 12. ($12 = 3 \times 4$.) The next number written twice is 24. The numbers increase by 12. So the question is how many multiples of 12 are there from 1 to 100. We can just write the numbers 12, 24, 36, 48 60, 72, 84, 96. That is 8. Or we can divide 100 by 12 and ignore the remainder; 100 divided by $12 = 8$ without the remainder.

53. **(B)** Solving this problem involves a little trial and error. Start to eliminate answers. Multiply each term of the ratio by an estimated factor and add to see if you can get 28.

(A) Try 5 as the factor $(5 \times 2) + (5 \times 3) = 25$. No factor will get us to 28.
(B) Try 4 $(4 \times 3) + (4 \times 4) = 28$. This is the correct ratio.
(C) Try 3 $(3 \times 4) + (3 \times 7) = 33$. No factor will get us to 28.
(D) Try 2 $(2 \times 5) + (2 \times 7) = 24$. No factor will get us to 28.
(E) Try 2 $(2 \times 6) + (2 \times 10) = 32$. No factor will get us to 28.

54. **(E)** Half off the listed price means the same thing as 0.5 times the listed price or $\frac{1}{2}$ times the listed price.

Choice (E) is $\frac{L}{0.50} = \frac{L}{\frac{1}{2}} = 2L$. That is twice the listed price.

The other choices all show half the listed price.

(A) $0.50 \times L = 0.5L$ – one half the listed price

(B) $L - .50L = 0.5L$

(C) $\frac{L}{2} = L \times \frac{1}{2} = 0.5L$

(D) $\frac{5L}{10} = \frac{5}{10}L = 0.5L$

55. **(C)** One mile is about 1.6 kilometers so the correct answer will represent $1.6 \times 40 = 64$.

Choice (C) is correct. It is best to rearrange it as $32 \times \frac{1}{10} \div 2 \times 40 = \frac{3.2}{2} \times 40 = 64$. The other answers are incorrect.

(A) $\frac{16}{100} \times 40 = 0.16 \times 40$ is incorrect.

(B) 0.6×40 is incorrect.

(D) $0.6 \times 10 \times 40 \times \frac{1}{10} = 0.6 \times 40$ is incorrect.

(E) $\frac{60}{10} \div (\frac{1}{40} \times 30 \times 2) = \frac{3}{4} \times 2 = \frac{6}{4} = \frac{3}{2} = 6 \times \frac{2}{3}$ is incorrect.

56. **(A, C)** Choice (A) is correct because a chord is a line segment connecting two points on a circle. Choice (C) is correct because a radius is a line segment connecting the center of a circle to a point on the circle. Choice (B) is incorrect because $\overline{AE}$ does not connect the center of a circle to a point on the circle. Choice (D) is incorrect because $\overline{AB}$ does not connect two points on a circle and pass through the center. Choice (E) is incorrect because $\overline{BD}$ does not connect two points on a circle.

Index